SPECIFIC LEARNING DIFFICULTIES

(DYSLEXIA)

A HANDBOOK FOR STUDY AND

PRACTICE

Gavin Reid

SCOTTISH DYSLEXIA TRUST

This publication has been funded by the Scottish Dyslexia Trust. The Trust was set up in 1988 to encourage the development of teacher training, so that all teachers will eventually have a grounding in recognition and teaching of dyslexic children.

Other Titles

Course Reader   –   Specific Learning Difficulties (Dyslexia)
Perspectives on Practice
edited by Gavin Reid

Course Text   –   Specific Learning Difficulties (Dyslexia)
A Handbook for Study and Practice
Gavin Reid

Module Coursebooks   –   An Overview
Assessment Process
Curriculum Perspective
Research Project
Gavin Reid

Study Guide   –   Open Learning Courses in Specific Learning
Difficulties (Dyslexia)
Gavin Reid and Fernando Almeida Diniz

ISBN: 0 90 158 060 0

First published 1994

Reprinted 1996

© Moray House Institute of Education 1994

Printed and bound by Bell & Bain Ltd., Glasgow

Open Learning Courses
in Specific Learning Difficulties

General Editors: – Gavin Reid and
Fernando Almeida Diniz

Course Handbook
A HANDBOOK FOR STUDY AND PRACTICE
Gavin Reid

Moray House Publications, Edinburgh,

Acknowledgments

THIS handbook is part of the Open Learning Course materials for Post Graduate Awards in Specific Learning Difficulties offered by Moray House/Heriot-Watt University.

I would like to acknowledge those who have supported the development of the course materials and the initiation and development of the Centre for Specific Learning Difficulties at Moray House.

Thanks are due to The Scottish Dyslexia Trust and the Scottish Office Education Department for providing the funding for the Centre and its work, and for advice on the development of the Centre in the fulfilment of its aims.

Considerable gratitude is also due to colleagues in the Centre: Fernando Diniz, Margaret Crombie, Alison Closs and Pat Hill the Centre Administrator.

Support has also been offered from teachers and advisers in regional authorities, psychological services, voluntary associations and within Moray House itself. This has been greatly appreciated.

I am also indebted to Pat Hill for typing the manuscript for this publication; Rita Dunn for her advice on the chapter on learning styles; learning support staff from Madras College for relevant comment; Margaret Crombie and Stephen Iliffe for specialist editing of the content; Fernando Diniz for general editing; Sionah Lannen, Maggie Nicholson and Janet Hunter for support and advice; Dave Aikman and Aileen Robertson for typesetting, page make-up and graphics and Tanja Lannen for the cover design.

Sincere thanks are also due to the authors and publishers who have kindly allowed their work to be reproduced in this publication.

Since the Centre opened in 1991, a number of modules and courses have been run both at Moray House and within different regions in Scotland. I would like to thank those who have participated in these courses, not only for their enthusiastic and conscientious application which in itself provides enormous satisfaction to any course developer, but also for their positive and informative feedback which has helped shape the finished product.

Gavin Reid
Centre for Specific Learning Difficulties.

Contents

Foreword

MORAY HOUSE was commissioned by the Scottish Dyslexia Trust to provide a coherent and professionally relevant package to support teachers, psychologists and allied practitioners to respond to the particular needs of pupils who may experience barriers to learning associated with specific learning difficulties (dyslexia). Emphasis was to be given to disseminating good practice whilst also capitalising on our current research evidence.

The modular programme was devised to meet this need. It is an example of co-operation between the voluntary and higher education sectors, resulting in the first university validated course leading to postgraduate awards in specific learning difficulties (dyslexia) in Scotland.

The course handbook is the second in a series of publications and is designed to offer practitioners an up-to-date coverage of theoretical perspectives which underpin the development and delivery of the curriculum. Gavin Reid has consulted widely, within the United Kingdom and internationally, in writing this text.

I wish to congratulate him on his achievement and am confident that the handbook will be well received by all who are involved in the education of dyslexic pupils.

Fernando Almeida Diniz
Head of Department;
Chairperson,
Advisory Committee for the Centre for
Specific Learning Difficulties (Dyslexia),
Moray House Institute, Edinburgh.

Section 1 –

Introduction

Chapter 1

Specific learning difficulties

Introduction

THE FREQUENT use of the terms 'dyslexia' and 'specific learning difficulties' to describe the population of learners with distinctive or unexpected literacy difficulties begs some answers to the following questions – what do these terms mean? how do they differ? in what way do the children described by these terms differ from other children with literacy difficulties and how discrete is the population of children defined by these terms?

It is hoped this handbook will provide some insight into these questions and allow readers to draw their own conclusions about the whole phenomenon of specific learning difficulties and dyslexia. It is, however, important to note that in discussing this area careful attention should be directed to the needs and the individuality of the learner: whatever perspective one adopts in relation to dyslexia, the individual differences of learners need to be appreciated, including the individual profiles, learning preferences and educational and emotional needs.

This chapter will highlight the particular issues which serve as an introduction to this field and pave the way for the chapters which follow, providing the reader with a comprehensive familiarity with the principal aspects of dyslexia and its implications for the teacher, learning and the learner. The chapter will therefore focus on the following:

- definitions and terminology;
- perceptions of professionals and parents;
- perspectives on dyslexia: neurological, psychological and educational, and the implications of these perspectives for practice in schools.

Definitions and terminology

Until recently the most prevalent definition of dyslexia was that given below:

Dyslexia is a disorder manifested by difficulty in learning to read despite conventional instruction and sociocultural opportunity. It is dependent upon fundamental cognitive disabilities which are frequently of constitutional origin.

World Federation of Neurologists (1968)

This definition, however, has been subject to considerable criticism due to its vagueness and generality.

For example, what does 'conventional instruction' mean? The phrase 'sociocultural opportunity' is also open to interpretation. What are 'fundamental cognitive disabilities' and what is meant by 'constitutional origin' ?

These points have resulted in debate and controversy regarding the notions of dyslexia and specific learning difficulties and have been reflected in a number of educational reports. Examples are given below with reference to the Tizard and Warnock Reports.

Since the term 'Dyslexia' . . . used so very loosely . . . we think it would be better to adopt a more usefully descriptive term, specific reading difficulties to describe the problems of the small group of children whose reading abilities are significantly below the standards which their abilities in other spheres would lead one to expect.

Tizard Report (DES, 1972)

Although there are no agreed criteria for distinguishing those children with severe and long-term difficulties in reading, writing and spelling from others who may require remedial teaching in these areas, there are nevertheless children whose disabilities are marked but whose general ability is at least average and for whom distinctive arrangements are necessary.

Warnock Report (DES, 1978)

Both these reports suggest the use of caution in using the term dyslexia and in defining the population of children who experience these difficulties. While the reports do not deny the existence of children with specific learning difficulties in literacy, there is a reluctance to specify how one might attempt to identify this group except perhaps by the use of discrepancy criteria. The following examples from the Tizard and Warnock Reports highlight the emphasis placed on discrepancies between reading ability and other abilities. The reports suggest that *reading abilities are significantly below the standards which their abilities in other spheres would lead one to expect* (Tizard Report) *and disabilities (in literacy) are marked but general ability is at least average* (Warnock Report).

The reports themselves, by describing the difficulty in such a loose and vague manner, left more questions unanswered than answered and arguably set the scene for confusion and controversy, anomalies in regional education authority policies, disparate provision, and bewildered and anxious parents. This is indeed reflected in the studies which have followed focusing on policy, practice and provision (Pumfrey and Reason, 1991: Riddell, Duffield, Brown and Ogilvy, 1992) which illustrate the disparate views among different groups and the geographical and philosophical discrepancies which exist in relation to practice and provision.

The Dyslexia Institute (1989), however, provided an expanded and clearer definition which highlights the range of difficulties such children may experience.

Specific Learning Difficulties can be defined as organising or learning deficiencies which restrict the students' competencies in information processing, in motor skills and working memory, so causing limitations in some or all of the skills of speech, reading, spelling, writing, essay writing, numeracy and behaviour.

Dyslexia Institute (1989)

This is a much broader definition than that used by the World Federation of Neurologists (1968) and represents the generally broader concept of specific learning difficulties which is reflected in the wider range of resources and strategies now being suggested for children with specific learning difficulties.

This broader concept has provided the general model for the definition developed by the Moray House Centre for Specific Learning Difficulties which, following discussions with a wide group of professionals, conceptualises specific learning difficulties as follows:

Specific Learning Difficulties can be identified as distinctive patterns of difficulties, relating to the processing of information, within a continuum from very mild to extremely severe, which result in restrictions in literacy development and discrepancies in performances within the curriculum.

Moray House Centre for Specific Learning Difficulties (1993)

It is important to note that this definition suggests that although children may present different types of difficulties, there are distinctive patterns which suggest the presence of specific learning difficulties. It is important to appreciate that different pupils may show widely differing degrees of difficulty and that these should become evident in their performances and discrepancies within the curriculum. The patterns of difficulty, however, can be highlighted by different characteristics centring on the auditory/phonological, visual, motor and/or cognitive processing. Thus this definition emphasises the notion of constellations of dyslexia (Vail, 1993) and supports the view that different dyslexic children can display different patterns of difficulties.

Specific learning difficulties and dyslexia

Another recent trend is the merging of the two labels 'specific learning difficulties' and 'dyslexia'.

The definition of 'dyslexia' supported by the British Dyslexia Association (1989) is as follows:

Dyslexia can be defined as a specific difficulty in learning, constitutional in origin, in one or more areas of reading, spelling and written language which may be accompanied by difficulty in number work. It is particularly related to mastering and using written language (alphabetic, numerical and musical notation) although often affecting oral language to some degree.

This definition is quite closely related to that of specific learning difficulties previously offered by the Dyslexia Institute (1989), although it will be noted this definition makes reference to dyslexia being 'constitutional in origin' without defining what is meant by this phrase.

It has been recognised (Pumfrey and Reason, 1991) that the two concepts specific learning difficulties and dyslexia are becoming closer in interpretation; indeed the expansion of the two definitions has contributed to the two labels being used interchangeably. Hammill (1990) sees a consensus emerging within the field, although in a study of the literature he found eleven different definitions.

Irrespective of the manner in which 'dyslexia' or 'specific learning difficulties' may be conceptualised, defined or understood, such children have a significant special educational need, particularly in the acquisition of literacy. This is highlighted by the description of Special Educational Needs taken from the Education Act 1981:

A special educational need exists *where a child has a significantly greater difficulty in learning than the majority of children of his age or has a disability which either prevents or hinders him from making use of educational facilities of a kind generally provided in school.*

HMG (UK) (1981)

The educational implications of this can be wide ranging, depending on whether one views specific learning difficulties as a discrete entity or as a variation of normal reading difficulties. These differences can be reflected in the following contrasting views:

Children who experience difficulty in learning to read are frequently called dyslexic, but their difficulty does not arise because they are dyslexic . . . they are dyslexic because they cannot read . . . and therefore the cure for dyslexia is to learn to read.

Smith (1971)

Dyslexia is a discrete condition which cannot be regarded as a normal variation of reading performance.

Miles (1983)

Stanovich (1988) adopts the commonly held view that dyslexia is essentially a phonological deficit and that the variable severity of this definition creates a graded continuum of performance from poor reader to good reader.

Stanovich proposes a Phonological Core Variable Model which describes dyslexia as essentially a phonological difficulty which can be accompanied by secondary problems. The core problem, however, is a phonological one, although this can be seen within a continuum from, on the one hand a phonological difficulty as the core difficulty to, on the other hand, a 'garden variety poor reader' showing a 'host of cognitive deficits'.

Stanovich argues that this does not necessarily undermine the concept of dyslexia and he suggests that such a theory would produce 'galaxies of dyslexic and non-dyslexic readers' rather than discrete sub-groups. He concludes, therefore, that the concept of dyslexia exists and that it is different from 'garden variety' poor readers, although there may be common elements within both categories.

This view, however, can be challenged. McDougall, Ellis, Hulme and Monk (1994), who examined the reading characteristics of dyslexic and other groups of readers, found no evidence of a specific phonological deficit in dyslexic readers.

Perceptions of parents and professionals

The attitudes and perceptions which people bring to a task or profession is of significant importance, in this case to the educational progress of the child. The results of recent surveys which examine these issues hold more than a passing interest.

Parents

Extensive research (Pumfrey and Reason, 1991; Riddell, Duffield, Brown and Ogilvy, 1992) and increasing coverage in the media suggest that key elements relating to parents' attitudes and perceptions of specific learning difficulties are those of effective communication and guidance. The research conducted by Pumfrey and Reason (1991), mainly in England and Wales, found that the areas of frustration experienced by parents of dyslexic children concerned delays in identification and assessment, provision available and the shortage of teachers who had undertaken advanced courses of training in specific learning difficulties.

Parents were, however, quite realistic in their expectations and generally accepted that their child's progress would be slow in most cases, irrespective of where the child was educated (Pumfrey and Reason, 1991). Similarly, Scottish research conducted by Grampian Region (1987) showed that 75% of the parents of children with specific learning difficulties were realistic in their expectations and that 85% had accurate perceptions of their children's difficulties. This research found that parents and psychologists typically held similar views regarding the likely pace of progress and the most appropriate educational provision for individual children, although Thomson (1990) reports that parents often feel dissatisfied with the lack of follow-up communication after psychological assessment.

In their research project Riddell, Duffield, Brown and Ogilvy (1992) examined policy, practice and provision for specific learning difficulties in Scotland. Parents and parent representatives were among those interviewed. It was found that parents favoured the use of the term 'dyslexia' rather than 'specific learning difficulties' and also voiced concern that teachers were not as alert to early identification of specific learning difficulties as perhaps they should be. This consequently delayed formal assessment. The parents also believed that teachers lacked knowledge of specialised teaching methods and they (the parents) were not kept fully informed about the nature of their child's difficulties and the school's strategy in dealing with these difficulties. They also felt that their children received insufficient individual tuition.

There are issues stemming from the outcomes of these studies which underline the need for effective communication between all groups and individuals involved. It is interesting that, in the research conducted by Pumfrey and Reason (1991) and Riddell et al (1992), there are clear indications that parents preferred to use the term 'dyslexia' rather than 'specific learning difficulties'. The research indicates that this preferred use of the term 'dyslexia' by parents may be on grounds of social acceptability, or perhaps as a means to access resources. Effective communication could circumvent the desire for a label to access appropriate provision and resources. Recognising and discussing how the curriculum could be accessed to meet the child's needs could be a more effective strategy than a separate diagnosis by an expert from another body of professionals from outwith the educational authority, which can result in anxiety and confrontation between parents and school. It is important therefore that effective communication be established and maintained from a very early stage.

Teachers

There is a growing awareness among all sectors of the teaching profession of the problems associated with specific learning difficulties. This increased awareness, according to the United Kingdom Reading Association (Pumfrey and Reason, 1991) would be enhanced by linking research and teacher education; it could be further enhanced by multi-professional and parental collaboration, emphasising whole-school approaches to tackling the difficulties.

Research has, however, highlighted some confusion (among teachers) about definitions, assessment and teaching approaches. Reid (1990) found a high level of awareness among teachers regarding the problems associated with specific learning difficulties. The majority felt labels such as 'dyslexia' or 'specific learning difficulties' were useful in helping to provide the basis for a framework within which they could operate and devise individual programmes. Although the teachers in this study supported the principle of integration and adopted the concept of cooperative teaching, they still felt withdrawal from class and individual tuition were necessary for children with specific learning difficulties. They were, however, aware of the danger of creating an 'exclusive' role for some teachers and of highlighting a 'special' category of pupil.

The study conducted by Riddell, Duffield, Brown and Ogilvy (1992) indicated that the term 'specific learning difficulties' was accepted by most learning support teachers and two thirds used the term 'dyslexia' on some occasions. The responses from learning support teachers indicated that they perceived cooperative teaching and consultancy as the most important aspects of their role and that most of the provision for children with specific learning difficulties was provided within the mainstream class. There was, however, some withdrawal for individual tuition although this was more common in primary than secondary schools. This study also revealed that learning support teachers felt too many demands were being made on them and that they had to establish their own priorities in relation to limited resources and the wide range of special educational needs they encountered. This is consistent with the conclusions of a study of learning support teachers which examined role factors; considerable levels of role conflict, role ambiguity and role overload were reported by this sample of learning support teachers who experienced high levels of perceived stress in the implementation of their roles (Reid, 1991).

In relation to assessment, Pumfrey and Reason (1991) found some teachers placed great emphasis on looking for some kind of discrepancy in the learners' performances in classroom activity while others suggested the use of standardised tests. Others still were committed to curriculum-based assessment combined with qualitative error analysis.

This view is also supported by research in one Scottish region (Reid, 1989) where it was found that differences existed regarding methods of assessment and identification. In this study, half the educational psychologists felt assessment for specific learning difficulties should be curriculum-based although slightly more than half felt standardised tests would provide some useful information and should be considered as a starting point. As a follow up to this study, a series of workshops for psychologists and teachers was held. It highlighted some evidence of a mismatch between the expectations of teachers and that of educational psychologists (Reid, 1989). These included a lack of agreement regarding the criteria for identification of specific learning difficulties; teachers perceiving psychologists as 'back-up' persons who were capable of conducting individual assessments whilst psychologists preferred to operate on a consultancy basis with intervention being in the form of project work rather than on an individual basis. This confirms the change in emphasis of psychologists' working practices from individual child referrals to consultancy, preventative intervention and collaborative involvement with schools (O'Hagan and Swanson, 1983; Imich and Kerfoots, 1993).

An examination of the research, perceptions and practice evident within the field of specific learning difficulties highlights at least three general perspectives. The neurological perspective which focuses on the child; the psychological perspective which highlights how the child utilises capacities for learning, and the educational perspective which highlights curriculum access and provision as the important elements (see Fig. 1).

Neurological perspective

This perspective has generated an abundance of relevant research, despite some criticisms voiced against the neurological position (Whittaker, 1992). Some promising directions of research include studies in genetics (De Fries, 1991), hemispheric asymmetry and cerebral blood flow (Duane, 1993; Galaburda, 1993), residual primitive reflexes (Blyth, 1992), and aspects involving visual acuity and stability (Pavlidis, 1989; Stein, 1992). Galaburda's studies (1991,1993) reveal dyslexic brains are 'different' in relation to the pattern of cell organisation which occurs during the pre-natal period of cell migration. Some cells migrated to the 'wrong' area and thus affected reading development. Additionally, in these persons areas of the right hemisphere, which would influence visual, aesthetic, mathematical and mechanical abilities were proportionately larger. The influence of neurological aspects in relation to dyslexia is still an area of vigorous research and can provide pointers towards effective programmes. Examples of such programmes have been described by Dobie (1993) and Blyth (1992). These consist of a series of physical exercises which, according to Blyth, help to inhibit primitive reflexes and thus facilitate neuro-developmental progress which in turn facilitates skills in learning and literacy.

Psychological perspective

This perspective relates to how children process information. Cognitive aspects of learning which involve skills in attention, concentration, memory, phonological decoding, auditory and visual discrimination, automatization and problem solving are well documented in the literature (Seymour, 1987; Stanovich, 1992; De Bono, 1986 and Fawcett, 1989). The efficiency with which the child relates to stimuli is important and the use of skills with cognitive aspects such as memory and attention will have effects on the output whether in written work, speech or in reading or spelling. Inefficiency in the processing of information has been the focus of studies which have provided pointers for teaching programmes in relation to overlearning, phonological skills, sequential learning, study and thinking skills.

Educational perspective

This perspective adopts a curriculum centred approach and attempts to match the curriculum to the needs of the child irrespective of the difficulties displayed. There are many excellent examples of curriculum differentiation (Dodds, 1993; Russell, 1992) and of programmes and strategies (Barthorpe and Visser, 1991; Russell, 1993). The emphasis here is not on the child's deficits or difficulties but on adapting the delivery of the curriculum to suit the child. This does not mean that a different curriculum is offered – the curriculum content should be the same for all, but the means and mode of teaching used to achieve this will differ from child to child. It includes examination of the learning behaviour of the child, the learning styles and the error behaviour in the child's performances within the classroom (Clay, 1989; Keefe, 1987; Given, 1993).

Since the educational perspective attempts to ensure that the child has full access to the curriculum, teaching and learning usually occur within the mainstream classroom although specific programmes such as paired reading (Topping, 1992 and 1993) can provide an additional focus to help the child overcome a particular difficulty. This, however, should not be at the expense of, or a substitution for, any particular area of the curriculum.

Fig. 1

PERSPECTIVES OF SPECIFIC LEARNING DIFFICULTIES

PRODUCT   –   NEUROLOGICAL PERSPECTIVE

- Hemispheric Asymmetry
- Genetic Factors
- Cerebral Blood Flow
- Visual Instability
- Residual Primitive Reflexes
- Faulty Cell Migration

PROCESS   –   PSYCHOLOGICAL PERSPECTIVE

- Information Processing
- Phonological Coding
- Memory
- Attention/Concentration
- Laterality
- Metacognition

PROVISION   –   EDUCATIONAL PERSPECTIVE

- Curriculum Differentiation
- Curriculum Delivery
- Language Experience
- Peer Support
- Linking Assessment and Teaching

The three broad perspectives summarised in Figure 1 may be viewed in relation to aspects of the **product, process** and **provision** in dealing with difficulties associated with dyslexia. The neurological perspective refers to the **product** – what the child brings to the learning situation; the psychological perspective refers to the **process** – how the skills and abilities develop and are utilised; and the educational perspective links with the **provision** – how the learning and curriculum needs of the child are met by the educational system (Diniz and Reid, 1994). These perspectives also provide a general pointer to some of the conflict and controversy which are evident in this area, and which are supported in the responses from 'policy makers' in a research study looking at policy, practice and provision (Riddell, Duffield, Brown and Ogilvy, 1992). In this study some policy makers took an anti-categorisation stance, and viewed the educational task as providing curricula for all; they anticipated that skilled teaching and knowledge of the learner would facilitate curriculum differentiation and this would allow all learners, despite any specific difficulties they may display, to have full access to the curriculum. Other policy makers, however, recognised the need for specific approaches, because they saw 'specific learning difficulties' either within a continuum of learning difficulties or as a discrete difficulty; this group therefore justified additional focus being placed on supporting the learner, and the capacity and skills of the learner to process information which would enable at least some degree of curriculum access.

These variations and different opinions on the concept of dyslexia and suitable teaching approaches are also evidenced by research (Pumfrey and Reason, 1991) in which voluntary groups and associations were interviewed, in addition to professionals. It is quite interesting to look at some of the responses from these groups which highlight different perspectives.

We recommend that every effort be made to link research and teacher education with INSET related to the National Curriculum, and that there is increased awareness not only of what specific learning difficulties are like for the child and teacher, but of what can be done to adapt teaching to meet the special educational needs of such pupils.

United Kingdom Reading Association

We regard it as of vital importance that children with specific learning difficulties are given support both in the normal classroom and by having access to a support tutor outside the classroom.

British Dyslexia Association

The range of teaching provision to be made for students with specific learning difficulties will be wide and varied. For the majority of students this can be arranged and managed in the ordinary school. Others with greater difficulty will need to be withdrawn to a unit for small group teaching. A few will have such serious difficulties that they cannot sustain the broad curriculum of the ordinary school.

Dyslexia Institute

Differences, of course, can appear within the same group of professionals. This is quite obvious in the following two responses from educational psychologists in the same piece of research (Pumfrey and Reason, 1991). The responses were in relation to assessment for specific learning difficulties.

I feel very strongly that an individual test of intelligence should be used . . . It is not possible to identify all pupils with specific learning difficulties on the basis of attainments only.

I am looking for performance discrepancies rather than hypothetical abilities.

Pumfrey and Reason, 1991

This national enquiry highlighted some of the differences which are evident among groups of professionals and groups of parents in areas related to definitions, assessment and teaching of children with specific learning difficulties.

Despite this the situation is far from doom and gloom. Collaboration between educational authorities, schools and parents now appears to be much closer than before although tensions are clearly evident. Riddell et al (1992) identified a number of such tensions (see Fig. 2).

Fig. 2

SPECIFIC LEARNING DIFFICULTIES – AREAS OF CONFLICT AND TENSION

1   Friction between competing policies which reflect different ideological stances.
2   Economic argument that education authorities have responsibilities and concern for all children.
3   Nature of specific learning difficulty.
4   Recognition of specific learning difficulty.
5   What constitutes effective provision.
6   Conflict of emotions between interest groups.

Source: *Specific Learning Difficulties Policy, Practice and Provision*
Riddell, Duffield, Brown and Ogilvy, (1992)

Their research has a number of implications, including the need for clear operational definitions of specific learning difficulties to enhance an awareness of the phenomenon. It was clear that confusion and uncertainties exist with the result that teachers, and in some cases specialist teachers, are uncertain of 'appropriate identification and assessment procedures'. Other aspects of note include the worrying practice of late identification and the restrictive use of assessment strategies which provide a rather narrow focus on the whole area of assessment. The research also stressed the need for evaluative studies in order to gather data on examples of practice which appear to be effective.

In relation to provision, not all schools clamoured to utilise the resources and expertise in the specialised reading centres. Some schools were regular users of the centre, other schools not at all. One must ask the question – why ? In other words, how did the schools who did not use the centre deal with the difficulty? It is unlikely that they had no children on their roll with specific learning difficulties. This type of information would be of enormous value. Hard data and qualitative studies are required on the effectiveness of all types of programmes and provision, including those used in mainstream classes.

Above all, this research highlighted the need for training both during initial teacher training and for practising and experienced teachers. Although there has been some progress in recent years, there is still some way to go before all class teachers are aware of the needs of children with specific learning difficulties, and are able to deploy appropriate support strategies.

The responses from both the Pumfrey and Reason study and the Scottish Research (Riddell, Duffield, Brown and Ogilvy, 1992) do seem to suggest that much still needs to be achieved in the area of early identification and preventative intervention. These aspects will be considered in subsequent chapters in this Handbook. It seems also that evaluative studies are still required in relation to effective practice. No single programme, assessment tool or education provision can be said to hold all the answers to the phenomenon of specific learning difficulties.

The following chapters will therefore outline a variety and range of approaches and perspectives. They will emphasise the need to perceive dyslexic children as individuals, and dyslexia as a learning difficulty which requires special consideration to achieve the desirable aim of a *curriculum for all*.

Chapter 2

The acquisition of literacy

There is no one method, medium, approach, device or philosophy that holds the key to the process of learning to read.

Bullock Report, 1975

Introduction

WHAT is reading? This question, despite its apparent simplicity, can provide some insight into how reading is perceived by the learner, and some answers as to why, for a significant number, the acquisition of reading skills is an arduous and sometimes deflating process.

This chapter will examine the issue, *What is reading?* Analyse the difficulties some dyslexic children have with reading and suggest how reading can be made more accessible to them.

The same piece of text can relate a different message to different readers. This is illustrated in the text on page 16 (see Fig. 3). It is clearly possible for two readers to extract different meanings from this same piece of text. Both are reading, but they may obtain different messages from the same print. In the process of reading, the reader interprets the text and the text (or the print) relates a message to the reader.

Fig. 3: Text

PACKING FOR THE FAMILY HOLIDAY

Everything had to be in the right place – nothing could be forgotten, otherwise mother would be angry. Even the shirts, blouses and bed linen had to be folded. Just as well this does not happen a lot. True, people will be inspecting it but they are not interested in whether the garments are correctly folded. Naturally, everything had to be cleaned and dusted – the whole house from top to bottom and, of course, the whole family would need to be on their best behaviour. Politeness was to be the order of the day, no speaking out of turn. This episode really was going to be fun!.

SELLING OUR HOUSE

Everything had to be in the right place – nothing could be forgotten, otherwise mother would be angry. Even the shirts, blouses and bed linen had to be folded. Just as well this does not happen a lot. True, people will be inspecting it but they are not interested in whether the garments are correctly folded. Naturally, everything had to be cleaned and dusted – the whole house from top to bottom and, of course, the whole family would need to be on their best behaviour. Politeness was to be the order of the day, no speaking out of turn. This episode really was going to be fun!

The above texts serve to underline the interactive nature of reading. This interactive aspect is extremely important as it combines the reader's background experience and previous knowledge with the 'new' text to be read. This interaction provides the reader with meaning and interpretation. Reading, therefore, is an interaction of previous knowledge involving the use of semantic and syntactic cues and accuracy in the decoding of print. It is important that in teaching reading all these aspects are considered. It is likely the child with specific learning difficulties will find this interactive process difficult as his efforts and cognitive capacities are directed to either mechanically decoding the print or obtaining the meaning from print – simultaneous interaction of these processes is not easily accomplished.

The two key elements of reading therefore are the understanding of print and the message (purpose) of the print (Fig. 4). They both have to be carefully considered in the selection and development of reading programmes and strategies for children with specific learning difficulties.

Fig. 4: Reading skills

UNDERSTANDING OF PRINT	PURPOSE OF PRINT
• Alphabet skills • Organisation of letters and words • Visual features of letters and words • Phonological skills • Word rules • Understanding of syntax	• Semantic understanding • Vocabulary skills • Use of inferences • Comprehension skills • Prediction skills • Concept and schema building

How do children perceive reading? This question was put to a sample of children aged between 7 and 10 years (Reid, 1993) and the responses illustrate the different perceptions and beliefs children hold of reading.

The main dichotomy drawn from the responses related to aspects of the **task** of reading rather than the **function**. Those who focused on the 'task' highlighted aspects such as the decoding of words and the learning of these words. A typical response from the 'task' group was 'Reading is when you look at words and you say them in your mind'. The 'function' group recognised reading as an activity from which they derived pleasure and the purpose of reading was to obtain meaning from text.

Why do children perceive reading in such vastly different ways? Does the answer to this question lie in the method and strategy used to teach children reading? Or perhaps the answer to this is related more to the child's skills and abilities and how easy and accessible learning to read is for the child. Whichever way one might be inclined to argue, there is something fundamentally amiss if the child perceives reading as an arduous and laborious exercise – a product of classroom routine and relentless practice. If this is the child's perception of reading, then surely the real meaning of reading is lost and books then become a confusing contradiction between the pain and pleasure of acquiring knowledge.

Children with specific learning difficulties seldom have a perception of reading which reveals the pleasure of books and the real meaning of print. They often perceive reading as a dreaded exercise, calling for skills in precision and accuracy – an exercise which appears to stretch their natural and accessible competencies.

The challenge for teachers of children with specific learning difficulties is to teach the basic fundamental structure and framework for the understanding of print, but at the same time to provide an enriched and meaningful language experience to facilitate and encourage access to books, thus helping the child gain some real appreciation of the message and pleasure of books.

The facilitation of reading

The skills used in reading are little different from many of the skills used in other aspects of learning.

For example, linguistic, visual and auditory skills are all essential for access to reading. These skills are also used in other learning activities such as speech, listening, creative and visual work. These skills develop independently of reading because they are used in learning activities other than reading. This does not necessarily imply that coaching in reading sub-skills promotes proficiency in the practice of reading. Rather the view could be held that actual practice of reading fosters reading skills and therefore reading practice is essential to develop skills as a reader (Smith, 1983; Clay, 1989).

An examination of the linguistic, visual and auditory factors associated with reading reveals the areas of difficulty dyslexic children meet when learning to read (see Figs. 5 and 6).

Fig. 5

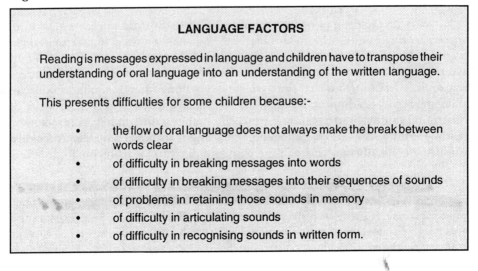

LANGUAGE FACTORS

Reading is messages expressed in language and children have to transpose their understanding of oral language into an understanding of the written language.

This presents difficulties for some children because:-

- the flow of oral language does not always make the break between words clear
- of difficulty in breaking messages into words
- of difficulty in breaking messages into their sequences of sounds
- of problems in retaining those sounds in memory
- of difficulty in articulating sounds
- of difficulty in recognising sounds in written form.

Fig. 6

VISUAL FACTORS

Some of the most important visual factors include:

- recognition of visual cues
- left to right orientation
- recognition of word patterns
- recognition of letter and letter shapes

AUDITORY FACTORS

These include:

- recognition of letter sounds
- recognition of sounds and letter groups or patterns
- sequencing of sounds
- corresponding sounds to visual stimuli
- discriminating sounds from other sounds
- discriminating sounds within words

Many of the above visual and auditory aspects of reading do not develop spontaneously in children with specific learning difficulties. These skills need to be taught, and usually in a sensitive and structured manner.

Lovegrove (1993) highlights the importance of visual factors in poor readers. He comments on the two visual sub-systems – the transient and the sustained systems. The transient system which is sensitive to contrast and more suited to identifying the general form of objects has a fast transmission time, and deals with peripheral vision. The sustained system is sensitive to black and white, detailed stimuli and is slow to change. It has a slow transmission time and deals with the central vision.

The key feature in relation to these systems is that both systems inhibit each other – that means that they do not operate simultaneously. Lovegrove's studies show that poor readers have a weak transient system and a normal sustained one. This results in interference between the two systems and has implications for the processing of visual stimuli in reading, since reading involves the synchronisation

---

of both transient and sustained systems. This may therefore have implications for masking parts of a page which are not being focused on at that time. It certainly has implications for allowing sufficient processing time for poor readers.

Reaซ.ng is essentially therefore an integrative activity and these skills need to be acquired in an integrated manner. One such documented approach (Reason and Boote, 1986) appears to do this by identifying stages in developing reading skills:

> pre-reading; beginning to read;
> intermediate; mastering of basic reading skills.

For example language development is considered and integrated. It is provided with a focus throughout by integrating it with concepts, visual word recognition and phonics at all the stages considered by Reason and Boote, above.

Reading development

Frith (1985) identifies the following developmental stages in the acquisition of reading skills.

Logographic stage

The child makes use of visual recognition of overall word patterns – thus he/she is able to recognise words as units. This may not necessarily mean the child can reproduce these words accurately (this would be an alphabetic skill) and as a result the child can easily misspell words they are able to read.

Alphabetic stage

The child tackles the sound/symbol correspondence and one can identify if children possess this one-to-one correspondence between the letter and the sound.

Orthographic stage

The child possesses and comprehends knowledge of letter-sound relationship as well as structure and meaning. Thus as well as being aware of rules the child can use cues and context.

It has been argued that children with specific learning difficulties can find the alphabetic stage difficult because the sound/symbol correspondence rests to a great extent on skills in phonics. Before children, therefore, acquire a competent understanding of the relationship between letter units (graphemes) and sound units (phonemes) they need a degree of phonological awareness (Frith, 1980; Snowling, 1987).

Frith (1985) puts forward the view that writing and the desire to write helps to enhance the alphabetic stage of reading because spelling is linked more directly to the alphabetic principle and letter-sound relationships. This view is also supported by the work of Bradley and Bryant (1991) who found that beginner readers in the process of acquiring the skills of the alphabetic stage use visual strategies for reading but phonological strategies for spelling. In their study children read correctly words which were visually distinctive such as 'school' and 'light' but failed to read simpler words like 'bun' and 'sit'. Yet these children tended to spell correctly words they had failed to read such as 'bun' and 'sit' and spell incorrectly words they had read by focusing on the visual patterns (school, light).

The alphabetic reader according to Snowling (1987) may also find difficulty reading words which have inconsistent orthographic patterns but which are pronounced in the same way. Similarly, irregular words are **mis**pronounced e.g. 'island' would be pronounced 'is-land'.

This developmental aspect of reading serves to illustrate the importance of the procedure of error analysis and identifying the type and pattern of errors made by children with difficulties in reading.

Seymour (1993) highlights individual variations and reaction times among dyslexics. Referring to a number of studies, he argues that the variations among dyslexics in visual, semantic and phonological processing can be partly accounted for by the different reaction times in the processing of information.

Dreary (1993) identifies the problem of rapid integration of sensory information and relates visual and auditory 'inspection time' processing speed. He argues that children who require less inspection time in tasks score higher in verbal tasks and so highlights the correlation between verbal ability and auditory inspection time.

Reading in practice and models of reading

One's reading improves every time one reads. (Marie Clay)

This comment implies that the important aspect of reading is the experience of reading and of language. While this is a valid point and language enrichment and reading experience can increase interest, skill and motivation for reading, it can only effectively do so once the child has reached a certain level of reading. Indeed Marie Clay argues that there is a reading level below which the child may lose his skill if he is not provided with the opportunity of the experience of reading and of language. Clay argues that this is around the level of 10-11 year old level of reading achievement. Thus it is necessary for children below this level of achievement to practise reading every day or they may lose some of their reading skill.

Reading models

There are two principal models of the reading process. These have come to be known as 'Bottom-up' (i.e. data driven) and 'Top-down' (concept driven) (see Fig. 7).

Fig. 7

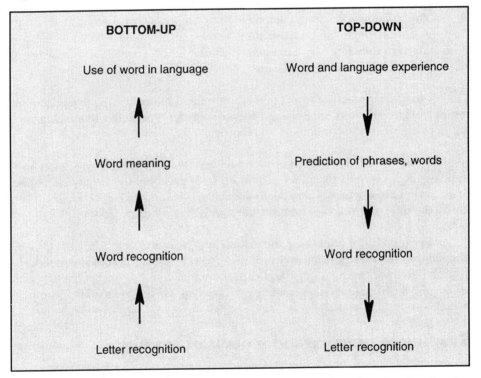

BOTTOM-UP	TOP-DOWN
Use of word in language	Word and language experience
↑	↓
Word meaning	Prediction of phrases, words
↑	↓
Word recognition	Word recognition
↑	↓
Letter recognition	Letter recognition

The 'Bottom-up' model suggests that first we look at the stimulus, i.e. the components of the letters and then move to the meaning.

This emphasises the need to translate:

- written symbols to sound

- sound to meaning.

'Bottom-up' theorists argue that the brain attends to every bit of available information, thus we read letter-by-letter so quickly that it becomes automatic.

The 'Top-down' model is concept driven. The reader attempts to absorb the meaning of the text from the cues which are available. These cues can include:

- the context of the passage being read:

    this relates to the syntactic context, i.e. the structure of the sentence, and semantic context, i.e. the anticipated meaning of the passage;

- the graphic information available:

    i.e. what the word looks like, the reader anticipates the word or sentence from these descriptive cues (see Fig. 8).

Fig. 8

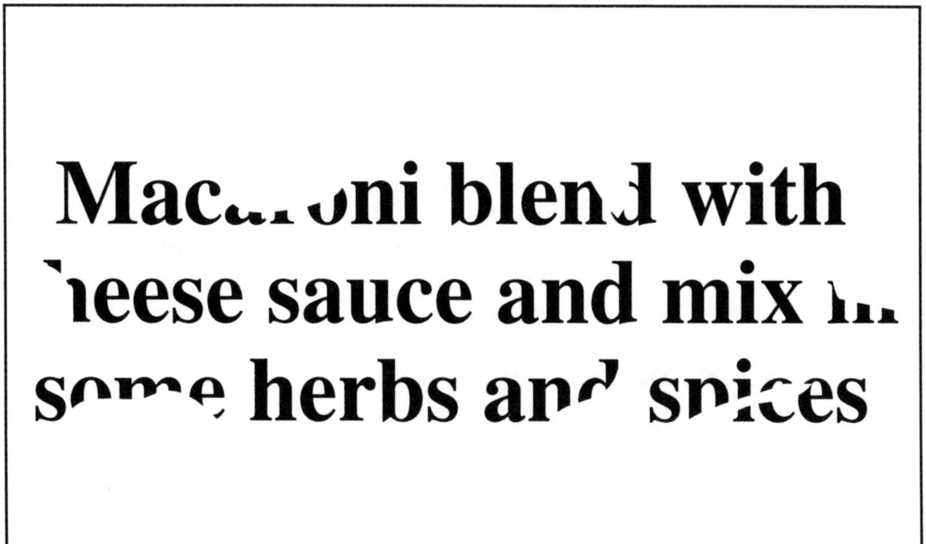

Mac... oni blend with 'ieese sauce and mix h.. some herbs and spices

The interactive compensatory model

Both 'Top-down' and 'Bottom-up' models have limitations in terms of an understanding of the reading process because clearly readers draw on both these processes when reading. The Interactive Compensatory Model attempts to explain how these dual processes work.

This model acknowledges that reading involves recognising words based on information provided simultaneously from both the text and the reader, and as proposed by Stanovich (1980) focuses on the following assumptions:

- readers use information simultaneously from different levels and do not necessarily begin at either the graphic (Bottom-up) or the contextual (Top-down) level;
- during their development of reading skills, readers may rely more heavily on some levels of processing than on others, e.g. they may use context to greater or lesser extents;
- the reader's weaknesses are compensated for by his/her strengths.

Stanovich casts doubt on the view that good readers use the Top-down model more than poor readers. Indeed research shows that good readers pay more attention to graphic detail and poor readers rely more on context. Thus higher level processing of text does not necessarily need the completion of all lower levels of processing.

Stanovich's model, therefore, takes account of the fact that many poor readers have developed strategies for compensating for their information processing difficulties. Clay (1979) suggests that the cues from language are supplemented by learning in other areas such as letter knowledge, word knowledge and letter-sound associations.

Considerations on reading models

Models of reading need to take into account the following:

Print
- logographic stage
- alphabetic stage
- orthographic stage

Language

- communicative aspects of print
- structure of language
- meaning

Context

- prediction
- life experiences
- knowledge
- pleasure and purpose

Most models of reading are derivations from the 'Top-down' or 'Bottom-up' processes.

Holistic nature of reading

It should be recognised, however, that reading is a holistic activity. This means that in order to engage successfully in the reading process the learner must utilise a range of cognitive and learning skills. Thus reading depends on:

- the use of skills associated with the verbal and auditory domain, such as language knowledge and language use;
- perceptual and spatial domain, in relation to letter and word recognition;
- segmentation of words and sentences;
- contextual factors which may relate to the reader's previous knowledge and cognitive development.

The reader not only reads for meaning and for accuracy, but also reads for 'thought'. This means that aspects including personality, experience and imagination are all related to the holistic learning activity of reading.

For the teacher the implication of this is that the learner needs to be considered as an individual in relation to reading. It is important to ensure that the general context is appropriate and suited to the individual's style and interests. Interest level, organisation of learning and careful balance between group and individual attention are important factors in the development and integration of skills necessary for reading.

The most popular models used by teachers in the teaching of reading include the following:

- psycholinguistic
- phonic
- look and say
- language experience
- psycholinguistic model.

Advocates of this approach suggest that, when reading in context, readers use syntactic and semantic cues to help them predict forthcoming words – thus decoding is less relevant to reading than more general language aspects. Goodman (1976) put forward the theory that reading is essentially 'hypothesis testing' and the reader attempts either to confirm or to disprove the prediction. Goodman advocates that skilled readers are better at using context in a predictive way than beginner readers. Thus this model of reading views the process as a 'Top-down' one relying on a knowledge base rather than on the data-driven view of 'Bottom-up' theorists.

Phonic model

The phonic method highlights the importance of phonology and the sounds of letters and letter combinations.

There are a number of structured phonic programmes in existence which can teach children to distinguish the 44 phonemes or sound units of English, by using a variety of strategies. These strategies may include colour-coding and marks to indicate short or long sounds.

Although phonic programmes are structured, and structure is beneficial for children with specific learning difficulties, there are also difficulties associated with such programmes. The most important of these include the possibility that:

- they may increase the burden on children's short and long term memories by increasing what the child needs to remember;
- there are still words which need to be taught as sight vocabulary because they do not fall into the 'sound blending' category, such as 'one' and 'many'.

Phonic methods can help children who have an obvious difficulty in mastering and remembering sound blends and vowel digraphs and have difficulty in synthesising them to make a word. At the same time they present additional learning which may be seen to be meaningless and out of context. Some difficulty may be identified in merging the two components, i.e. knowledge of sound and knowledge of language, together to facilitate a meaningful reading experience.

Snowling (1993) distinguishes between phonological dyslexia, where children have poor processing skills and poor phonological representations, and surface dyslexia, where children have adequately specified phonological representations but can still display phonological processing problems. The difference between phonological and surface dyslexia rests on the severity of the reader's phonological problems and how the reader uses the strategies and skills available to him/her.

Look and say model

Look and say methods emphasise exposure to print on the grounds that children will become familiar with words and build up a sight vocabulary with increased exposure. The emphasis is therefore on meaningful units of language rather than sounds of speech.

This type of method therefore requires attractive books which can become progressively more demanding. The use of flash-cards and pictures can be used in the initial stages. The method, however, assumes a good memory for shapes of letters and words as well as the ability to master many of the irregularities of spelling and sound-symbol correspondence. This, of course, may be difficult for children with dyslexic difficulties, particularly since their memory may be weak and can rapidly become overloaded. Some elements of the phonic approaches can accompany most look and say methods.

Language experience model

Language experience methods focus on the use of language, both oral and written, as an aid to learning to read through various modes of language enrichment. This helps the reader develop important language concepts and schemata which in turn help to bring meaning to print. Although the child may have a decoding problem the experience gained in language can help to compensate for this and bring some meaning to the text.

This model engages the child in the process of going from thought to speech and then to encoding in print and from print to reading.

The reading debate

The teaching of reading has been subject to historical debate. Theories and methods have been reviewed and revised often following the revelation of dismal and disappointing attainment scores in national surveys. The 'Head Start Programme' in the United States and the resultant DISTAR approach to the teaching of reading, emanated from such concerns and alarm over low standards of literacy.

The issue of reading standards is still a national concern and a national debate. Turner (1991) cites the concern over reading standards as a phenomenon which can be largely explained by the trend from phonic instruction to that of whole language, language experience and 'real' books. This argument gains some credence from the widely accepted view that beginning readers need to possess at least a basic knowledge of phonological skills, before they can effectively benefit from enrichment through literacy and associated language activities.

Wray (1991), however, challenges this view by arguing that the evidence for suggesting that a decline in reading standards is due to the move towards a whole-language approach is not strong. He suggests that the whole-language movement is not practised widely enough to account for such a decline in reading standards. He further suggests that the criteria for assessing reading attainment needs to be questioned since it raises the fundamental point 'What is reading?'

At the same time it might be argued 'What is whole-language?' Bergeron (1990) attempted to obtain a consensual definition of whole-language from the literature and found whole-language was defined as an approach, a philosophy, an orientation, a theory, a theoretical orientation, a programme, a curriculum, a perspective on education and an attitude of mind. It is difficult either to promote or to criticise a movement when it is so loosely defined.

To attempt to find the positive aspects of this loose interpretation called 'whole-language' one can look for some common factors in Bergeron's responses. Adams (1991) argues that some commonalities include:

- construction of meaning from text
- developing and explaining the functional dimensions of text
- pupil-centred classrooms
- integration of language arts.

These points can be complementary to any education system and might be described as the flip side of the whole-language movement. The other side, promoted by Smith (1971,1973) and Goodman (1973) suggests that skilful readers do not process individual letters, spelling-sound translations are irrelevant for reading, and it is therefore not necessary to teach spellings and sounds.

Smith (1971) therefore argues that phonics teaching should not be emphasised because the child has to learn phonic rules by himself and can only do this through experience in reading. Thus phonics teaching, according to Smith, can lead to too deliberate decoding and as a result the meaning of the text will be lost. He argues that decoding is a classroom induced behaviour, not a natural one, and that skilled and even beginning readers only use it to a limited extent.

There are considerable arguments against this (Adams, 1991; Turner, 1991) centering on the need for children to read words before they can obtain meaning from a text. Adams (1991) in fact argues that automaticity develops from actually reading words and not by ignoring or guessing them.

Smith, (1993), however, illustrates how reading in fact relies on a combination of word-centred and meaning-centred approaches and therefore assessment of reading clearly requires to account for these two aspects, in order fully to assess reading and evaluate reading programmes. Smith in fact contends that the important point is that a reading approach should be clear and have a 'firm sense of purpose'. Teachers should be aware of the approach they are using and why they are using it.

Bryant (1994) contends that both forms of linguistic knowledge, constituent sounds and language experience, play an important part in children's acquisition and development of reading and writing skills. He reports on a longitudinal study in which children's scores in phonological tasks predicted the progress they made in learning about letter-sound associations, and that scores in semantic and syntactic tasks were good predictors of children's ability to use context and decipher difficult words within a meaningful context. Bryant concludes that each form of linguistic knowledge makes an independent and specific contribution to the reading process, particularly since the children's scores in the phonological task did not predict the children's success in the use of context, and similarly scores in the semantic and syntactic tasks were not significant in predicting phonological skills.

Clearly a balanced approach is necessary when looking at the teaching of reading. Both the phonic method and the 'whole-language' movement have many commendable aspects – both should be utilised in relation to the needs of the individual reader.

Individual preferences

Some mention should be made of the differences which exist between children and particularly groups of children with specific learning difficulties. Stanovich argues for the notion of 'galaxies' of dyslexics, implying that it is not necessarily a 'unitary condition' but a cluster of symptoms which produce different 'galaxies of dyslexics'. Some support for this view is found in the work of Snowling (1990) who discusses two distinct patterns of reading performance

An avoidance of phonological strategies

This group have difficulty with grammatical endings such as -ing, -ly, -ed, BUT they are able to read familiar words with meaning. They may make visual errors for example reading 'cheery' as 'cherry' and may also make derivational errors such as reading 'appeared' as 'appearance'. This group has been described as showing 'phonological developmental dyslexia '(Seymour, 1984).

The reliance on phonological strategies

The children in this group place a heavy reliance on reading by sound and thus are able to read regular sounding words such as 'fresh', 'dance' and 'treat' more easily than irregular words such as 'broad', 'pint' and 'great'.

For example, 'broad' may be read as 'brode' and 'great' as 'greet'.

This group has been likened to 'surface' dyslexia in adults (Coltheart, 1983) or of morphemic dyslexics (Seymour, 1984).

Snowling (1993), however, argues that although children from both these groups are clearly slower in developing literacy skills and thus have specific learning difficulties, their development seems to be progressing 'along normal lines'.

Phonics and phonology

Snowling highlights the importance of making explicit the nature of the phonological deficits displayed by individual children. For example, some children can have difficulties with phoneme awareness, phoneme segmentation and verbal memory which affect the manner in which their whole phonological system can be accessed.

These difficulties can be observed by examining children's spelling errors. Children with short-term memory problems may write down the last phoneme first, whilst children with difficulty in phoneme segmentation often have difficulty with words of more than three syllables and therefore segment syllables inappropriately. Snowling argues that the extent and the severity of a child's phonological difficulty will greatly influence the development of that child's reading and spelling.

It should be noted, however, that the possession of adequate phonological skills does not necessarily ensure that reading and spelling will be successfully acquired. Snowling argues that in some cases superior decoding can be a hindrance because some children may rely too heavily on letter-sound rules which can produce excellent decoding of single words but may prevent reading with understanding.

Children with specific learning difficulties often find considerable difficulty in mastering the use of phonics and in remembering phonic rules. While it is necessary to provide some structured teaching in the use of phonics, too heavy a reliance on this approach can be counter-productive, since it encourages the use of just one language cue system – the grapho-phonic system, and this may make the reading for meaning difficult.

Hulme (1993) argues that speech rate and phonological awareness independently offer significant predictors of reading ability. Speech rate in fact, according to Hulme, is a better predictor than memory span performance. Of the phonological awareness tasks, phoneme deletion, that is identifying a word from another word, e.g. 'ice' from 'nice' was the best predictor of reading ability.

Reading strategies

Context

The art of becoming a fluent reader lies in learning to rely less and less on information from the eyes.   Frank Smith

Readers can utilise two principal types of context

- **Syntactic context**
  i.e. the grammatical structure of sentences and clues from prefixes, punctuation, word endings and word order;

- **Semantic context**
  i.e. the meaning of words and the meaningful relations between words.

Contextual cues can be of considerable benefit to the learner. Such cues can be seen in the form of syntactic and semantic context.

Syntactic context helps the reader predict the written word. If the child is reading only key words he will not be able to draw on syntactic context for meaning. Fig. 9 below illustrates the importance of syntactic context.

Fig. 9

This is how the billboard on the newsagent's street-stand may read. It can be read easily because the vocabulary is simple; but the phrase is lacking in syntactic cues, e.g. does it mean 'two raiders in bank robbery' or 'two banks have been robbed'? The lack of syntax may therefore change the meaning. If the reader is not competent at reading all the words, then some of the syntactic cues could be lost. This could result in the reader being deprived of some essential semantic cue, consequently restricting meaning and comprehension.

For many readers, therefore, a sentence from a newspaper article would be easier to process than the headline of the article. This is because:
- the headline would have no developed context to provide the reader with some clues;
- often headlines use 'eye-catching' phrases and do not utilise grammatical structure so the reader cannot rely on syntactic cues.

Semantic context relates to the meaning of words and how they convey messages. This acts as a powerful aid to reading and many readers with poor decoding skills can rely, perhaps too much, on the use of semantic context. Using inferences and even accurate guessing can be a powerful aid to dealing with the written word. It is important, therefore, that learners develop skills in using inferences and identifying the main theme and points in a particular story. The use of Schema (see Chapter 12) is a useful strategy for improving semantic context. Simple exercises such as the one below can help develop semantic context.

Fig. 10

THE BLUE BUS DROVE INTO THE G.........A.......E.

THE PEN HAD NO I........

In these examples the learner has to infer the correct response from the semantic context.

Context therefore as a reading strategy can be important and is evident in the following ways:

- within the sentence, i.e. before and after the word being read;
- within the text, i.e. before and after the sentence being read;
- within the reader, i.e. entire store of knowledge and experience.

To utilise fully the benefits of contextual reading it is also important for the reader to have a stock of sight words in order that the context can be accurately obtained. It has been argued, for example, by the proponents of the language experience approach, that instead of helping children build up a stock of sight words in order to read, perhaps teaching should be directed to help children read in order to build up a stock of sight words. This would mean that sight words can be built up gradually within the context of reading itself.

A classic dilemma is exemplified here between encouraging, indeed insisting on, reading accuracy of all the words, and accepting the accurate reading of the key words, which should be sufficient through the use of semantic cues for comprehension acquisition. The reading of every word, although it may help the reader obtain the full use of the benefits of syntactic cues, can restrict the reader's use of prediction and inferences because attention and concentration are absorbed in accurate decoding. Although accuracy may help aid comprehension, an understanding of the text is possible without full accuracy. Therefore if the child has difficulty with accuracy, it is important that efficient use of semantic context is encouraged, although in the pursuit of this accuracy should not be totally ignored, but carefully considered alongside the need for efficient use of the semantic cues available.

Contextual strategies can be summarised thus:
- words are easier to identify in context than in isolation;
- beginning readers can often identify words in context that they cannot identify in isolation;
- to identify words we use preceding syntactic and semantic cues to predict what might be coming next;
- grapho/phonic cues can help to identify words;
- syntactic and semantic context can help to confirm or correct these identifications;
- efficient readers use a maximum of context and a minimum of visual information.

Conclusion

This chapter has looked at some principles in the acquisition of literacy and has examined a variety of reading approaches by discussing some of the problems children with specific learning difficulties may display in relation to reading. Since the concept of dyslexia is essentially a multi-faceted one with neurological, psychological and educational perspectives, it follows that the teaching of reading should be flexible and should consider the child's learning difficulties and preferences, in the educational context. In the next section it will be argued that assessment is essentially hypothesis generating, so that teaching interventions need to be designed, tried, evaluated, revised and tried again (Smith, 1993). Clearly no one approach can be singled out and a combination of methods involving the teaching of sight words, phonics and context is preferable. At the same time one must also look at what the child brings to the situation and have some knowledge of the child's background knowledge and preferred learning styles and strategies. All of these aspects are important to facilitate the acquisition of literacy.

Section 2 –

Assessment

Chapter 3

Aims and rationale

Introduction

THE PROCESS of identifying and assessing specific learning difficulties is a matter of some debate (Pumfrey and Reason, 1991). This, however, should not necessarily prevent the teacher from identifying those children whose literacy problems are severe, unusual and unexpected. There are various identification and assessment strategies which can be used by the teacher, some of which will be discussed in the next chapter. It is, however, useful to reflect on some issues relating to identification and assessment and how these may influence assessment outcomes. Before examining these it is worthwhile to reflect on the overall aims of conducting an assessment for specific learning difficulties. There are a variety of reasons why an assessment should be undertaken. It may be to identify the appropriate level of text and learning materials for the child, or to diagnose a difficulty or perhaps to review progress. Whatever the reason it is important to have clear aims when conducting an assessment.

Fig. 11 below highlights some of these aims.

Fig. 11

AIMS OF ASSESSMENT

- identification of the learner's general strengths and weaknesses;
- an indication of the learner's current level of performance in attainments;
- an explanation for the learner's lack of progress;
- identification of aspects of the learner's performance in reading, writing and spelling, which may typify a 'pattern of errors';
- identification of specific areas of competence;
- an understanding of the student's learning style;
- an indication of aspects of the curriculum which may interest and motivate the learner.

In some cases the aim of the assessment may be to confirm what the teacher already suspects, for example by identifying areas of competence. It may already be obvious to the teacher that the child is quite proficient in, for example, oral communication skills, but an assessment may still be worthwhile since it can reveal additional competences which have not been obvious in the day-to-day work in the class. The child may well be proficient in oral communication skills, but not have appropriate opportunity to display these skills. The assessment may therefore identify aspects of the learner's cognitive functioning or performances in the curriculum which need some attention in order for the student's abilities to be fully utilised.

Children's strengths and weaknesses may be obvious to the class teacher who is in daily contact with the child and who can readily assess the particular areas of the curriculum with which the child has difficulty or indeed those areas which can be coped with comfortably; but the assessment should also reveal **why** the child is coping or is not coping with a particular piece of work.

The assessment can, therefore, hope both to uncover some explanation for children's difficulties and to look for particular patterns, such as errors, which seem to be predominantly due to visual or auditory difficulties. These may be identified as a specific pattern. The unearthing of a pattern of difficulties can help the teacher decide on the nature of the child's difficulty and so can assist in the planning of appropriate programmes of work.

Assessment, however, should aim not only to assess the child, but also to assess the curriculum to analyse which factors motivate the child and help to promote development in thinking and progress in attainments. Similarly it is important to analyse the child's learning style, looking at how the learner relates to the classroom, the task and the curriculum in general. All children have a preferred style of learning. The research studies which have been conducted and replicated (Keefe, 1988; Dunn and Dunn, 1991 and 1992) seem to indicate that learning styles analyses can help to answer the important question – Why is this child not performing?

The key questions in relation to assessment relate to the what, why, how and the effect of assessment.

What?

What aspects of the child's cognitive abilities or curriculum performance are to be assessed?

There is a fairly long-standing debate regarding the role of sub-skills of reading and their importance in relation to the actual process and product of reading (Smith, 1988; Seymour, 1987). Irrespective of the particular standpoint which is adopted, it may be necessary to examine the development of some specific sub-skills of reading, such as auditory or visual discrimination, letter recognition and phonological awareness in order to provide some insight into a diagnosis of the child's difficulties. Such a diagnosis can provide pointers to the child's strengths and weaknesses and consequently can help to direct the teacher to preferred learning strategies and appropriate teaching material. There is also considerable debate in relation to the whole question of assessing ability, the role of IQ in assessment and the use of IQ tests. IQ tests aim to measure a child's intellectual functioning, a measure which is often misused by suggesting that IQ is predictive of the child's potential. The research evidence on this is inconclusive and some doubt must be cast on any discrepancy between IQ and attainments as evidence that the child has a specific learning difficulty (Stanovich, 1991).

Siegal (1989) argues that the discrepancy definition between achievement and intelligence which has traditionally been of significance to the concept of specific learning difficulties is not a valid one. She supports her argument by disputing the relationship between IQ and reading by citing examples of children with low IQ scores who can display good mechanical reading skills, as evidence that low IQ scores do not necessarily result in poor mechanical reading.

This criticism of a discrepancy definition between IQ and reading attainment is also supported by Stanovich (1990) who argues that the key to reading disability relates to the problem of phonological processing and is therefore independent of intelligence.

The most commonly used IQ test is the Wechsler Intelligence Scale for Children (W.I.S.C.) from which a great deal of information can be gleaned. The actual administration of the W.I.S.C. can provide information in much the same way as an interview. Additionally the tester can note the various strategies the child uses in providing responses to the test materials.

The normative data which can be obtained from the W.I.S.C. can be in the form of verbal, performance and full scale IQ scores, but this is only one set of information and can be supplemented by observation from the actual administration of the test (Lannen and Reid, 1993).

Additionally, in deciding what is to be assessed, it may be prudent and worthwhile to focus on the child's learning strategies. Looking at how he/she learns can readily provide some direction to the development of a programme and also help to provide some diagnostic information on why the child may be encountering difficulty with the curriculum (see Chapter 11 on Learning Styles).

Why?

Why should an assessment be carried out and what purpose does this serve?

Although there may be a number of different reasons why an assessment is required there are usually some common factors. The assessment may be used for diagnostic purposes in order to provide information which may account for the child's difficulties in learning. At the same time the assessment may be used as a predictive tool – in order to obtain some information which can help the teacher predict how the child will cope with particular aspects of the curriculum. Used in this way, however, the information from the assessment may in fact be misused since it may lead to unnecessary curricular restrictions being placed on the child. This indeed is one of the misuses of IQ tests since the case may arise where a child assessed as having a low IQ is disadvantaged in terms of curricular access and expectation – this of course should be avoided at all costs.

The assessment may be used in a 'normative' way by comparing the child with his peers. Again some caution should be applied, although it may be useful to obtain some kind of data in relation to how the child is progressing in relation to others in the same chronological age range.

If the child has already been assessed, then further assessment can contribute to monitoring and review. This is an important element of any assessment since it assists in measuring the effects of teaching. Assessment should be linked to teaching, and there can be a prescriptive element to assessment in that it may offer some suggestions for teaching approaches or programmes.

How?

The issue of how an assessment should be conducted is an important one.

It may be advisable to use a range of assessment strategies and not simply opt for one particular type of assessment (Pumfrey and Reason, 1991). While norm-referenced assessment compares the child's performances with other children, criterion referenced assessment looks at the child's performances within a given task. Both of these strategies have a role to play in the assessment of children with specific learning difficulties.

Many forms of assessment can be described as static, in that they test what the child can do without assistance. Assessment, however, can also be provided with an additional dynamic dimension thus allowing the assessment process to be used more flexibly. It has been argued (Campioni and Brown, 1989) that when conducting an assessment the teacher should **not** be asking – '**what can the child do?**', but '**what do I need to do to help the child successfully complete the assessment?**'. The help which is necessary to facilitate the correct response from the child should be noted. Thus the teacher is focusing on the process of the assessment not the product or the outcome of the assessment.

The teacher may also wish to conduct the assessment from the perspective of the curriculum and examine how the child copes with different areas of the curriculum. At the same time it may also be possible to look at specific sub-skills of reading using an informal approach through the analysis of errors.

It is important to perceive assessment as a process. Similarly, the assessment should focus on the process of learning and observe and collect data on the child's learning style. This can be achieved through observation (Reid, 1992), through more formal assessment using a learning styles inventory (Dunn and Dunn, 1991), or indeed by error analysis using diagnostic assessment (see Chapter 4).

Effect

A consideration throughout the assessment process is the effect of the assessment – the assessment outcome. It is important to ensure that the assessment provides information which can be readily linked to a teaching programme or which can be used to help the child cope more effectively with the curriculum.

It is also important to bear in mind that a formal assessment, by necessity, provides a 'spotlight' on a particular child and the child understandably, quickly becomes aware of this. The assessment, therefore, should be implemented judiciously in order that the child is not exposed to any feelings of failure additional to those already resulting from his/her particular difficulties. The assessment should uncover data which will help in the development of a teaching programme. This ultimately will enhance the child's self-concept through academic success (Lawrence, 1987).

Theoretical considerations

Regardless of the specific aims selected as the principal goals of a particular assessment, and indeed the responses to the what, why, how and effect questions relating to the assessment, some particular theoretical issues will be evident.

The principal theoretical issues in assessment relate to the child, the curriculum and the process of learning.

Child-centred assessment

Child-centred assessment focuses on skills and abilities. It can aim to identify strengths and weaknesses. This form of assessment may be viewed as a deficit model because the implication is that the child's difficulty results from a particular deficit which in some way restricts the acquisition of skills necessary for tasks such as reading.

Child-centred assessment may include norm-based standardised assessments and may utilise some of the measures outlined below.

(a)   Psychometric measures

These involve the use of test materials to obtain some kind of measure of the learner's skills and abilities. These may include important sub-skills of learning such as memory, perception and auditory skills.

The Wechsler Intelligence Scale for Children (W.I.S.C.), is one such example of a psychometric test.

(b)   Attainment measures

These tests measure educational achievement and are usually standardised – reading, spelling and mathematics can be assessed in this way. They, therefore, provide normative scores such as reading ages, or percentiles.

They can also provide qualitative data which can give information on types of errors and pupils' performances.

(c)   Screening packs and checklists

These are usually criterion-referenced and focus on strengths and weaknesses in a child's performance. They commonly reflect factors which have been identified as significant indicators of reading learning or factors associated with dyslexia.

(d)   Neurological and physiological assessment

Assessment may focus on congenital abnormalities, and other areas such as visual acuity, hearing, attention concentration, and coordination.

Curriculum-based assessment

This type of assessment is conducted in relation to aspects of the curriculum. Assessment may be an integral part of the teaching, as in the learning outcomes in the 5-14 programme in Scotland or the National Curriculum in England, or in units of work related to the curriculum.

This type of assessment focuses on matching the child with the curriculum.

Process-focused assessment

This form of assessment looks at the processes involved in learning and enables the teacher to consider the child both in relation to the curriculum, and in terms of learning style and learning strategies.

Usually this form of assessment is integrated with teaching, and the process and interaction involved in undergoing the test is more important than the outcome. Thus the assessment in this situation is part of the child's learning experiences. Reuven Feuerstein's (1979) theory of Instrumental Enrichment includes one such example of a process-based assessment – 'Learning Potential Assessment Device' – which focuses on the abilities to grasp common principles.

Practical considerations

Conducting an assessment may rest more on practical than theoretical considerations. Ideally though one should be able to:

- justify the assessment approach in theoretical terms, and
- adapt the practicalities of the teaching or education setting to accommodate the theoretical approach.

This would imply that if the teacher felt that the child needed to be assessed in a one-to-one situation, outwith the classroom, arrangements and decisions would need to be made regarding:

- who was to conduct the assessment,
- how the results could be reported back to the relevant people,
- who were the relevant people, and,
- how the results would be related to the curriculum.

With any form of assessment, practical factors need to be addressed prior to selecting the assessment approach.

The identification and assessment of specific learning difficulties is of crucial importance, since proper assessment will facilitate the planning of appropriate intervention which will help to prevent the child from becoming engulfed by a feeling of learned helplessness. Preventing, or at least minimising, such failure removes the threat that intransigent learning difficulties will become so deeply embedded that they not only penetrate the affective domain but also result in inappropriate reading styles embedded within the child's learning pattern.

Clearly, therefore, assessment should consider the child's self-concept. Every effort should be made to ensure that the difficulties displayed by the child and the underlying problems do not detract from the development of skills in learning and in access to the curriculum.

It is vital that the approaches and strategies selected provide the data and information to facilitate an effective teaching programme, preferably within the context of the classroom and the curriculum. Careful preparation and planning are necessary before embarking on assessment and the questions relating to what, why, how and effect must be addressed at this planning stage and reviewed throughout the assessment.

Chapter 4

Assessment approaches and strategies

Introduction

IT IS NECESSARY to use a broad range of assessment strategies in order to ensure that adequate attention is given not only to the student's learning and cognitive profile but also to the process of learning itself and the context within which learning takes place.

Assessment for specific learning difficulties should consider three aspects – difficulties, discrepancies and differences. The central **difficulty** is clearly related to the decoding or the encoding of print, and this may be the result of different contributory factors. For example, some difficulties may include phonological processing, memory problems, organisational and sequencing difficulties, motor coordination, language problems, or perceptual difficulties of an auditory or visual nature.

The **discrepancies** may be apparent in comparing decoding and reading/ listening comprehension, between oral and written responses, and in performances within the different subject areas of the curriculum.

It is also important to acknowledge the **differences** between individual learners, including dyslexic children. An assessment, therefore, should also consider learning and cognitive styles. An appreciation of this can help to effectively link assessment and teaching, which should be a principal aim in assessing for specific learning difficulties.

A wide range of assessment strategies can be used to help recognise the **difficulties, discrepancies and differences** displayed by learners.

The range which will be discussed in this chapter is outlined in Fig. 12.

Fig. 12

• Standardised and diagnostic	• Metacognitive
• Criterion-referenced	• Diagnosis by exclusion
• Curriculum-based	• Components
• Behavioural	• Observational

Standardised and diagnostic

This form of assessment consists of standardised or norm-referenced tests which provide some form of score or measure which is compared with the average scores of a standardised sample. From this type of test one can obtain, for example, a reading age or IQ score. As well as providing an indication of the pupil's progress in relation to his peers, these tests can also provide information which can be used diagnostically and prescriptively. Important factors in standardised tests are the aspects of validity and reliability. Standardised tests must have a high validity and reliability so that the teacher can use the data from the test with confidence.

Validity: This refers to the design of the test and whether the test actually measures what it was designed to measure, e.g. IQ, decoding, verbal comprehension, etc.

Reliability: This refers to the reliability in obtaining the same responses from the test if repeated under similar conditions. Clearly the reliability of a test is limited by its validity.

Wechsler Intelligence Scale

One such standardised test in widespread use for the assessment of children who may have specific learning difficulties is the Wechsler Intelligence Scale for Children. This test was originally devised as an assessment tool for psychologists and psychometricians. It provides both an IQ and sub-test profile. It was revised and re-standardised in 1974 and a Scottish version with Scottish norms was issued in 1988. A new version with more modern and appropriate test materials was produced in 1992.

The use of ability measures such as the W.I.S.C. (or indeed the British Ability Scales (see page 49) according to Siegal (1989) rests on all or some of the following assumptions:

- that tests of ability or IQ are valid and reliable measures, so that there is some virtue in examining discrepancies between ability and achievement;

- particular sub-tests are valid instruments in the assessment of specific cognitive sub-skills;

- distinctive patterns may emerge which can be reliably correlated with specific learning difficulties;

- that IQ and reading share a causal dependency with IQ factors influencing reading ability.

Siegal, however, argues that the evidence in relation to these points is inconsistent. She argues that IQ tests do not necessarily measure intelligence, but in fact measure factual knowledge, expressive language ability, short-term memory and other skills related to learning. The implication of this for children with specific learning difficulties, is that because of the nature of their difficulty, their scores in relation to factual knowledge, expressive language and short-term memory will provide an artificially depressed IQ score.

This assertion clearly undermines the view that the sub-tests (see Fig. 13) and sub-test patterns can reveal useful information in the assessment of specific learning difficulties. Yet factor analytic studies of the W.I.S.C.-R (Lawson and Inglis, 1984-85) show that verbal skills can be isolated as a discrete factor. Interestingly, the sub-tests which had a high loading value for the factors Arithmetic, Coding, Information and Digit Span are those sub-tests which present problems for children with specific learning difficulties. This is consistent with the 'ACID' profile which identified the same set of sub-tests and provides some evidence for a distinctive dyslexic cognitive profile (Thomson, 1984).

Some studies have examined the clustering of specific abilities as measured by the W.I.S.C. sub-tests (Bannatyne, 1974; Thomson, 1984). These studies show spatial ability can be identified from data on the results of the Picture Completion, Block Design and Object Assembly sub-tests; sequencing ability from Digit Span, Picture Arrangement and coding and conceptualising from Comprehension, Similarities and Vocabulary.

These studies, therefore, support the view that it is possible to identify a pattern of difficulties from an analysis of sub-test scores (Thomson, 1989).

Using the British Ability Scales (BAS) (see Fig. 14), Tyler (1990) has identified sub-tests which can highlight a sequential processing deficit – a difficulty often associated with dyslexia. The scales of the BAS which highlight this are Information Processing, Recall of Digits, Basic Arithmetic, Immediate Memory for Visual Recall, and Delayed Memory for Visual Recall.

There is, however, strong evidence to dispute the assertion that IQ and reading ability share a causal dependency. Stanovich (1991) argues that the key to reading disability is related to the problem of phonological processing. This notion has indeed widespread support (Bradley, 1991). Stanovich further argues that phonological awareness and processing is independent of intelligence, and is in fact a specific skill and one which is not measured or directly taken account of in IQ tests.

The difficulty known as Hyperlexia (Aaron, 1989; Healy, 1992) can be used as evidence to dispute any valid association between IQ and reading attainment. Hyperlexia has been described as affecting those children with good decoding skills but poor comprehension indicating a low general IQ.

Siegal (1990) cites the existence of a hyperlexic group as further evidence of the need to disassociate IQ and reading attainment. It has been argued that listening comprehension correlates more highly with reading ability than IQ. The evidence from studies of hyperlexia (Healy, 1992) therefore suggests that children with low IQ scores can be good mechanical readers. This clearly indicates that a causal relationship between IQ and reading ability is a doubtful one.

Fig. 13

FEATURES OF W.I.S.C.

The W.I.S.C. consists of 10 main sub-tests which are sub-divided into verbal and performance scores.

Verbal Tests

Information (a general knowledge test)
Similarities (verbal concepts)
Arithmetic (basic mental arithmetic operations)
Vocabulary (ability to define words)
Comprehension (mental understanding of events)
Digit Span (auditory sequential memory) (Optional)

Performance Tests

Picture Completion (identify what is missing from a picture)
Picture Arrangement (re-arrange pictures to make a story)
Block Design (arrange blocks to make a pattern)
Object Assembly (form a picture with cut out pieces)
Coding (under timed conditions put symbols beside numbers)
Mazes (a pencil and paper maze test) (Optional)

The British Ability Scales

The BAS (see Fig. 14) consists of a set of 23 tests which provide data on a range of mental abilities. It also provides visual, verbal and general IQ scores. General IQ scores derived from the BAS correlate quite highly with independent measures of scholastic and academic attainment (Elliott, 1983).

The BAS has been widely and effectively used in identifying sub-groups of dyslexic children. For example, the sub-tests for information processing, recall of digits, basic arithmetic, immediate memory for visual recall, and delayed memory for visual recall, provide a collective grouping in relation to a sequential processing deficit (Elliott, 1983).

Since the tests also measure sequential processing and holistic processes, analyses of the results can provide some pointers regarding particular processing preferences. Elliott and Tyler (1986) found a cluster within a dyslexic sample who scored high on the holistic visual and verbal tasks such as block design, visualisation of cubes, matrices, recall of designs, similarities and word definitions, but scored low on immediate visual recall, recall of digits and speed of information processing.

Fig. 14

THE BAS DIVIDES INTO SIX AREAS:

Speed
- of information processing

Reasoning
- formal operational thinking
- matrices
- similarities
- social reasoning

Spatial Imagery
- block design, level
- block design, power
- rotation of letter-like forms
- visualisation of cubes

Perceptual Matching
- copying
- matching letter-like forms
- verbal tactile matching

Short-term Memory
- immediate visual recall
- delayed visual recall
- recall of designs
- recall of digits
- visual recognition

Retrieval and Application of Knowledge
- basic number skills
- naming vocabulary
- verbal compensation
- verbal fluency
- word definitions
- word reading

Appendix
- conservation items

Aston Index

The Aston Index was developed by Aston University in Birmingham. It consists of a series of tests which claim to be able to:

- identify children with potential language associated problems early in their education. (It can therefore be used as a screening device);
- be used to analyse and diagnose reading and language difficulties displayed by children who are experiencing difficulties in coping with basic attainments.

The Aston Index produces a pupil profile based on a number of tests.

The tests are divided into:

- General Underlying Ability and Attainment
- Performance Items.

The 'General Underlying Ability' section consists of tests on:

- picture recognition
- vocabulary
- Goodenough draw a man test
- Copying geometric designs
- Grapheme/phoneme correspondence
- Schonell Reading Test
- Spelling Test.

The Performance Items consist of tests on:

- Visual discrimination
- Child's laterality
- Copying name
- Free writing
- Visual sequential memory (pictures)
- Auditory sequential memory
- Sound blending
- Visual sequential memory (symbolic)
- Sound discrimination
- Graphomotor Test.

The tests within the Aston Index help the teacher diagnose the nature of the problem which may be preventing the child from achieving a satisfactory level in basic attainments. The Aston Index, however, has been the subject of criticism in relation to weaknesses in both construction and standardisation. There is also some doubt as to the potential of the test to discriminate between various groups of children experiencing specific learning difficulties (Pumfrey and Reason, 1991).

The Aston Portfolio Assessment Checklist is essentially a development from the Index and consists of assessment cards, checklists and teaching cards which help the teacher identify specific difficulties associated with attainments and suggest possible methods of dealing with this difficulty.

The Boder Test of Reading and Spelling Patterns

This test was constructed by Elena Boder, Professor of Paediatrics, University of California and Sylvia Jarnoco, Research Psychologist. It is intended to fulfil the need for a practical, direct diagnostic screening procedure that can differentiate developmental dyslexia from non-specific reading disorders. It attempts to classify dyslexic readers into one of three subtypes on the basis of their reading-spelling patterns. The unique feature of the test is that it jointly analyses reading and spelling as interdependent functions.

The key features of the test include:

- reading and spelling tests with equal numbers of phonetic and non-phonetic words;
- a reading test based on sight vocabulary and phonic attack skills;
- an individualised written spelling test based on the results of the oral reading test.

The authors claim that it is beneficial to examine two basic components of the reading-spelling process – the Gestalt and the analytic function. These correspond to the two standard methods of initial reading instruction – the whole word (look-say) method, which utilises visual/Gestalt skills, and the phonics method which relies on the student's ability to analyse words into their phonic components.

Furthermore, the authors argue that the strengths and deficits of the Gestalt and analytic functions of dyslexic children are displayed within three characteristic reading-spelling patterns. These are:

- The dysphonetic group. This type of reader has difficulty integrating written words with their sounds. Thus he/she will display poor phonic word analysis and decoding skills. Typical misspellings are phonetically inaccurate and misreadings are word substitutions, which can be semantic, e.g. 'bus' for 'car' and 'tree' for 'wood', or might be Gestalt substitutions, e.g. 'bell' for 'ball'. This category – the dysphonetic – is likely to be the largest among the dyslexic readers.

- The dyseidetic group. This group displays weaknesses in visual perception and memory for letters and whole word configurations. They may have no difficulty in developing phonic skills, but will have a weakness in the visual/Gestalt area. Their typical misspellings are phonetically accurate and can be decoded, e.g. 'wok' for 'walk', and their misreadings are good phonetic attempts and non-phonetic words such as 'talc' for 'talk'. Visuospatial reversals can also be seen in this group, e.g. 'dab' for 'bad' and 'for' instead of 'of'.

- Mixed dysphonetic and dyseidetic patterns. This group has difficulty in both the development of sight vocabulary and phonic skills.

Clearly, if learners from the dysphonetic group are identified, then their strengths will be on the visual side rather than phonic analysis skills. The implications of this for teaching may be a preference for a visual whole-word approach to help build a sight vocabulary before tackling the difficulty with phonics which will be very evident.

Dyseidetic readers are unable to perceive whole words as a visual entity. Although it is important to build up a sight vocabulary with this type of learner, reading skills can be more readily attained through a phonics programme.

For children who have difficulty with both visual and auditory stimuli, learning can be provided through the third channel – tactile-kinesthetic. Both phonic programmes and whole word techniques can be supplemented with an emphasis on the tactile-kinesthetic.

Teaching Reading Through Spelling

This programme produced by teachers at the Reading Centre at Kingston upon Thames (Teaching Reading Through Spelling) contains a very useful booklet on diagnosis of specific learning difficulties (Cowdery, McMahon, Morse and Prince, 1983).

The programme provides a very comprehensive diagnosis and assessment but both the time and the expertise required for such comprehensive assessment is likely to be outwith the scope of the class teacher. Some of the strategies, however, particularly in relation to informal testing and diagnosis can be readily utilised by the class teacher.

The assessment objectives outlined by the authors include compiling a case profile, obtaining sample data of the problems, obtaining criterion-referenced and diagnostic information and obtaining age-related data. The objectives are achieved through interview with parents and the child; observation; informal testing and diagnosis and standardised testing and diagnosis.

Each of the stages has a specific function. For example, the interview conducted in a 'relaxed and supportive manner' attempts to provide an initial estimate of the child's abilities and parent's perception of the problem. Observation can take account of aspects such as directional confusion, coordination, movement, attention span, eye movements and general level of activity.

The informal testing involves noting conversational and listening skills, noting errors, omissions and difficulties in conversation. Mispronunciation of words and asking for questions to be repeated or clarified can also be noted. In addition to conversational and listening skills, sequencing skills such as reciting days of the week, and months of year can be recorded as well as aspects of dominance – eye, ear, hand and foot – and directional aspects such as knowledge of left and right, below and above, and ability to mix laterality such as being able to touch the left ear with right hand.

Further information may be derived from observation of classroom activities by noting competencies in using different types of materials such as scissors, paints and paste, and observations can be made in physical education by noting general movement skills and motor coordination. The diagnostic programme provides some useful activities which the teacher can provide for the child in order to obtain further data, including threading a needle, dealing cards, throwing and catching a ball, kicking a ball, screwing a lid on a jar, tying a shoelace and doing up buttons.

The programme also provides pointers to the assessment of language skills by noting the child's word finding difficulties, vocabulary range, expressive difficulties, receptive language skills, phonological difficulties (such as the confusion of sounds), grammatical errors and articulation difficulties.

A very useful and comprehensive reading inventory is also provided (see Fig. 15) which can be used as a type of checklist by the teacher.

Fig. 15

READING INVENTORY

1. **Word Attack Skills**

   Can pupil guess from initial letters?

   Does s/he self correct?

   Are words divided into syllables or does s/he inappropriately sound out all the letter sounds?

   Any difficulty with particular sounds, blends or words?

   Is reading word by word?

2. **Comprehension**

   Are pictures used to aid comprehension, ignored or syntax and/or semantic context?

   Does s/he comprehend all or most of what is read?

   Is comprehension satisfactory at factual and inferential levels?

   Are any higher order comprehension skills discernible?

3. **Audience Effects**

   Is the reading in a monotone?

   Is the voice a strained and high pitched whine?

   Is reading according to units of meaning?

   Is there use of punctuation and appropriate pause, or is reading line by line ignoring punctuation?

   Is the reading too fast. Does it become jumbled and conceal misreadings?

4. **Contextual Factors**

   Is the child's language experience sufficient to understand what is contained in the text?

   Is the material stilted and not in everyday language?

   Is the story line trivial or unsuitable for the pupil's age level?

   Does the material contain stereotype details or social content which would be rejected by the child?

5. **Behavioural Aspects**

   Note the body posture and attitude, relaxed or stiff?

   Is the book held remarkably close or far away or in an odd position?

   Do you perceive any unusual mannerisms or habits?

6. **Emotional Factors**

   These may be observed in a fixed smile, eyes widened and whites showing over iris; rocking and jiggling continuously or when difficulties arise.

Reproduced by kind permission of the authors of Kingston Teaching Reading Through Spelling Programme

(Cowdery *et al*, 1987)

Specific Learning Difficulties (Dyslexia)

This programme clearly provides useful diagnostic information which can be utilised by both specialist teachers and adapted by class teachers.

Slingerland

The Slingerland Assessment (1974) is a diagnostic assessment which can provide data relating to both the child's skills in learning and preferences in learning style in relation to language and literacy.

The test has three components, each applicable to a different stage – Test A is directed at infants, Test B to middle primary and Test C to upper primary. The tests can be administered to a group or individually. There are nine sub-tests in the assessment and the tests can be administered over several sessions. There are also pre-reading screening procedures (1977) which can highlight auditory, visual and kinesthetic difficulties. These difficulties can be due to short attention span, faulty perception and recall of visual or auditory symbols and fine motor difficulties. As in other Slingerland tests this screening pack also attempts to highlight, for classroom teachers, the 'strengths and weaknesses of the learning modalities of their pupils'. As well as a pupil assessment booklet, the test also contains a teacher observation sheet. This observation sheet focuses on attention span, behaviour and social relations, general maturity and indications of mental growth, language factors, coordination in terms of gross movement and fine motor control and general information in relation to activity of modality preferences.

In the screening procedures test each of the sub-tests performs a different function but can be used to cross-check on data to confirm diagnostic opinions. For example, in Test A, Sub-test 1 focuses on the visual-kinesthetic area. It involves copying from the blackboard and can help to identify children with perceptual motor difficulties and visual scanning; because it is a visual coping task, it can also provide data on the linking of the child's visual-kinesthetic skills.

Sub-test 2 performs a similar task, except the 'model' is closer and comparisons between the results of this test and the previous one can be drawn.

Sub-test 3 looks at visual perception, visual discrimination and memory. It involves displaying a card with a written word to the child, then distracting him before asking him to identify the word from a number of words on the test sheet.

Sub-test 5 is similar, except that the child has to reproduce the word in writing, thus associating visual memory with the kinesthetic channel.

The other sub-tests focus on auditory memory, which involves listening to the word, then selecting it from the test sheet; visual discrimination and linking the auditory and visual channels through listening and looking activities to identify words.

The Slingerland Test has no norms. Its use, therefore, is diagnostic and the insight provided by the test into the student's strengths, weaknesses, modality preferences and modality integration can help the teacher identify appropriate teaching materials for the student.

Edwards Reading Test

This test, although providing data relating to a reading range, can be used diagnostically. It has the clear advantage of assisting in the assessment of reading skills using a range of criteria. Thus in addition to the Quick Word Screen Test there are also tests on oral reading, silent reading and listening comprehension. Scores can be recorded for comprehension, accuracy and speed. All the reading passages are graded in year level and recommended satisfactory scores for the year levels are provided.

The interesting and useful aspect of the Edwards Reading Test (1981) is that it enables the teacher to compare the child's performance in the decoding of single words free from context, with comprehension from passages read both orally and silently. This can provide useful information which may highlight discrepancies in a child's reading skills and performances.

Neale Analysis of Reading Ability

This revised edition (1989) consists of a set of graded passages for testing reading rate, accuracy and comprehension of oral reading, and can be used as an attainment test and a diagnostic test. A demonstration cassette is also included which provides useful extracts from test sessions. The test material has an appealing format – a brightly coloured book with pictures accompanying each of the graded passages.

There is also a Diagnostic Tutor Form with extended passages for further error analysis and Supplementary Diagnostic Tests focusing on discrimination of initial and final sounds, names and sounds of the alphabet, graded spelling and auditory discrimination and blending, which can provide very useful information to help the teacher both diagnose and prepare teaching programmes.

Miscue analysis during oral reading

The strategy known as miscue analysis is based on the 'Top-down' approach to reading which has developed from the work of Goodman (1972). Goodman argued that the reader first has to make predictions as to the most likely meaning of the text. Such predictions were based on how the reader perceived the graphic, syntactic and semantic information contained in the text. The reader, therefore, according to Goodman, engages in hypothesis testing to either confirm or disprove the prediction – this he named the 'psycholinguistic guessing game'.

It was, therefore, assumed that miscues occur systematically and occur whether reading is silent or aloud, and that the degree of sense the child makes of the material reflects his use of prior knowledge.

The marking system which is usually adopted in miscue analysis is indicated in Fig. 16.

Fig. 16

MARKING ERRORS OR 'MISCUES'	
Reversals:	Indicate reversals of word or phrase by 乙 e.g. 'will 乙 you' should be 'you will'
Omissions:	Circle all omissions, either of letters or whole words, e.g. he saw (the) car.
Insertions/Additions:	Use this sign ∧ if a word is inserted into the text.
Substitutions:	Cross out any word for which another is incorrectly substituted and write in the substituted word, e.g. above / about
Repetitions:	Draw a wavy line under any word that is repeated ∿
Hesitations:	Insert a diagonal slash when this occurs, i.e. / .
Non-response:	Indicate by dashed line beneath the word at which the child halts. ----------

It is important to observe whether the miscue is self-corrected, the graphic or phonemic similarly between the expected response and the observed response (what the child actually says) and whether the miscue produces syntactically or semantically acceptable text.

It is, therefore, possible to obtain useful data on the child's reading pattern by observing the reading errors and noting the significance of these oral errors (see Fig. 17).

Fig. 17

THE SIGNIFICANCE OF ORAL ERRORS

- **Omissions**

These may occur in relation to reading speed – for example, when the child's normal silent reading speed is used when reading orally. As the child progresses in reading ability and reading speed increases, omissions may still be noted as they tend to increase as reading speed increases.

- **Additions**

These may reflect superficial reading with perhaps an over-dependence on context clues.

- **Substitutions**

These can be visual or semantic substitutions. In younger readers, substitutions would tend to be visual and in older readers contextual. In the latter case they may reflect an over-dependence on context clues.

- **Repetitions**

These may indicate poor directional attack, and perhaps some anticipatory uncertainty on the part of the reader about a word to be read.

- **Reversals**

These may reflect the lack of left-right orientation. Reversals may also indicate some visual difficulty and perhaps a lack of reading for meaning.

- **Hesitations**

These can occur when the reader is unsure of the text and perhaps lacking in confidence in reading. For the same reason that repetitions may occur, the reader may also be anticipating a different word later in the sentence.

- **Self-corrections**

These would occur when the reader becomes more aware of meaning and less dependent on simple word recognition.

There are some specifically designed assessment materials to use with the miscue analysis strategy. Arnold (1984) has developed a series of graded passages which have been specially prepared with miscue analysis in mind (see Fig. 18). The graded passages range from reading levels 6 to 12 years. They vary in length and are written in autobiographical, narrative and informational styles.

The manual, as well as outlining the theoretical viewpoint and rationale for miscue analysis, provides a number of illustrative case studies with comments and suggestions of follow-up action. One example of this is illustrated in Fig. 18 on the following page.

Arnold (1992) has also produced a diagnostic reading record. This also contains case studies which highlight assessment through the use of miscue analysis. It also includes a teacher's handbook and pupil profile sheets and focuses on observations of reading behaviour and an examination of oral reading through discussion in order to obtain the child's level of understanding of the passage.

This can be a useful resource for the teacher and the reading passages are contained in photo-copiable masters.

Fig. 18

(The) Bad Dogs

Once there were two dogs. They lived in the same village. One was called Spot. The other was called Lassie. They liked each other. They went/for runs on their own. One hot day they went for a long run. They ran and ran. They came to a field. They sniffed new smells. They saw some white animals. They were not dogs. They ran round and round the animals. The animals made silly noises. The noises sounded like 'Baa-baa'. They were sheep.

Spot/said, 'We will chase them out of the field.' They did so. The sheep were frightened. Spot and/Lassie barked loudly. They felt very clever./ They thought the sheep were silly.

Then Lassie stood still. Her ears went up. 'A man/is/coming. He has a big stick.'

Coding Symbols

MISCUE TYPE	ORIGINAL TEXT	ACTUAL RESPONSE	SYMBOL
Non-response (refusal)	The other was called Lassie.	The other was called _ _ _ _ _ _ _	Lassie
Substitution	Once there were two dogs	On there were two dogs	On Once there were two dogs
Omission	they ran round and round the animals	they ran round the animals	they ran round (and round)
Insertion	– to a field. They sniffed	– to a field where they sniffed	Where to a field. They sniffed
Reversal	They did so	so they did	They did so
Self-correction	Then Lassie stood still.	Then Lassie stopped-stood- still	Then Lassie stopped stood still
Hesitation	They went for runs	They went for – runs	They went for /runs
Repetition	runs on their own	runs on their their own	runs on their own

Specific Learning Difficulties (Dyslexia)

Criterion-referenced assessment

This form of assessment examines particular skills and abilities against a set of criteria.

The criteria can include learning outcomes which are curriculum-based, or relate to particular aspects of learning in terms of skills or attainments.

One of the valuable aspects of criterion referenced assessment is that it can be adapted by the teacher to maximise the relevance of the assessment. The teacher therefore has to decide what kind of information is required and the criteria which need to be examined to obtain that information. For example, Fig.19 below looks at some general factors associated with reading and written work.

Fig. 19

**CRITERION REFERENCED ASSESSMENT FOR
READING AND WRITTEN WORK**

	VERY SEVERE	QUITE SEVERE	MODERATE
READING:			
Sight vocabulary	————	————	————
Sound blending	————	————	————
Use of contextual clues	————	————	————
Attempting unknown vocabulary	————	————	————
Eye tracking	————	————	————
Difficulty keeping the place	————	————	————
Speech development	————	————	————
Motivation in relation to reading material	————	————	————
Vocabulary	————	————	————
Naming deficit	————	————	————
Use of associative words	————	————	————

(tick if appropriate)

Fig. continued over

Fig. 19 (cont.)

CRITERION REFERENCED ASSESSMENT FOR
READING AND WRITTEN WORK

	VERY SEVERE	QUITE SEVERE	MODERATE
WRITTEN WORK:			
Articulation			
Directional configuration			
Difficulty in associating visual symbol with verbal sound			
Auditory discrimination of vowels			
Liability to sub-vocalise sounds prior to writing			
Bizarre spellings			
Inclination to persevere			
Lack of knowledge of serial probabilities			
Poor handwriting			
No joined handwriting			
Poor organisation of work on page			

Some specific factors which can be considered in reading include:

ADDITIONS

Puts in extra letters into words e.g. Sip read as snip			
Adds words which are not in the passage			
OMISSIONS			
Omits words			
Omits word endings			
Omits phrases			
Omits whole lines			

(tick if appropriate)

Specific Learning Difficulties (Dyslexia)

This form of assessment can provide some general data on the broad areas of difficulty experienced by the child. For example, the teacher may decide the child has a pronounced difficulty in the use of contextual cues, but this does not provide information as to why this difficulty persists and the kind of difficulties the pupil experiences with contextual cues. Does the child use contextual cues on some occasions, and under certain conditions? Clearly, this type of assessment, though useful, is limited and the teacher would be required to carry out further investigations to obtain a further picture of the difficulty.

The Bangor Dyslexia Test (Miles, 1983) is a commercially available example of a Criterion Referenced Test. This test was developed from work conducted at Bangor University and includes some diagnostic indicators. It might be argued, however, that many of these indicators can be symptomatic of other difficulties quite apart from dyslexia. The test has also been criticised on technical grounds (Singleton, 1988).

Although it does not offer a definitive diagnosis, the test may still be useful in providing some additional information towards a diagnosis.

Diagnosis by exclusion

Diagnosis by exclusion involves eliminating a number of factors which may account for the child's difficulty in reading. This is good practice and should be a preliminary step prior to formal assessment. Thomson (1988) outlines a number of criteria which should be considered and excluded before embarking on a full assessment. These include:

- no serious visual defect;
- no serious hearing loss;
- adequate school opportunity;
- no primary emotional disturbance;
- adequate family background;
- adequate intellectual ability to cope with written language;
- no serious general health difficulties;
- no well-documented brain injury.

It is interesting that medical officers report a continual flow of referrals for children with, or suspected of having, a specific learning difficulty (Riddell, Duffield and Brown, 1992). The medical officers interviewed in this study saw their role as 'ruling out' serious neuropsychological factors, such as abnormalities in relation to reflexes, coordination and attention. They would also examine visual, spatial and perceptual aspects, language functioning, gross motor abilities, and very likely perform a chromosome check.

It is important to ensure that the factors outlined above are not the primary difficulties which are affecting the child's performance in class.

Neurological aspects which can be associated with dyslexia have been widely researched. Pavlidis (1989) and Stein (1991) have documented the problems of eye tracking, convergence and visual acuity. DeFries (1990) has illustrated, using twin studies research, the importance of chromosomal factors in reading; pre- and post-natal biological factors affecting cerebral dominance have been highlighted by Geschwind and Galaburda (1985); Galaburda (1993); Sherman (1993) and Duane (1991b) has shown that hemispheric symmetry and cerebral blood flow are important considerations in relation to reading. Stephenson (1986) argues that motor difficulties need to be examined since they can highlight the apparent failure of the central nervous system to process and integrate information which can be the underlying cause of difficulties in reading, writing and spelling.

Exclusional criteria may be examined, either at the beginning of an assessment as a preliminary check or when, following other forms of assessment, no appropriate explanation can be found for the persistent difficulties displayed by the child.

Curriculum based assessment

Curriculum based assessment seeks to ensure that the assessment process is relevant to the actual curricula work with which the pupil is involved. This strategy has clear advantages including:

- teaching and learning aims easily identified;
- readily identifiable criteria for success;
- task matched to pupil's previous experience and present abilities;
- flexible teaching methods can be used to take into account pupil's approach to learning;
- progress can be easily monitored;
- tasks can be made challenging, and a problem solving approach can be encouraged.

Different modes and methods of assessment have been suggested to accommodate curriculum based assessment. The assessment document within the Scottish 5–14 programme suggests the following:

Fig. 20

- 'Staggered' assessment, i.e. the teacher does not necessarily assess all of the learning aims at once.
- Assessment through talk – this would include questioning pupils about their understanding and their ideas.
- Assessment through writing – this would include pieces of writing of different lengths, i.e. short answers and longer pieces of work.
- Assessment through practical activities – thus the skills involved in planning and carrying out experiments and in working with others would be assessed.

    (Assessment 5-14 Scottish Office Education Department, October 1991)

Thus by examining the child's progress in relation to the curriculum, one can:

- clearly identify the child's actual performance, i.e. what s/he can do;
- examine the nature of the curriculum presented to the child;
- identify what type of assistance/teaching the child requires to achieve the desired learning outcome;
- observe the child's learning styles and strategies.

In effect, therefore, curriculum based assessment means that assessment will be an integral part of the teaching and learning process. This clearly has many advantages, not least that assessment would occur on a day-do-day basis and involve recording the pupil's performances in a variety of modes: oral, written, and kinesthetic. A cautionary note however should be sounded to ensure that whilst assessment is an important issue, it should not necessarily dominate the teaching and learning process.

Behavioural approaches to assessment

This approach examines the child's learning behaviour through an analysis of the task. Data on the child's behaviour can be obtained through observations and through the use of checklists. This, in fact, is fairly consistent with the approach advocated by Marie Clay whereby the child's reading behaviour is recorded, described and quantified using a Running Record.

The task aspect of the behavioural approach involves describing the desired objectives which it is hoped will be achieved and a series of sequential targets to help achieve these objectives. This approach is similar to precision teaching; it provides definable objectives and progress can be readily observed by both the learner and the teacher.

Although there are a number of commercially produced programmes based on the precision teaching/task analysis methodology, materials for assessment can be developed by the teacher. Targets and objectives can be set to suit the purpose and task which has been identified as a learning task. Examples of this are described in the literature (Ainscow and Tweddle, 1984) and can be seen in commercially produced programmes such as DATAPAC (1983). Other adaptations have been devised, developed and used in different areas. These include the Phonic Codecrackers materials which are based on the principles of behavioural objectives and can be used as a whole-school approach to assessment and teaching.

While behavioural assessment may well reveal the precise difficulties displayed by children in relation to their performances, it does not provide information on the causes and the underlying difficulties which may account for the problem. The strength of the approach, however, lies in its linkage with teaching and in the way that assessment is curriculum based.

Dynamic and metacognitive tests

Essentially dynamic assessment is that which involves active participation from the learner. It focuses on the process rather than the product of learning, thus providing information which can help facilitate learning and also determine how change can best be accomplished (Lidz, 1991). It is essentially a diagnostic model which can be applied and adapted to different educational settings.

There are a number of different forms of dynamic assessment models, such as Feuerstein's Learning Potential Assessment Device (LPAD), which is inextricably linked to the Intervention Model – Instrumental Enrichment. The LPAD battery includes both verbal and non-verbal tasks, analogical reasoning, numerical reasoning, memory strategies, and conceptual categorisations; it also utilises Raven's Progressive Matrices as one of the measures. Extensive training is required to develop proficiency in the administration of the LPAD, although it has been described as the 'most comprehensive and theoretically grounded expression of dynamic assessment' (Lidz, 1991).

Campione and Brown's model

Campione and Brown (1989), dissatisfied with the limited information which can be obtained from normative procedures, have developed a soundly researched model for dynamic assessment, focusing on the task and the process of learning. They have also linked this form of assessment with the intervention model known as Reciprocal Teaching (see Chapter 12).

The focus of Campione and Brown's work relates to aspects of learning and transfer; the information obtained provides an indication of the nature and amount of help needed by the child, rather than the child's level of attainment or improvement. This can be revealed through 'prompts', memory tasks and help with developing learning strategies.

Campione and Brown argue that there should be a link between assessment and instruction. They argue that traditional tests are intended to be predictive and prescriptive BUT fail on both counts. Their argument rests on the assertions that children can be too readily mis-classified and that traditional tests do not really provide a clear indication of what is really required for instruction.

Campione and Brown argue that the context of assessment is important and divide assessment into two aspects:

Static tests. In these the child works unaided on sets of items and is given but a single chance to demonstrate his/her proficiency. Thus:
- no aid is provided;
- social interaction between the tester and the child is minimised;
- objective scoring systems can be readily implemented;
- norms can be available.

Although such tests may fulfil a purpose they have considerable shortcomings.

- They say nothing about the processes involved in the acquisition of the responses.
- Some children may get the right answer for the wrong reason.
- Students may be mis-classified because they have not yet acquired the competence but are in the process of acquiring it.

Dynamic tests

Dynamic type tests emphasise the individual's potential for change. Such tests do not attempt to assess how much improvement has taken place, but rather how much **help** children need to reach a specified criterion and how much help they will need to transfer this to novel situations. Such tests are therefore metacognitive in that they can provide information on how the child is learning. By noting the cues necessary to facilitate the correct response from the child, the teacher can obtain some information on how the child thinks and learns. Such information can be relayed back to the child to illustrate how he or she managed to obtain the correct response. Thus assessment is **a learning experience, not a testing one.**

Elliott (1993) maintains that dynamic assessment offers considerable promise by providing valuable information about children's true potential and can be used to help develop educational intervention programmes. He also argues, however, that because dynamic assessment research is in its infancy, and it represents more of a general concept than a specific technique, it does not readily fit into 'western models of professional thinking'. This thinking, according to Elliott, is characterised by the perseverance with familiar techniques because of time demands and the increasing number of formal assessments professionals need to undertake to assist in decision making regarding placements and resources. It is, however, unfortunate if the need for quantitative data overburdens professionals at the expense of developing and disseminating qualitative strategies, which can provide a real insight into students' learning skills and development.

Linking assessment and teaching

A components approach

The limitations of traditional assessment procedures such as intellectual/ attainment discrepancies and cognitive deficit diagnoses have led to the development of alternative criteria and procedures to assist in the diagnosis of reading difficulties.

One such approach, known as the 'components approach' (Aaron, 1989 and 1992), examines the components of the reading process and thus enables linking assessment and teaching.

The main aims of the 'components approach' to assessment are:

- to distinguish the dyslexic child from the 'slow learner' child who displays reading difficulties;
- to distinguish the dyslexic child from the child who has a comprehension deficit in reading;
- to adapt the assessment for classroom use, to make it available for the teacher and psychologist;
- to allow for a complete diagnostic procedure which would be comprehensive enough to include quantitative as well as qualitative information that is relevant to the reading process.

The main strands of the components approach are:

- the identification of the factors which determine performance;
- a description of the components of reading;
- an evaluation of the child's functioning in relation to these components.

Aaron (1989) describes four main components of reading:

- Verbal comprehension;
- Phonological awareness;
- Decoding speed;
- Listening comprehension.

It can be argued that decoding and comprehension are the two most important components of reading, representing visual and auditory processing skills together with meaningful comprehension. (This simultaneous processing involving decoding and comprehension may require hemispheric integration and justify the claim that reading is a holistic activity).

Decoding versus comprehension

In normal readers these two aspects should complement each other. Thus as a child reads (decodes the print) meaning is simultaneously expressed.

Research suggests that:
- COMPREHENSION is a controlled process, i.e. is attention-demanding, with limited capacity.
- DECODING is an automatised process, i.e. not attention-demanding, and does not require reader's conscious control.

It is known that for dyslexic children decoding does not readily become automatised (Fawcett, 1990) and therefore requires:
- attention-demanding operations;
- conscious control from the reader.

These are also factors in comprehension and hence it is argued that dyslexic readers, when decoding, draw on some of the capacities which should be focusing on comprehension and thereby weaken their potential for comprehension while reading. This suggestion is supported by work on visual imagery in reading (Bell,

1990) which claims that the decoding process weakens the dyslexic child's gestalt (right hemisphere) and consequently comprehension.

Aaron (1989) suggests that differences in reading achievement are due to factors associated with either decoding or comprehension or a combination of both. To differentiate between these two abilities, it is necessary to assess them independently. Thus reading comprehension has to be assessed without involving the decoding of print.

Reading comprehension and listening comprehension

Some researchers suggest that reading comprehension and listening comprehension share the same cognitive mechanisms and that the two forms of comprehension are related. Palmer (1985) obtained a highly significant correlation between these two forms of comprehension and states that 'reading comprehension can be predicted almost perfectly by a listening measure – therefore a test of listening comprehension can be used as a measure of reading comprehension.'

In the early reading stages there seems to be a close relationship between decoding and reading comprehension, so one can use a decoding assessment procedure in the early years. One must, however, attempt to use a task which is closely related to decoding but not influenced by environmental or contextual factors.

It has been shown that phoneme analysis skills (phonological awareness) are a good predictor of reading ability (Bradley and Bryant, 1990.

Therefore a components approach to assessment which can be readily carried out by the teacher can include the following:

- decoding test (non-words reading test;
- word reading test;
- phonological awareness test;
- listening comprehension test;
- reading comprehension test.

Aaron (1989) has indicated four different categories of reading disorders (see Fig. 21).

Fig. 21

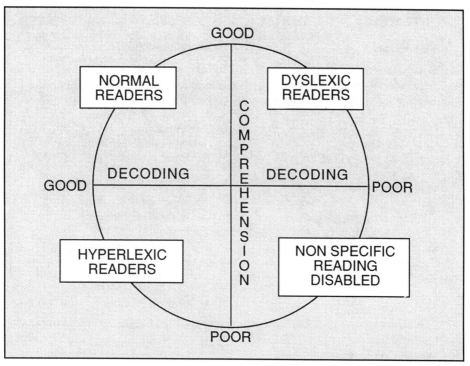

Reproduced by permission of P. G. Aaron
(Aaron, 1989)

An interesting difference is drawn here between hyperlexic readers and dyslexic readers. Hyperlexic readers are those who can decode and are therefore good at mechanically reading while dyslexic readers are poor at decoding and read inaccurately but can perform better in reading comprehension tasks.

Hyperlexia

This term was initially used by Silberberg and Silberberg (1967). In Aaron's view these children lie at the other end of the continuum of reading difficulties from 'dyslexia'. Aaron suggests the comparison shown below (see Fig. 22) as illustrating the two extremes of reading disorder.

Fig. 22

DIFFERENCES BETWEEN HYPERLEXIA AND DEVELOPMENTAL DYSLEXIA	
Hyperlexia	**Developmental Dyslexia**
Good decoding	Poor decoding
Poor listening comprehension	Adequate listening comprehension
Reading comprehension inferior to decoding	Reading comprehension superior to decoding
Spelling above average	Spelling below average
Below average IQ	Average or above average IQ
Bottom-up processing, data driven	Top-down processing, concept driven
Use of grapheme-phoneme relational rules and word-specific addressing of pronunciation	Use of print-to-meaning; direct access and word-specific addressing of pronunciation
Clinical neurological symptoms often present	Clinical neurological symptoms usually absent

Reproduced by kind permission of P. G. Aaron
(Aaron, 1989)

This emphasises that the key components of the reading process which are to be assessed are:

- decoding;
- listening/reading comprehension.

The components approach is a diagnostic procedure which does not rely solely on norm-referenced, standardised tests, but can be applied with locally developed assessment materials from which programmes can be developed in the context of the curriculum and the classroom activities.

Aaron and Joshi (1992) contend that a measure of listening comprehension is more appropriate in diagnosing reading difficulties than, for example, an IQ measure. Listening comprehension tests do not possess the same drawbacks as IQ measures (Siegal, 1989) and the diagnostic findings can link directly to teaching procedures.

Observational assessment

There are a number of different forms of observational assessment. Some of these are in the form of checklists, such as the sample on early indicators of phonological difficulties (see Chapter 5).

This approach can provide important data and also offer some pointers as to appropriate teaching strategies. Checklists, however, do fall short in that they say little of how the student arrived at his or her response. In other words little information is provided to understand how the student learns or why the student is having success or difficulty with different items in the checklist.

An observation schedule can be constructed to take account of these factors. A number of benefits of observation schedules can be identified, for example they can be flexible, adaptable to different situations, and placed within the context of the learning situation. Hopefully a 'natural' response will then be recorded free from the influence of 'test contamination' factors. In the case of specific learning difficulties a framework can be developed.

Throughout the observation it is important to record not only what the student does or can do but how the response is achieved – the cues required, level and extent of the assistance needed at the stages the student needs to go through to solve a problem or obtain a response.

With increased importance being placed on early identification and metacognitive aspects of learning, procedures such as observational criteria can have an important role to play in the assessment process.

Observational framework

In this framework one is looking at a broad range of areas which can relate to some of the difficulties experienced by children with specific learning difficulties. One is clearly looking for factors which may suggest that the child is having difficulty in the learning situation.

It is important to gather information which relates to the child, the learning situation and context. The aim is not just to find out how or why the child is having difficulty, but to gain some insight and understanding into the strategies and processes of learning for that child (Lannen and Reid, 1993).

A framework for observational assessment for specific learning difficulties can therefore include the areas listed below.

Attention
- Length of attention span?
- Conditions when attention is enhanced?

- Factors contributing to distractability?
- Attention/distractability under different learning conditions?

Organisation

- Organisational preferences?
- Degree of structure required?
- Organisation of work, desk, self?
- Reactions to imposed organisation?

Sequencing

- Able to follow sequence with aid?
- General difficulty with sequencing: work; carrying out instructions; words when reading; individual letters in written work?

Interaction

- Degree of interaction with peers, adults?
- Preferred interaction – one-to-one?
                          small groups?
                          whole class?
- How interaction is sustained?

Language

- Expressive language?
- Is meaning accurately conveyed?
- Spontaneous/prompted?
- Is there appropriate use of natural breaks in speech?
- Expressive language in different contexts, e.g. one-to-one, small group, class group?
- Errors, omissions and difficulties in conversation and responses, e.g. mispronunciations, questions to be repeated or clarified?

Comprehension

- How does the child comprehend information?
- What type of cues most readily facilitate comprehension?
- Use of schema?
- What type of instructions are most easily understood – written, oral, visual?
- How readily can knowledge be transferred to other areas?

Reading

- Reading preferences – aloud, silent?
  Type of errors:

Visual, e.g.

- Discrimination between letters which look the same?

- Inability to appreciate that the same letter may look different, e.g. 'G' 'g'?
- Omitting or transposing part of a word (this could indicate a visual segmentation difficulty)?

Auditory, e.g.
- Difficulties in auditory discrimination?
- Inability to hear consonant sounds in initial, medial or final position?
- Auditory sequencing?
- Auditory blending?
- Auditory segmentation?

Motivation/initiative
- Interest level of child?
- How is motivation increased, what kind of prompting and cueing is necessary?
- To what extent does the child take responsibility for own learning?
- What kind of help is required?

Self-concept
- What tasks are more likely to be tackled with confidence?
- When is confidence low?
- Self-Concept and confidence in different contexts?

Relaxation
- Is the child relaxed when learning?
- Evidence of tension and relaxation?

Learning preferences
These include the following learning preferences:
- Auditory?
- Visual?
- Oral?
- Kinesthetic?
- Tactile?
- Global?
- Analytic?

It is important, therefore, to note in observational assessment the preferred mode of learning. Many children will of course show preferences and skills in a number of modes of learning. Multi-sensory teaching therefore is crucial in order to accommodate as many modes as possible.

Learning context

When assessing the nature and degree of the difficulty experienced by the child, it is important to take into account the learning context. This context, depending on the learner's preferred style can either exacerbate the difficulty or minimise the problem (Reid, 1992 and 1994). The contextual factors below should therefore be considered.

- classroom
- role of teacher
- task
- materials/resources.

Observation and assessment therefore needs to adopt a holistic perspective i.e.:

- observing components within a framework for learning;
- observing some factors within that framework associated with specific learning difficulties;
- observing preferred styles of learning;
- acknowledging the importance of the learning context;
- observing the degree of match or mis-match between the learner and the context.

Conclusion

Clearly, no one approach can provide both sufficient data to identify and assess specific learning difficulties and a sufficient and effective linkage with teaching. Different factors need to be taken into account and all assessment procedures discussed in this chapter have considerable merits. The factors which determine what approach or approaches should be used relate to the reasons for the assessment and the purposes for which the information is to be put. It is, however, important to bear in mind that different children may well display different profiles and still meet the criteria for specific learning difficulties. Ideally, the assessment should link with teaching and if this is a successful outcome of the assessment for specific learning difficulties, then it will indeed have been a valuable and worthwhile exercise.

Chapter 5

Process and procedures

Introduction

DIFFERENT approaches to assessment together with the practicalities of implementing appropriate and effective assessment help to determine 'how', 'when' and 'if' the 'high risk' child is identified and appropriately assessed for specific learning difficulties. One of the key issues in the assessment process is that of early identification. How such identification should take place and when it can most effectively, and most sensitively, be conducted are matters of some debate. The debate can be highlighted by examining some current models of identification and assessment, such as a 'stage-process' model and a 'whole-school interactive model'. These models will be discussed later in this chapter, but a number of clear issues become evident when the process and procedures of identification and assessment are examined. Some of the most important of these issues are listed below.

Initial identification
- When should this take place, how should it be conducted and by whom?
- What criteria should be used at this early stage in relation to specific learning difficulties ?

Whole-school involvement
- What are the advantages of whole-school involvement?
- How can this be successfully and effectively conducted?

Multi-professional assessment
- How can the different professions coordinate their roles in relation to assessment?
- What are the roles of the speech therapist, educational psychologist, school medical officer, learning support teacher and class-teacher?

Linkage with teaching

- How can identification and assessment be most effectively related to teaching and in particular the curriculum?
- How appropriate is assessment outwith the context of the curriculum?

Consistency and uniformity

- How can the unfortunate situation be prevented whereby pupils with specific learning difficulties are not identified until the point of transfer to secondary school? (Riddell, Duffield, Brown and Ogilvy, 1992).
- How can procedures become consistent, and uniform from school to school and region to region?

Training

- The importance of training in relation to assessment must be emphasised. Training should not only be provided for a select few, who are subsequently over-stretched because of the demands being placed on them. Training needs to be provided for all professionals involved in assessment, particularly the class teacher – who is often overlooked.

Early identification

Failure to read does not end in spontaneous recovery.   (Marie Clay)

The implication of this is that for some children who are failing to read, considerable and appropriate intervention must be carried out in order to:

- assess how they read;
- analyse the difficulties they are experiencing with reading;
- decide which strategies can be utilised to help the child overcome the reading difficulty;
- ascertain how such problems could have been prevented.

Clay asserts that early intervention is crucial since it is more difficult to help a child once he/she has established a consistent pattern of error behaviour, yet delays in early intervention appear all too common. Such delays may be due to reluctance to label a child too early, or indeed label a child at all. While it can be appreciated that it is not wise to unnecessarily and prematurely diagnose a difficulty, this must be balanced with the need to identify difficulties in order to provide appropriate early intervention which can prevent the difficulty from becoming too entrenched.

If delays do occur in early identification the result may be that:

- the gap in literacy between the child who is failing and his peer group will widen;
- deficits transfer to other areas of the curriculum;
- the difficulties begin to manifest themselves in the affective domain;
- poor self-concept and impaired emotional development will have an additional adverse effect on learning (Lawrence, 1987).

Clay (1985) believes that by the end of the first year at primary school the teacher can identify the children who are failing in literacy. This can be achieved through the administration of a systematic observation technique focusing on children's reading behaviour.

Systematic observation of children's learning behaviour

Marie Clay argues that to do this one must:

- observe precisely what children are saying and doing;
- use tasks which are closely related to the learning tasks of the classroom;
- observe what children have been able to learn;
- identify from this the reading behaviour they should now be taught;
- focus the child's general reading behaviour to training on reading tasks rather than on specific sub-skills such as visual perception or auditory discrimination.

In order to achieve the above Marie Clay has developed a 'diagnostic survey' (The Running Record) which looks at directional movement, motor coordination, reading fluency, error behaviour, oral language skills, letter identification skills, concepts about print and writing skills.

This latter aspect is particularly important as writing skills may provide some indication of any reading problems, e.g. a poor writing vocabulary may indicate the child is taking very little notice of visual differences in print. The weakness in visual discrimination may be because the hand and eye are not complementing each other and this is an important aspect of early writing. Additionally, in writing, other factors such as language level and message quality are also important to note. In writing, children are required to pay attention to details of letters, letter sequences, sound sequences and the links between messages in oral language and messages in printed language.

In addition to this structured observation technique, other types of observation can also be carried out in a more informal and less structured way. This 'flexible observation' can be developed to encompass a range of learning activities including metacognitive aspects such as the child's learning style.

Early identification can be attempted by carrying out formal screening, informal testing or observational assessment. It is important, however, that some attempt is made to ensure such early identification takes place. It is therefore a cause for concern that recent research findings appear to indicate that early identification is not widespread; indeed in some cases identification for specific learning difficulties occurs around transfer to secondary school (Riddell, Duffield, Brown and Ogilvy, 1992).

Bradley (1989) highlights linguistic and phonological aspects of early identification and subsequent early intervention programmes. She highlights the aspect of rhyming and contends that a lack of awareness of rhyme is correlated to subsequent reading proficiency. Thus, using this criterion, one is seeking to identify children who have difficulty reciting rhymes, appreciating the breaks in words, and have little general awareness of natural breaks in sentences. Bradley's studies show that children with these difficulties will experience problems matching alphabetic letters with phonological sounds, in connecting speech which is continuous with written words which are segmented, and in blending letters in a smooth, continuous manner, being inclined instead to overlap the sounds.

Lindberg's study (1988) which involved training six-year-old children, through a series of daily sessions of games and metalinguistic exercises showed that such exercises can significantly improve reading and spelling. Lindberg's programme included:

- rhyming games;
- games segmenting sentences into word units;
- encouraging children to clap their hands to the syllables of their own names;
- the use of exaggerated repetition to identify phonemes in words.

Farrer (1993) asserts that decoding is only one aspect of reading and writing and the child needs to learn to understand and formulate written language. Additionally she argues that even mild difficulties in phonological skills in spoken language can cause considerable difficulties in reading and spelling. She lists the most common language deficits in dyslexic students to include sound segmentation and sound blending difficulties; difficulties in auditory short-term memory and difficulties in word fluency.

The Kingston Programme of Teaching Reading Through Spelling (see Chapter 4) contains a useful checklist of early indicators of phonological difficulties.

Early indicators of phonological difficulties.

- Difficulty segmenting initial sounds from words – (d) – (og).
- Inability to appreciate rhyme and alliteration.
- Inability to clap the beats in their own and others' names (given no motor impairment).
- Reversing letter and word order – 'on' for 'no' and 'was' for 'saw'.
- Difficulty sequencing the alphabet.
- Difficulty differentiating between letter names and sounds.
- Difficulty relating a spoken sound to a written symbol.
- Difficulty relating a written symbol to a spoken sound.
- Difficulty with specific sounds – especially short vowels and voiced/unvoiced consonants.
- Difficulty segmenting sounds within words.
- Difficulty in memorising and sequencing sound segments.
- Difficulty in blending sound segments to synthesise whole words.
- Inability to determine where the articulators (tongue, teeth, lips) are when producing sounds.
- Incorrect sequencing of sounds in words, e.g. 'flutterby' for 'butter-fly'.

Reproduced with permission
(Cowdery, McMahon, Morse and Prince (1987)

Muter (1993) reports that children's knowledge of letter names and their phonological awareness are the best predictors of success or failure of early reading. General intelligence as measured by IQ is in fact not a good predictor of reading progress. This is consistent with the views of Siegal (1989) (see Chapter 4). In relation to phonological awareness tests, Muter (1993) argues that segmentation skills (measured by tests of syllable and phoneme, counting, sound blending or phoneme deletion, and rhyming skills) measured by recording children's accuracy at reciting nursery rhymes or being able to identify rhymes, are the most effective measures.

Screening

The screening of children, at virtually any stage in education, is an issue which has aroused considerable debate and controversy. Three main questions can be raised in relation to screening:

• What is the most desirable age (or ages) for children to be screened?
• Which skills, abilities and attainments in performances should children be screened for?
• How should the results of any screening procedures be used?

Additionally, the benefits of screening need to be weighed against the costs in terms of staff and resources which are necessary to implement effective screening procedures. This raises the issue as to whether screening should be for all children, or only for those who do not appear to be making satisfactory progress.

One education authority which operates a very comprehensive screening procedure at the early age of six (Evans, 1991) accepts the criticism levelled at such time-consuming procedures. Evans acknowledges that it may not be necessary to test all children with all the tests in the screening battery; that training of class teachers to recognise the 'at risk' children may circumvent the need for some of the screening tests; and that the issue of screening, or indeed early identification, could be viewed as a school responsibility and not necessarily the exclusive remit of the learning support specialist.

If one examines the actual screening procedures described by Evans, it becomes fairly obvious that, although the importance of early identification cannot be minimised, screening of all children may be an unnecessary extravagance. The procedure outlined by Evans includes a standardised reading test and an opportunity for the child to read from a familiar reader; a reading comprehension test; a vocabulary score; colouring a picture of a clown; free writing; printing and writing own name; copying a sentence and a phonics test, using phonically regular nonsense words.

From the initial battery of tests, high risk children are identified and undergo further diagnostic testing. The essence of this type of screening procedure is to highlight discrepancies. Such discrepancies include differences between reading level and vocabulary score, and discrepancies between performances in some of the other tests such as vocabulary and copying. In this context it appears Evans, in using the vocabulary score (BPVS) as a measure of ability, may well cast some doubt on the value and the validity of the discrepancies revealed by these procedures. Without doubt, however, such a comprehensive assessment should at least reveal the 'high risk' children. The question of the role of the class teacher is still relevant, however. Should not he or she be able to assemble the information revealed by the screening without necessarily adopting sophisticated, formal and time-consuming procedures?

Dyslexia early screening test

Nicolson and Fawcett (1993) are currently developing a series of tests to provide an objective and valid early screening for dyslexia. The assumption made is that it is possible to identify early warning signs of dyslexia during the pre-reading period. These tests (see Fig. 23) examine performances in a range of activities not dependent on taught skills such as reading.

Fig. 23: Dyslexia early screening test

TESTS ADMINISTERED	
Method	**Test**
Paper	B.P.V.S.
Paper	British Ability Scales (10 sub-scales)
COMB	Non-Word Repetition
COMB	Phonological Discrimination
Verbal	Prepositions
COMB	Rhyming Task
Verbal	Word Segmentation
Video	Blindfold Balance
COMB	Articulation Rate
Beads	Beads Task
Pencil	Draw-a-Person
Board	Pegboard Task
Paper	Visual Search
COMB	Simple Reaction
COMB	Choice Reaction
COMB	Lexical Access
COMB	Naming
* COMB = Combination of Methods	

Reproduced by permission of Angela Fawcett and Rod Nicolson
(Nicolson and Fawcett, 1993)

Models of identification

Pumfrey (1990) contends that the concept of diagnosis and treatment is based on a medical model and is not therfore appropriate to the education context. Teachers, Pumfrey asserts, ought to be wary of moving down the classification escalator, which he describes as moving from individual differences to deviations, difficulties, disabilities, deficits and eventually to defects.

Yet while this 'classification escalator' is clearly something which ought to be avoided, and something which underlines the inherent dangers of hasty diagnosis or perceiving lack of attainments as a within-child difficulty which requires diagnosis, it is still beneficial to implement early identification procedures, despite these risks. It has been well argued that the intricacies of the reading process result in significant numbers of children adopting ineffective reading strategies which need to be identified and modified by the teacher lest the error behaviour becomes too entrenched thus placing a restriction on further progress (Clay, 1989; Pumfrey, 1990). To ensure, however, that a medical diagnosis-treatment model is not perceived as the principal assessment strategy, it is important that assessment is undertaken by the class teacher, using informal strategies, and that this assessment is linked to teaching and the curriculum. This type of model has some advantages over formal assessment by specialist teachers, but if difficulties do persist there is a definite role for utilising the expertise of specialist teachers.

Assessment has been described as 'hypotheses generation followed by intervention' (Pumfrey, 1990), but before hypotheses can be generated in even a vague way, a high degree of awareness and training is necessary. Research findings, however, indicate that teachers, and even in some cases, specialist teachers, feel inadequately trained in relation to the assessment process (Pumfrey, 1990,1991(b); Riddell, Duffield, Brown and Ogilvy, 1992).

It is beneficial, therefore, for assessment procedures and models of identification to be encapsulated into the context of the curriculum and the classroom. It is also important that such models and training should be included in the training of other professionals, such as speech therapists and educational psychologists.

It is perhaps quite alarming that around 15% of children with specific learning difficulties are not identified until they reach secondary education, and around 40% are identified between Primary stages 4 and 7 (Riddell, Duffield, Brown and Ogilvy, 1992).

Fig. 24 and Fig. 25 illustrate two possible models of identification. Fig. 24 focuses on the needs of children, while Fig. 25 predominantly focuses on the curriculum and training aspects. It can be argued that the Stage Process Model (Fig. 24) is a reactive one since assessment and intervention develop throughout a period of stages – beginning with the class teachers' observations and leading to multi-disciplinary meetings to monitor progress.

The whole school interactive model (Fig. 25) focuses on training, the curriculum and consultancy. The rationale for this model is clearly one of early identification through training of class teachers and indeed of student teachers undergoing teacher training courses. It matches the curriculum with the learner in order to maximise the learner's potential for success. It also includes regular consultancy arising **not** out of a need to discuss problems but out of a desire to share professional expertise for the benefit of the school as a whole. This can help to produce a productive and efficient school system within an atmosphere of collaboration and empathy.

Clearly both models may operate simultaneously within schools, but professionals must be flexible and practise in ways which can accommodate both models while ensuring that an acceptable measure of consistency and effectiveness is achieved.

Models of intervention

Fig. 24: Stage process model

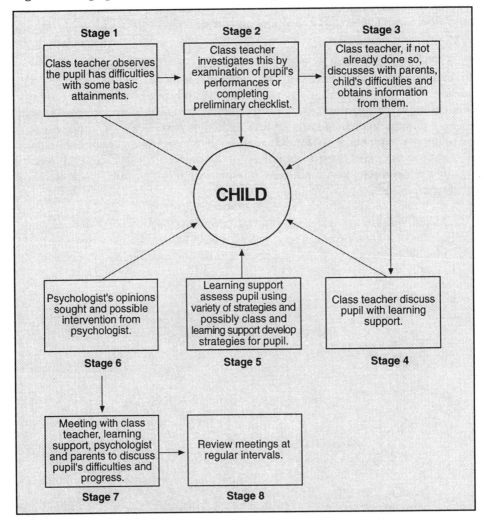

This model is essentially a reactive model because one is focusing on the child's difficulties as they become obvious. The procedure and the stages may take time. This model, therefore, does not readily facilitate early identification, unless the class teacher has a sound awareness of the difficulties associated with dyslexia.

Fig. 25: The whole-school interactive model

The focus for this model is the school, not necessarily the child, and it can be illustrated in the following way:–

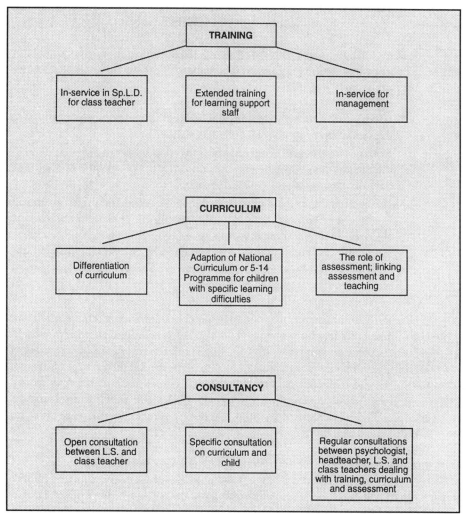

The above model may enable the philosophies concerning individual needs and whole-school approaches to interact effectively, minimise the role conflicts and misconceptions between professionals and provide appropriate and effective support for children with specific learning difficulties, teachers, parents and other professionals.

Conclusion

This chapter has focused on issues of early identification and on the processes and procedures of implementing assessment. It is necessary that local groups of professionals working together in this field have some common aims and an agreed rationale in identification and assessment.

Pumfrey and Reason (1991), following their national survey, suggest a number of recommendations regarding assessment. Four of these which may be considered particularly useful are outlined below.

- Identification procedures should include consideration of the child's previous learning history.
- Both normative and criterion-referenced assessment of specific learning difficulties should be supplemented by the observations of pupils, parents, teachers and psychologists.
- In identifying pupils with specific learning difficulties, attention should be given to the strategies, strengths and weaknesses that children bring to their attempts to read and write.
- The symbiotic relationship between assessment and teaching should be appreciated by all practitioners involved with pupils identified as having specific learning difficulties.

These four points assume assessment as a process and accept the importance of the child's previous learning history. It is also acknowledged that no one form of assessment is suitable, but that different forms of assessment should be used to complement each other. The value of multi-professional involvement is also recognised and the different aspects which each professional can bring to the assessment is appreciated. Importantly, it recognises the individual nature of children. Every child has an individual learning preference and this must be recognised in the assessment.

Finally, it is of extreme importance that the link between assessment and teaching is appreciated, and that assessment should centre on the child's performances within the class, on the appropriateness of the demands and presentation of the curriculum.

Section 3 –

Teaching and the Curriculum

Chapter 6

Programmes and strategies

Introduction

THE RANGE and variety of programmes and strategies which have been developed to help teachers deal with the difficulties displayed by children with dyslexia may at first glance seem to be an extraordinary virtue for the teacher who is coping with seemingly intransigent, and at times, insurmountable problems. Yet on closer examination it becomes evident that, firstly many of these programmes show considerable similarities and adopt the same principles; and secondly, many cannot naturally and easily be accommodated within the school curriculum and the mainstream class. The range, and indeed thoroughness, both in rationale and development of these programmes do however warrant an awareness and consideration of these programmes by the teacher. This may lead to dilemmas regarding selection and application but at the same time it does exert welcome pressure to ensure that the assessment process is thorough, that the child's problem is clearly defined, and that appropriate teaching materials are selected.

In determining the most appropriate programmes and strategies for children with specific learning difficulties, a number of factors must be considered, the most important of which are:

- the context
- the assessment
- the learner
- the curriculum.

The context

The context relates to the classroom, the school and the teaching situation. The issue of one-to-one tuition and that of mainstream provision for children with specific learning difficulties has been the subject of considerable research, and indeed heated controversy (Pumfrey and Reason, 1991; Riddell, Duffield, Brown and Ogilvy, 1992).

In many schools, learning support teachers work cooperatively with class teachers, and clearly intervention in this case may be of a different nature to that where support teachers withdraw children for individual tuition. Both these systems can be effective. It is important therefore that the teacher uses the context to its maximum benefit through the provision of materials and teaching programmes that can be effectively adapted to different teaching situations and contexts.

Materials need to be individualised to meet the needs of individual children. This involves considering the strengths and weaknesses, as well as the learning style and strategies, of the child and attempting to match this to the teaching programme. For example, the learner who appears to benefit from peer support and collaborative learning may also prefer to accept responsibility for learning and clearly this should be encouraged. If the learning environment is modified to accommodate the learner to a teaching programme which requires some 'withdrawal' from class, the teacher will need to exercise sensitivity and consideration to prevent disillusionment and demotivation. It is therefore unwise to suggest that a particular programme is the most suitable and useful in accommodating the needs of dyslexic children. Clearly an awareness of, and indeed some competence in the alphabetic and phonological aspects of letter, sound and word recognition are of prime importance and therefore would be considered as an important need, but the context for learning must consider how best that need can be met for that particular child. Blanket policy or statements which assume a commonality for all dyslexic learners as regards the most appropriate context for teaching may be unnecessarily restrictive and indeed disadvantageous to the development of the individual's learning skills.

The assessment

One of the objectives, perhaps the principal objective, of an assessment is to provide some guidance to help in the development of teaching programmes. One must therefore attempt to find out from the assessment:

- the nature of the difficulties presented;
- some reasons for those difficulties;
- the child's pattern of strengths/weaknesses;
- the child's interests;
- the child's level of motivation;
- the child's self-concept;
- the type of teaching which has previously been attempted;
- the type of intervention which might be more successful and what has been found to be successful.

It is therefore important to examine the assessment findings in a holistic manner by looking at all aspects of the assessment, such as strengths, weaknesses, self-concept, interest and learning preferences and to link these factors to an appropriate teaching programme. This is consistent with the aims and rationale for assessment which were outlined in Chapter 3. Once again as with context, the individual needs of the learner need to be considered and the assessment should be able to provide this type of information.

The learner

It is important to adopt a holistic perspective, looking not only at the learner's strengths and weaknesses, but the preferred learning style, i.e. under what conditions would the child be most likely to learn. Which approaches may be preferred by the learner? In what way would these approaches help to maintain the learner's interest and motivation as well as enhancing self-esteem?

These questions must be considered before deciding on appropriate intervention and teaching programmes. Although children with specific learning difficulties have some common core difficulties (Stanovich, 1990) they do not represent an identical discrete entity with identical profiles. Therefore intervention and teaching programmes will be tailored to the profile of needs of the individual learner and this will vary depending on the preferred learning style and cognitive profile of each dyslexic child. It will be recalled that in the previous chapter it was similarly advocated that assessment should be linked to teaching in order that a holistic profile of the child can be obtained. The knowledge of the learner which can be most readily recorded by the class teacher is, therefore, of extreme importance in order to successfully match the needs and learning style of the child with the teaching and the requirements of the curriculum.

Programmes and strategies

There is a wide choice of specific programmes, and of useful strategies which often utilise some of the key principles of these programmes. The teacher can use these to help support children with specific learning difficulties.

The various types of programme available are outlined below.

Individualised programmes
*   These are highly structured, can be seen as essentially free-standing and form a central element of the overall strategy for teaching children with specific learning difficulties.

Support approaches and strategies
*   these may utilise the same principles as some of the individual

programmes, but can be used more selectively by the teacher thus making it possible to integrate them more easily within the normal activities of the curriculum.

Assisted learning techniques

• These strategies utilise different and various methods but a central, essential component is the aspect of learning from others. These programmes could therefore involve either peer or adult support and interaction and utilise some of the principles of modelling.

Whole-school approaches

• These recognise that dyslexic difficulties are a whole-school concern and not just the responsibility of individual teachers. Such approaches require an established and accessible framework for consultancy, whole-school screening, and monitoring of children's progress. Early identification is a further key aspect of a whole-school approach.

Some examples of these programmes and strategies are shown below.

Fig. 26

1 INDIVIDUALISED APPROACHES	2 SUPPORT APPROACHES AND STRATEGIES
Alphabetic Phonics	Aston Portfolio
Alpha to Omega	Simultaneous Oral Spelling
Bangor Dyslexia Teaching System	Counselling Approaches
DATAPAC	** Phonic Codecracker
DISTAR	Microcomputer Software Programmes
Hickey Language Course	Neuro-Motor Programmes
* Letterland	Reason and Boote—Reading and Spelling
Reading Recovery Programme (Clay)	Study Skills
* Spelling Made Easy	Quest Materials
Slingerland	Visual Acuity Activities
Orton-Gillingham Method	
Teaching Reading through Spelling (Kingston)	
3 ASSISTED LEARNING PROGRAMMES	4 WHOLE-SCHOOL APPROACHES
Apprenticeship Approach (Waterland)	Counselling Strategies
Paired Reading	Screening materials
Peer Tutoring	Study Skills Programmes
Reciprocal Teaching	Thinking Skills
Cued Spelling	Consultancy

* These can also be used as the main teaching programme for the whole class.
** This can also be used as an individualised programme.

There are considerable benefits from using individualised approaches, but often they require some additional training in addition to the instructions in the programme manual, although many such as the Hickey Course (Augur and Briggs, 1992) are now becoming more teacher-friendly.

The range of support approaches and strategies available (see Fig. 26) clearly demonstrates the different types of difficulties children may present. Some of the support approaches use the same principles of over-learning and multi-sensory strategies as the individualised approaches, and may similarly focus on developing phonological awareness and alphabetic skills. Some, however, such as cued spelling, adopt a behavioural perspective while some of the neuro-motor programmes focus on physical activity.

Recently much activity and development work has been on-going in the area of information technology and many appropriate programmes have been developed for children with specific learning difficulties (Singleton, 1990; Duggan and Turner, 1993). These can help children's word and sentence building skills and can aid both comprehension and spelling. Additionally, the microcomputer offers the child the opportunity for self-learning, control and pleasure from learning experiences. This area will likely show considerable further development in the coming years.

Programmes such as Paired Reading and Peer Tutoring (Topping, 1993), which enhance confidence and self-motivation, may offer considerable benefits and, therefore, these strategies should be given some consideration. The benefits of constructive interaction between adult and child, one of the features of paired reading, is also the key feature in reciprocal teaching, in which the teacher and child engage in a 'scaffold' building dialogue to help the child's comprehension and development of appropriate schema for the task (see Chapter 12).

Although whole-school approaches may be more difficult to administer and effectively organise, they are of the utmost importance. They require the support of all teachers and of the school management to develop a school framework for identification, assessment and consultancy. All teachers require an awareness of specific learning difficulties while some require more specialised knowledge and training. Training of the school management team ensures a framework for assessment which facilitates early identification, classroom observation, specialised assessment when necessary, monitoring and review procedures, and liaison with parents and other agencies. This helps to ensure that the full curriculum can be appropriately accessed by all children with specific learning difficulties. A whole-school strategy within an ethos of support and security, can help develop confidence, self-esteem and success for the child with specific learning difficulties.

It is important to consider the rationale for using particular programmes and strategies. Within the areas mentioned here of individualised learning, support approaches and strategies, assisted learning and whole-school approaches, many quality and effective means of dealing with the dyslexic-type difficulty are at the teacher's disposal. Therefore the criteria for selection – the context, the assessment, the learner and the curriculum – must be carefully considered. These factors are as influential in the selection of teaching approaches as the actual programme or strategy itself.

It is important not only to focus on what a programme does, but how it achieves its aim. The purpose of the following chapters is to assist in understanding some of the principles involved in particular approaches in order that the teacher can consider programmes and strategies in an enlightened and informed manner.

Chapter 7

Individualised programmes

Rationale

IT HAS BEEN argued that children with specific learning difficulties benefit from highly specialised, individualised programmes (Hornsby, 1990; Miles, 1990). Such programmes usually focus on the child's difficulty and aim to help him/her overcome that problem. Objections which can be raised to this are that firstly there is no certainty that the programme will achieve this aim; secondly, it may not be desirable to focus on a child's difficulties and thirdly, there needs to be convincing evidence that the gains made in the individual programme will be transferred to other areas of the curriculum and be sustained once the programme has been discontinued.

These issues are indeed relevant to the development of any programme, and do not necessarily mean that an individual specialised programme is not worthwhile. Indeed for some children, depending on factors such as the context, the difficulty, the assessment and the learner, such a programme may indeed be desirable.

There are a number of quality, established programmes in existence which have been successfully used for children with specific learning difficulties (dyslexia). The important point to bear in mind is that a specific programme used in isolation will not completely remedy the difficulties associated with dyslexia – certainly such programmes may alleviate some of the adverse effects of the difficulty, but any remedy will not be fully effective if used in isolation and an appreciation of the whole curriculum and of how the programme can fit into the curriculum are important.

One of the consequences of using specific programmes, however, is that the child may need to be withdrawn from the class group. Much criticism has been voiced regarding the adverse effects of this, particularly relating to the fact that teaching then takes place outwith the context of the classroom and that withdrawal can be socially and emotionally damaging to children. Yet evidence can be found to counter this claim. Payne (1991) in a survey of sixty articles and books, found little hard evidence of the damaging effects of withdrawal on pupils. This aspect therefore, is not clear cut and strong arguments can be put forward for both views.

Principles

Most individualised programmes incorporate some, or all, of the following principles and approaches.

- multisensory
- over-learning and automaticity
- highly structured and usually phonically based
- sequential and cumulative.

Multisensory methods utilise all available senses simultaneously. This can be summed up in the phrase 'hear it, say it, see it and write it'. These methods have been used for many years and have been further refined by Hornsby and Hickey in phonic structured programmes which incorporate multisensory techniques.

Over-learning is deemed necessary for children with dyslexic difficulties. The short- and long-term memory difficulties experienced by dyslexic children mean that considerable reinforcement and repetition is necessary.

The structured approaches evident in programmes of work for dyslexic children usually provide a linear progression, thus enabling the learner to complete and master a particular skill in the reading or learning process before advancing to a subsequent skill. This implies that learning occurs in a linear developmental manner. Although there is evidence from learning theory to suggest this may be the case, there is still some doubt in the case of reading that mastery of the component sub-skills results in skilled reading. In reading, a number of cognitive skills such as memory and visual, auditory and oral skills interact (Ellis, 1989). This interaction is the key feature so it is therefore important that the skills are taught together and purposefully with the practice of reading as the focus.

Sequential approaches are usually appropriate for children with specific learning difficulties because it may be necessary for them to master sub-skills before moving to more advanced materials. Hence a sequential and cumulative approach may not only provide a structure to their learning, but help to make learning more meaningful and effective.

Many of the individual programmes, however, have been evaluated fairly positively. For example Hornsby and Miles (1980) conducted a series of investigations examining 'dyslexia-centred teaching' programmes with the aim of evaluating how effective these programmes were in alleviating dyslexia. This study and a follow-up study (Hornsby and Farmer, 1990) indicate that the programmes did result in an improvement in terms of pupils' reading and spelling ages. The extent of the transfer of skills to other areas of the curriculum should also, however, be considered and this aspect has not been effectively measured in evaluative studies.

Programmes in practice

Below is a survey of some of the individualised programmes which may be utilised for children with specific learning difficulties.

Letterland

The Letterland material produced by Lyn Wendon is essentially a programme for the teaching of reading although it is currently being extended to include a writing programme which also assists with spelling and uses the same principles as the reading programme (see Fig. 27 and Fig. 28). Resources are also available which are specifically intended as support materials for parents to use at home.

Fig. 27

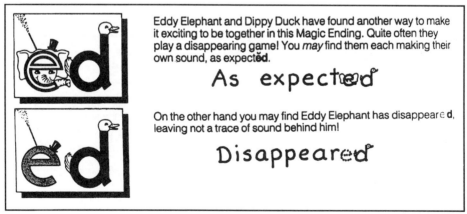

Eddy Elephant and Dippy Duck have found another way to make it exciting to be together in this Magic Ending. Quite often they play a disappearing game! You *may* find them each making their own sound, as expected.

As expected

On the other hand you may find Eddy Elephant has disappeare d, leaving not a trace of sound behind him!

Disappeared

An example of an activity from *Letterland*. Reproduced with permission.
(Wendon, 1987)

Fig. 28: Letterland

Every time I begin a sentence or a name I sit on end.

Ee:1

Eddy Elephant sitting on end   Eddy Elephant   Eddy Elephant sitting on end   Eddy Elephant

E E E !   e e e)

Egg Egg !

egg egg)

Ever Ever !

ever ever)

End End !

end end)

Name

Reproduced by kind permission of Lyn Wendon
(Personal Communication, 1994)

Specific Learning Difficulties (Dyslexia)

Letterland encompasses a number of teaching elements based on recognised and essential components of the teaching of reading. The major elements are language, with an emphasis on listening, speaking and communicating; phonic skills; whole word recognition skills; sentence awareness; comprehension; reading and spelling connections and preliminary skills in creative writing.

Thus Letterland focuses on letters and sounds and by using pictograms encourages children to appreciate letter stages and sounds, thereby reinforcing both shape and sound of letters and words. Integrated within this, however, are the programmes and exercises on whole word recognition, reading for meaning, spelling and creative writing. Spelling is not presented as a series of rules but instead through a story approach, focusing on the Letterland characters.

Progress through the Letterland programme is by a series of steps. These steps can provide the teacher with choice and flexibility and the programme can be implemented to the whole class, in small groups or individually.

There are a number of aspects about Letterland which make it useful for some children with specific learning difficulties. These include the use of pictograms – which can be particularly beneficial to the learner with difficulties in phonological awareness and auditory skills. The use of the story approach to reading and spelling which encourages the processing of information using the long-term memory, is particularly beneficial to dyslexic children whose short-term memory is generally weak. The range of activities which incorporates different approaches allows the learner to develop imagination and creativity in the use of letters and words. Other useful aspects include the focus on the context aspects of reading and the use of syntactic and semantic cues. It is likely that the learner with pronounced difficulties would enjoy this type of teaching programme.

Alpha to Omega

This is a phonetic, linguistic approach to the teaching of reading and can be used as a programme or as resource material. It is highly structured and follows a logical pattern of steps which promote the acquisition of phonological and language skills.

There is an emphasis on learning the 44 phonemes from which all English words are composed. These consist of the 17 vowel sounds and the 27 consonant sounds. There is also an emphasis on the acquisition of language structure, focusing on content words – nouns, verbs, adjectives and finite words – prepositions and participles. There is, therefore, an emphasis on using words in the context of a sentence. The programme provides a highly structured format for the teaching of sentences and for grammatical structure.

There are also three accompanying and very useful activity packs designed for different stages. These packs provide appropriate back-up exercises to reinforce the teaching programme (see Fig. 29).

Fig. 29

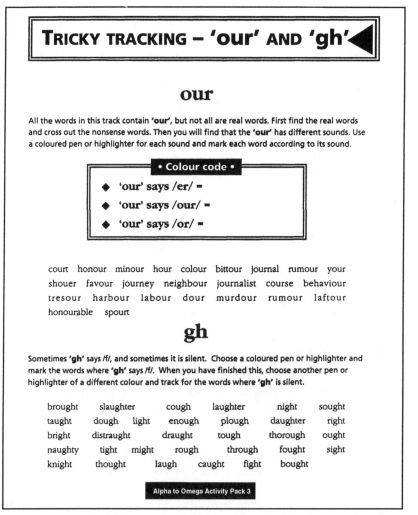

Illustration reproduced by kind permission of the publishers (Hornsby and Pool, 1989)

Specific Learning Difficulties (Dyslexia)

Orton-Gillingham

Programmes based on this approach have become a central focus for multisensory teaching. The programmes offer a structured, phonic-based approach which incorporates the total language experience and focuses on the letter sounds and the blending of these sounds into syllables and words. The approach rests heavily on the interaction of visual, auditory and kinesthetic aspects of language.

Clark (1988) describes the Orton-Gillingham approach as one which adopts the following sequence.

- Letters or phonograms are introduced as visual symbols on cards.
- The letter name is introduced and the teacher says the letter name; the child then repeats it.
- The letter sound is taught in the same way as the letter name.
- The teacher then says the letter sound and asks the child for the letter name. (According to Clark this helps to establish auditory to auditory associations).
- The teacher then writes the letter explaining how it is formed. The pupil traces the letter, copies it and eventually writes it from memory. (This establishes the visual-kinesthetic connection).
- The teacher then gives the letter sound and asks the pupil to write the letter which gives that particular sound. (This helps to form the auditory-kinesthetic association and is reinforced by the pupil saying the letter name simultaneously with the writing of the letter).

Introduction of letters

This is a carefully sequenced procedure and is carried out in the following way:

- to begin with ten letters are taught – two vowels (a, i) and eight consonants (f,l,b,j,h,m,p,t);
- each of the letters is introduced with a key word;
- the difference between vowels and consonants is taught together with the position of the mouth in the pronunciation of the sounds (different coloured cards are used for vowels and consonants).

Blending

Once the child has mastered the letter name and sound, the programme then advances to introduction of blending the letters and sounds. This begins with simple three-letter words and the child repeats the sounds until the word is spoken without pauses between the constituent sounds.

The visual-kinesthetic and auditory-kinesthetic associations are formed by the pupil tracing, saying, copying and writing each word.

Reading of text

Reading of text begins after the pupil has mastered the consonant-vowel-consonant words to a higher automatic level, i.e.. when the pupil can recognise and use these words.

The initial reading material is taken from the programme and contains words the pupil has learnt from the teacher's manual.

Other aspects of the programme

The programme gives considerable attention to the learning of dictionary skills as well as development of written language from pictographs to ideographs and eventually to the alphabet.

The programme does appear to be more suited to a one-to-one situation and it would be difficult to integrate the programme within the school curriculum. As in many programmes derived from the Orton-Gillingham approach, the key principles of over-learning, automaticity and multisensory approaches are very apparent and these principles **can** be utilised within the classroom curriculum.

Hickey Multisensory Language Course

The Hickey Multisensory Language Course (Augur and Briggs, 1992) recognises the importance of the need to learn sequentially the letters of the alphabet. The dyslexic child, however, will usually have some difficulty in learning and remembering the names and sequence of the alphabetic letters as well as understanding that the letters represent speech sounds which make up words.

The programme is based on multisensory principles and the alphabet is introduced using wooden or plastic letters; the child can look at the letter, pick it up, feel it with eyes open or closed and say its sound. Therefore the visual, auditory and tactile-kinesthetic channels of learning are all being utilised with a common goal.

The programme also suggests some activities to help the child become familiar with the alphabet. These include:

- learning the letters sequentially;
- positioning of each letter of the alphabet;
- naming and recognising the shape of the letters.

These programmes involve games and the use of dictionaries to help the child become familiar with the order of the letters and the direction to go, e.g. he needs to know that 'I' comes before 'K', the letters in the first half of the alphabet and those letters in the second half. The alphabet can be further divided into sections, thus it will be easier for the child to remember the section of the alphabet in which a letter appears, for example:

A B C D
E F G H I J K L M
N O P Q R
S T U V W X Y Z

The Hickey Programme suggests activities related to sorting and matching the capital, lower-case, printed and written forms of the letters; practising sequencing skills with cut-out letters and shapes; and practising positioning of each letter in the alphabet in relation to the other letters (this involves finding missing letters and going backwards and forwards in the alphabet).

The programme also indicates the importance of recognising where the accent falls in a word since this clearly affects the spelling and rhythm. The rhyming games can be developed to encourage the use of accent by placing the accent on different letters of the alphabet. This helps to train children's hearing to recognise when a letter has an accent or is stressed in a word.

The programme includes reading and spelling packs which focus on securing a relationship between sounds and symbols. This process begins with single letters, and progresses to consonant blends, vowel continuations and then to complex letter groupings.

The reading packs consist of a set of cards; on one side the lower-case letter is displayed in bold with an upper-case (capital) letter shown on the bottom right-hand corner, in order to establish the link between the two letters. The reverse side of the card indicates a key word which contains the sound of the letter with the actual sound combination in brackets. Rather than providing a visual image of the key word, a space is left for the child to draw the image. This helps to make the image more meaningful to the child and also utilises and reinforces visual and kinesthetic skills.

The spelling pack is similar in structure to the reading pack. On the front of the card the sound made by the letter is displayed in brackets, while the back contains both the sound and the actual letter(s). Sounds for which there is a choice of spellings will in time show all the possible ways in which the sound can be made. Cue words are also given on the back as a prompt, in case the child forgets one of the choices.

Spelling is seen as being of prime importance by the authors of the programme since they view it as an 'all round perceptual experience'. The multisensory method used involves the following process:

- the child repeats the sound heard;
- feels the shape the sound makes in the mouth;
- makes the sound and listens;
- writes the letter(s).

This process involves over-learning and multisensory strategies.

Fig. 30: An example of a worksheet from the Hickey Language Training Programme

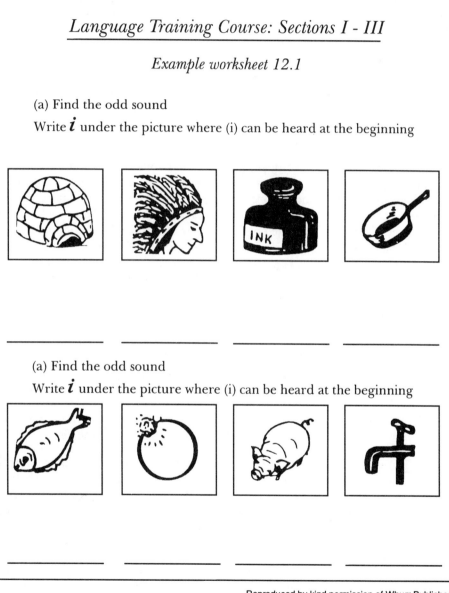

Language Training Course: Sections I - III

Example worksheet 12.1

(a) Find the odd sound

Write *i* under the picture where (i) can be heard at the beginning

(a) Find the odd sound

Write *i* under the picture where (i) can be heard at the beginning

Bangor Dyslexia Teaching System

This system (Miles, 1992) is a structured, sequential teaching programme developed for teachers and speech and language therapists involved in supporting children with dyslexia.

A useful aspect of this programme is the division between primary and secondary pupils. Although it is acknowledged that some secondary pupils are still 'beginning' readers and need to go through the same initial stages of acquiring literacy as beginning readers in the primary school, the programme makes some special provision and adaptations for secondary students. This helps to make the secondary material more age appropriate.

The basic philosophy of the programme is not unlike that of other structured, phonic programmes for dyslexic children. It centres around the issue of phonological difficulties and the problems dyslexic children have in mastering the alphabetic code. The programme attempts to provide children with some competence, at the earliest stage possible, in recognising and categorising speech sounds. Miles (1992) argues that it is not possible for children to benefit from 'top down' language experience approaches to reading if they have not mastered the basic principles of literacy. Some of these principles, which the programme for primary aged children focuses on, include: the teaching of basic letter sounds and the structure of words, long vowels, common word patterns, irregular words, alphabet and dictionary skills, grammatical rules and silent letters.

The programme attempts to acknowledge that dyslexic children may have difficulties with both visual and auditory processing. The issue of auditory processing, particularly relating to the acquisition of phonic skills, is well documented (Frith, 1986; Stanovich, 1991) and some recent studies (Stein, 1990, 1991, 1993) have helped to reawaken the debate on visual aspects of reading and the difficulties some dyslexic children may have in picking out visual letter patterns.

The programme shares the same principles as that utilised by other similar programmes for dyslexic children. It is highly structured and the teacher has to proceed systematically through the programme. The aspect of over-learning is acknowledged to be important and therefore revision of material already learned occupies an important place in the implementation of the programme.

One of the difficulties inherent in following the principle of over-learning is the aspect of boredom, which may result from repetitive revision of material already learnt. This programme acknowledges that pitfall, and suggests ways of overcoming it through the use of games and other adapted materials.

The multisensory teaching element is also crucial in this programme. Some of the exercises attempt to engage all the available senses simultaneously, thus acknowledging the accepted view that dyslexic children benefit from multisensory learning.

The programme also utilises the particular benefits of mnemonics for dyslexic children as well as the notion of reading and spelling as an integrated activity. Some emphasis is also placed on encouraging dyslexic children to use oral language to plan their work. It is felt that such verbalisations help children clarify their thoughts and planning before embarking on a course of action There is also a useful appendix containing guidance on handwriting, alphabet and dictionary skills.

The secondary component of the programme provides useful advice on dealing with the problem of teaching basic literacy to older students. Miles suggests that the material for older pupils should include words of more than one syllable, even though the student is at the early stages of literacy. Some effort is made to ensure that the student is familiar with polysyllabic words in order that the potential for creative writing is not unduly restricted. At the secondary stage the aspect of reading for meaning is of great importance in order to ensure sustained motivation. The Bangor Dyslexia Teaching System acknowledges this and suggests a range of techniques which can help to support the student through the decoding difficulty in order that maximum meaning and pleasure can be derived from the text. Such suggestions include: supplying difficult words; introducing the story and the book's background and characters; pointing out clues such as capital letters and titles; encouraging fluency by reading from one full stop to the next; omitting words which are difficult, thus encouraging the use of context to obtain meaning; practice; and reading rhymes and limericks which aid sound and syllable awareness.

The programme for secondary students, although less structured than that for primary, includes sections on syllabification and stress, plurals, short and long vowel patterns, silent letters, prefixes and suffixes (see Fig. 31).

The Bangor Dyslexia Teaching System clearly attempts to teach the dyslexic child the basic rules of literacy and the English language. Although the programme can stand on its own, it would be advisable for the teacher to attempt to integrate and relate the programme within the child's class work. This can be possible by selecting aspects of the programme which are most useful and would be particularly appropriate for secondary students of whose learning priorities Miles acknowledges the teacher would need to take account.

Fig. 31: Bangor Dyslexia Teaching System

SYLLABIFICATION AND STRESS

Clear articulation and counting of the successive 'bits' of a word help pupils not to omit parts of a word in writing. The syllables can be tapped out before the word is commenced. It is also useful practice to divide up words either with dividing lines or physically, with scissors, when they can also be reassembled. It is, however, possible to put the dividing lines at slightly different points according to the principle of division:

1. To reflect the way in which we naturally say the word. This would probably involve dividing the word 'extra' *e-xtra*, but such a division does not particularly help spelling because the consonant combination is then even more difficult to sort out, and identification of the prefix is obscured.

2. To assist the identification of long and short vowels, diphthongs, 'r' combinations etc. it is convenient to classify syllables into six categories:

(a) Closed syllables – where there is a consonant at the end of the syllable and the vowel is usually short, e.g. 'con/tent'.

(b) Open syllables – where there is a vowel at the end of a syllable, and the vowel is usually long, e.g. 'pi/lot'.

(c) Vowel - consonant - e – where the vowel is usually long, e.g. 'state/ment'.

(d) Diphthong – where the vowel is usually long, e.g. 'plea/sing'.

(e) -le syllable – e.g. 'ta/ble'.

(f) 'r' combination – where the *r* affects the vowel pronunciation; 'w' combination – where the *w* affects the vowel pronunciation; 'y' combination – where the *y* affects the vowel pronunciation; e.g. 'for/tune', 'aw/ful', 'pay/ment'.

This particularly assists reading since it makes the consonant combinations more manageable and helps decisions on vowel pronunciation. It does not fit well with words of foreign origin which do not follow a doubling principle (particularly words derived from Greek); such words often contain just one consonant after a single vowel pronounced short, e.g. 'comic', 'camel'. (See lists in 'Doubling' section, p. 80.) It may also conflict with recognition of suffixes, e.g. 'stan/ding'.

3. It is helpful, particularly at the secondary stage, to divide words into prefix-root-suffix, perhaps in order to compare the same root in different words, thus dividing the word into *morphemes*, e.g.

se-*par*-ate	a-*spir*-ate
dis-*par*-ate	in-*spir*-ation
pre-*par*-ation	con-*spir*-acy

where division according to principles in (2) above would be less helpful.

It is important sometimes, also, for the pupil to consider where the stress falls on a word. The doubling of consonants after a short vowel is a practice that applies to syllables which are stressed. Stress or lack of if changes the pronunciation of vowels in prefixes and makes them difficult to identify; suffixes lose clarity or pronunciation and vowel sounds and consonant sounds are corrupted by lack of stress, common in the last syllable of a word.

Dyslexics often find this matter of stress difficult, as they do not consciously reflect on speech characteristics.

Reproduced by kind permission of the publishers
(Miles, 1992)

Alphabetic Phonics

The key principles found in the majority of individualised programmes for dyslexic children – multisensory techniques, automaticity and over-learning – are all found in the Alphabetic Phonics programme. Additionally, the programme also recognises the importance of discovery learning. Opportunities for discovery learning are found throughout this highly structured programme.

The programme, which stems from the Orton-Gillingham multisensory approach, was developed in Dallas, Texas by Aylett Cox. She has described Alphabetic Phonics as a structured system of teaching students the coding patterns of the English language (Cox, 1985).

Cox asserts that such a phonic based programme is necessary because around 85% of the 30,000 most commonly used English words can be considered phonetically regular and therefore predictable. Thus learning phonetic rules can allow the child access to the majority of the commonly used words.

Alphabetic Phonics provides training in the development of automaticity through the use of flash cards, and over-learning through repetitive practice in reading and spelling until 95% mastery is achieved.

The programme also incorporates opportunities to develop creativity in expression and in the sequencing of ideas.

The programme is highly structured with daily lessons of around one hour. Lessons incorporate a variety of tasks which help to keep the child's attention directed to the activities and prevents tedium or boredom. A typical lesson may include the activities outlined in Fig. 32.

Fig. 32: Alphabetic Phonics

1.	An alphabetic activity, which emphasises sequence and directionality.
2.	Introduction of a new element or concept, which begins with discovery and is reinforced with multisensory techniques.
3.	Training in automatic recognition of letter names, through flashcard presentation (Reading Decks).
4.	Training in recognition of letter sounds, by having students pronounce the sounds for a letter or letters presented on flashcards (Spelling Decks) and then naming and writing the letter or letters.
5.	Practice in reading and spelling (10 minutes allotted for each). Each task is continued until student reaches 95 percent mastery, as measured by the Bench Mark measures.
6.	Handwriting practice.
7.	Practice in verbal expression, first oral and later written, focusing on various skills (e.g., sequencing ideas, creative expression, vocabulary, syntax).
8.	Listening to good literature and building comprehension skills, while reading instruction focuses on decoding skills.

Reproduced by kind permission of publishers
(Cox, 1985)

In this programme reading comprehension instruction does not begin until the student has reached a minimal level of accuracy in relation to decoding skills. Cox, however, does recognise that children will learn and retain new vocabulary more effectively and efficiently through experiential learning, and that this is particularly applicable to dyslexic children.

Although a number of studies have claimed impressive results using the Alphabetic Phonics Programme (Ray, 1986; Frankiewicz, 1985) it has been asserted that the research methodology used and the lack of effective control groups somewhat diminish the impressive results of these studies (Clark, 1988). Additionally, in order to teach the programme effectively, it has been maintained that 480 hours of teacher training is required, based on knowledge of the structure of the English language, knowledge of phonetic rules and patterns in spelling and integration of these activities into a structured, hierarchical curriculum. An accompanying text (Cox, 1992) *Foundations for Literacy*) does however provide an easy to follow lesson guide for the teacher (see Fig. 33).

In the programme Cox suggests a number of linkages between multisensory activities and the letter such as association of cursive shape, speech sound, graphic symbol and kinesthetic memory. An example is provided below:

Fig. 33: Multisensory introduction of a letter

Linkage 2 – Association of student's kinesthetic memory of letter's cursive shape (in hand and arm) with its name. Teacher demonstrates already learned approach strokes in the same order daily. Student chooses the one that fits best. All letters begin on baseline and are written left-to-right.

1.   Teacher prints a three-inch 'reading' letter on board and writes cursive letter over it, showing the relationship of 'writing' letter to 'reading' letter. The letter is then erased.

2.   Teacher places small arrow at starting point and writes large cursive letter carefully on board (one to three feet high) while describing strokes and rhythm. Student observes closely. Leave model on board.

3.   Student sky-writes letter several times in the air (facing chalk-board), naming letter just before writing it every time. He always points his index finger toward the arrow and names letter before he starts. Teacher emphasises stop to promote rhythm. Right hander begins sky-writing at mid-line and moves toward the right. Left hander begins to the left of the body and moves toward mid-line.

4.   Student traces large model of letter several times on paper (first with finger tip) until he has the 'feel' in his muscles. He always names letter aloud before he begins to write its approach stroke.

5.   Student copies letter once with model in view.

6.   Student writes large letter twice from memory, always naming letter first.

7.   Student writes large letter twice with eyes closed or averted, each time 'telling his hand' the letter's name before beginning the approach stroke. He develops independent follow-through without the need for teacher's oral directions.

Reproduced by kind permission of publishers
(Cox, 1992)

The principles and practices of this programme, such as structure, multisensory technique, emphasis on automaticity, emphasis on building comprehension skills, experiential learning and listening skills, and in particular recognition of letter sounds, can have desirable outcomes. These can readily be adapted and implemented into teaching programmes devised for different needs and contexts.

The Slingerland Programme

The Slingerland Programme is an adaptation of the Orton-Gillingham Programme. Essentially, the programme was developed as a screening approach to help minimise the difficulties experienced by children in language and literacy. The Slingerland Screening Tests accompany the programme and are usually administered in the early stages of education.

The programme shares similar features with other programmes. Multisensory teaching permeates the programme which begins by introducing letters of the alphabet.

The programme follows the format below.

Wr\iting

This is the first step and usually uses the following order:
- tracing
- copying
- writing in the air
- simultaneously writing from memory and saying the letter.

Letter sounds

This involves naming the letter then the key word associated with the letter and then the letter sound.

Blending

This is introduced with oral activities and may involve repetitive use and blends with kinesthetic support to reinforce the material being learnt.

Decoding

In decoding, students begin with three letters c-v-c, e.g. words such as 'bay' and way'. They are required to:

- pronounce the initial consonant,
- then the vowel
- then blend the two
- and pronounce the final consonant
- and say the whole word.

Vowel digraphs and vowel-consonant digraphs are taught as units, although Slingerland maintains that consonant blends are usually learnt more easily.

Reading for meaning

Once decoding has been sufficiently mastered a whole-word approach is encouraged in the reading of text.

Initially, students undergo a 'preparation for reading' lesson when some time is spent producing, recognising and reading words and the students become familiar with the image of the word.

There is also some emphasis on teacher modelling by reading aloud. To foster reading comprehension skills, the teacher cues in appropriate clues into the questioning technique, e.g. which seven words tell us where the house was – 'it was built on a high hill'.

The Slingerland Programme is highly specific and highly structured and contains some useful strategies and ideas (see Fig. 34).

Fig. 34: An example of an activity from the Slingerland Programme

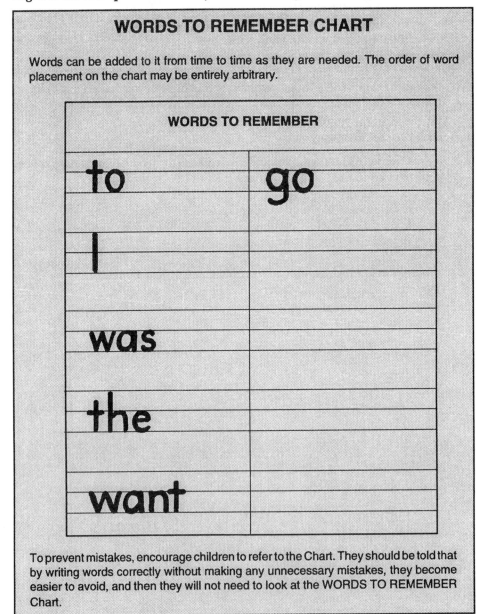

WORDS TO REMEMBER CHART

Words can be added to it from time to time as they are needed. The order of word placement on the chart may be entirely arbitrary.

WORDS TO REMEMBER	
to	go
I	
was	
the	
want	

To prevent mistakes, encourage children to refer to the Chart. They should be told that by writing words correctly without making any unnecessary mistakes, they become easier to avoid, and then they will not need to look at the WORDS TO REMEMBER Chart.

Reproduced by kind permission of the publishers
(Slingerland, 1993)

Research into the effectiveness of the Slingerland Programme indicates that it can produce significant gains in a number of language aspects, such as listening comprehension, punctuation, grammar, syntax, spelling and study skills. Gains have also been noted in vocabulary and the use of inference in reading (Wolf, 1985; McCulloch, 1985).

Project Read

This programme shares similarities with the Reading Recovery Programme (Marie Clay). It attempts to provide effective reading instruction for those students who are not progressing adequately with reading.

Devised by Enfield and Greene, who now consider the programme an alternative approach to the teaching of reading as well as one which provides remediation (Enfield and Greene, 1981), it is designed essentially for the classroom teacher.

The programme is divided into three phases – phase one highlights the use of phonics; phase two looks at reading comprehension, and phase three concentrates on written expression. The programme also incorporates the principles of multisensory learning, over-learning and automaticity.

Phase one

This focuses on the systematic teaching of phonic skills. Multisensory strategies are used: for example, whilst saying the letter children trace it in the air or on a table, then identify the picture which contains the letter. Attention is also given to mouth positions in the voiced and unvoiced sounds.

Over-learning occurs through a review of previously learned material at the beginning of each lesson, and automaticity is encouraged through the use of flash cards for letter sounds and the writing of the letter symbols in response to the teacher saying the sound.

Sounds are introduced in a structured manner, and usually the student will be familiar with a sound, the letter symbol and the use of the letter symbol and sound in a word before embarking on a new sound.

In order to provide some success, 'reinforcement reading', which consists of students reading texts which contain in the main phonetically regular words, is included in the programme.

Phase two

This phase focuses on reading comprehension and vocabulary development. The programme presents a sequence of comprehension skills which include identifying the subject of the text; selecting and explaining the meaning of unfamiliar words; identifying aspects of punctuation and the reasons for those particular aspects; noting the nature of the text material (for example, whether it is fiction, non-fiction); the use of inferences contained within the text; the conclusions which one could draw from the text; and the organisation of the text.

Students are encouraged to look for clues in the text which can help to support the conclusions which are drawn from the inferences made from the content. The teacher, therefore, makes a statement which contains inferences and asks students to find clues which can support this inference. Models are provided for demonstrating the structure of a story plot, such as the conflict, preliminary activities prior to the action, the action, the aftermath of the action and the conclusion.

Phase three

This phase looks at written expression. It focuses on the teaching of sentence structure and paragraph development. Considerable attention is given to creative writing experiences and the identification of ideas and concepts which are found in creative writing.

The Project Read Programme appears to possess some interesting elements. The focus on creative writing for example, is an aspect which can sometimes be lost in the quest to ensure that children with dyslexia are taught the essential decoding skills.

DISTAR

DISTAR (Direct Instruction System of Teaching Arithmetic and Reading) was originally designed for socially disadvantaged children in the United States as part of the Project Follow Through scheme launched by the Government in 1968. The programme is orientated to achievement in basic attainments and tasks and skills to enhance effective learning.

Some of the features of DISTAR include the transfer of learning from specific examples to general concepts; continual, positive reinforcement to enhance motivation and success; and the monitoring of progress through the use of criterion-referenced assessment. In addition to reading skills, the current DISTAR programme covers language, spelling and arithmetic (Engelmann and Bruner, 1983, SRA).

The reading programme, which commences at pre-school level, incorporates both decoding and comprehension lessons. The programme includes elements of pre-reading skills, pronunciation of letter sounds, different types of sounds, oral blending activities, rhyming activities, sound associations and sequencing skills. The individual lessons utilise a variety of teaching methods including games. These games aim to develop various strategies to help in the retention of letter sounds.

The programme is interspersed with activities to monitor progress in relation to reading accuracy, speed and comprehension.

Evaluation studies display impressive progress in attainments among students undertaking the DISTAR programme – results which appear to continue through to secondary education (Meyer, 1984). Some criticism, however, has been raised that the teacher's manual is too prescriptive and places too much restriction on teachers (Becker, 1977). The focus of the programme on transferring skills from the specific to the underlying general task concepts is indeed commendable and can make the DISTAR materials a useful resource.

Reading Recovery

Reading Recovery is an early reading and writing intervention programme, developed by Marie Clay, which focuses on children who after one year at school have lagged significantly behind their peers in reading and writing. Marie Clay originally introduced the programme in New Zealand, but it has now been shown that the programme can be successfully transferred to other countries and contexts (Pinnell, Lyons, Deford, Bryk and Seltzer, 1988, 1991; Wright, 1992).

The programme aims to boost the reading attainments of the selected children over a relatively short period, around twelve to twenty weeks, with specially trained teachers carrying out the programme, seeing children on an individual basis for thirty minutes daily. The programme centres around the individual child's strengths and weaknesses as assessed by the actual reading programme. It is not, therefore, structured around a set of principles and practices to which the child has to be accommodated, but rather the programme adapts itself to the child's specific requirements and needs. It utilises both bottom-up and top-down reading approaches and therefore encourages the use of decoding strategies through the use of phonics, and awareness of meaning through an awareness of the context and language of the text.

The programme aims to produce 'independent readers whose reading improves whenever they read' (Clay, 1985). There is an emphasis, therefore, on strategies which the reader can apply to other texts and situations, and there is evidence that gains made in the Reading Recovery Programme will be maintained over time.

For some children the Reading Recovery Programme may need to be supplemented by additional sessions which could include:

- re-reading familiar books
- taking a running record
- reinforcing letter identification
- writing a story, thus learning sounds in words
- comprehension of story
- introducing new book.

It is also important that the child is helped to develop a self-improving system. This would encourage the child to:

- be aware of his own learning
- take control and responsibility for his own learning.

The goal of teaching reading is to assist the child to produce effective strategies for working on text, and according to Clay this can be done through focusing on the practices of self-correcting and self-monitoring.

The main components of the programme include:

- learning about direction
- locating and focusing on aspects of print
- spatial layout of books
- writing stories
- learning sounds in words
- comprehension and cut-up stories
- reading books
- using print as a cue
- sound and letter sequence
- word analysis
- fluency.

A typical Reading Recovery lesson would include the analysis of the child's decoding strategies, the encouragement of fluent reading through the provision of opportunities to link sounds and letters, the reading of familiar texts and the introduction of new books.

Identification

Since the programme provides an intensive input to those children lagging in reading, it is vitally important that the identification procedures are sound in order to ensure that the children who receive the benefits of this programme are those who would not otherwise make satisfactory progress.

The lowest achieving children in a class group, after a year at school at around six years of age, are admitted into the programme. Clay believes that by the end of the first year at primary school it is possible to identify children who are failing. She suggests that this can be achieved through systematic observation of children's learning behaviour, together with a diagnostic survey.

The systematic observation takes the form of noting precisely what children are saying and doing in relation to reading, so the focus is on reading tasks rather than specific sub-skills such as visual perception or auditory dissemination. In order to identify the child's reading behaviour Marie Clay has developed a diagnostic survey which involves taking a 'Running Record' of precisely how the child is performing in relation to reading. This type of analysis of children's errors in reading can provide clues in relation to children's strengths and weaknesses in reading.

The diagnostic survey includes directional movement (which looks at general directional concepts, including motor coordination, impulsivity and hesitancy), error behaviour (focusing on oral language skills, speed of responding and the use of semantic and syntactic context), the use of visual and memory cues, the rate of self-correction, and the child's preferred mode of identifying letters (alphabetic, sound or cueing from words). The survey also includes details of the child's writing skills. This is particularly important since it may provide some indication of any reading problems as well as language level and message quality.

Evaluation of the Reading Recovery

Much of the research evidence which examines the effectiveness of this programme is impressive. The participating children appear to display gains which allow them to reach average levels of performance in reading within a relatively short period (Wright, 1992). There are, however, a number of studies which are critical of the programme.

Meek (1985) argues that the programme is rather restrictive in that it does not allow for children's reading preferences in relation to choice of material, and

Adams (1990) observes that the phonics element in Reading Recovery is not systematic and does not emphasise structures such as 'word families'. The programme, according to Topping and Wolfendale (1985), does not make adequate allowance for the effective role which parents can play in enhancing literacy skills, and Glyn et al (1989) argue that many of the gains made by children who have participated in the Reading Recovery Programme have disappeared after a year. Johnston (1990) feels that programmes such as Reading Recovery are only necessary because of the trend from phonics-focused programmes, and she concludes that 'rather than wait until children fail in a non-phonics programme, it would be very much better for them either to be taught routines in a reading programme which emphasises phonics as well as reading for memory, or for the class teacher to have such a scheme available for those who are making very slow progress'.

Dombey (1992), arguing on behalf of the National Association for the Teaching of English, puts forward some doubts about the efficacy of Reading Recovery because it focuses on one particular age group – six year olds – and because it requires intensive training of a few specialists with little opportunity for dissemination of the skills of these specialists so that the effects of the programme do not fully percolate into mainstream classes.

Dombey further argues that it could be more cost effective to study the existing provision for the teaching of reading, and to identify ways in which this could be improved, for example by ensuring that all teachers of young children have the time needed to teach reading thoroughly, and to provide those teachers with adequate training in the teaching of reading for all children.

The introduction of the Reading Recovery Programme in Surrey has shown that the programme can be readily adapted to the UK classroom context. Wright and Prance (1992) provide an illustrative case study of one six-year-old girl, the lowest progress reader in the class group. At the start of the programme this girl displayed 75-97% accuracy in reading three one-line caption books and was able to write accurately thirteen of the thirty-seven words on a dictation passage. By the end of the programme the girl had progressed to 98% accuracy on more demanding readers and scored full marks on the dictation passage. In addition the girl displayed considerable gains in the full battery of reading tests administered at the end of the programme. Wright and Prance also acknowledged some qualitative improvements in the girl's reading behaviour, for example she began to recognise similar patterns between words. This is a good example of the application of word knowledge which could be transferred to other contexts – a difficulty, in fact, which seems to pervade children with dyslexia and prevents effective transfer of word knowledge to other contexts. The general monitoring of her own work appeared to improve, something which was highlighted by the increase in her self-correction rate and in the use of the strategy of scanning the print before summarising to read aloud.

Longitudinal studies in Ohio and New Zealand showed that the gains made by children after three to six months of the programme were maintained: the former Reading Recovery pupils were still functioning within the average band at age nine (Clay, 1985; Delford et al, 1987).

A further evaluation conducted by Wright (1992) showed that in Surrey, the gains made by children participating in the Reading Recovery Programme were impressive. Ninety-six of those participating reached average levels of attainment in literacy after around seventeen weeks of the programme.

The study did reveal marked differences between schools, which reflected the difficulty some teachers had in seeing the pupils every day.

Only three of the 82 children taken into the programme did not achieve average levels for their classes after twenty weeks. This appears as an impressive statistic when it is considered that at the start of the programme the participating children were only able to read their names or a short sentence, displayed poor recognition of letter names or sounds, and could write only five words unaided in ten minutes. The results are broadly similar to those gains achieved in the New Zealand and Ohio studies (Clay, 1985; Pinnell et al, 1988) and Wright therefore concludes that the Reading Recovery programme was successfully imported to the Surrey context. Indeed, the Surrey children made greater gains than the New Zealand children in all areas except sight vocabulary, although the former did remain in the programme on average several weeks longer than the New Zealand children. Clearly, further research needs to be carried out to assess whether the gains made are maintained in the same manner as those made by the New Zealand children.

Teaching Reading Through Spelling

This programme produced by staff at the Kingston Reading Centre (Cowdery et al, 1984-88) provides a very detailed and comprehensive analysis of the diagnosis of specific learning difficulties and programmes of remediation.

It is based on the original Orton–Gillingham Programme and follows the same basic principles as those adopted by other specific programmes recommended by the British Dyslexia Association. The programme is, therefore, phonically based, structured and cumulative. These principles ensure that the programme has a coherent organisation and a progression through alphabetic knowledge to sounds, leading to sound/symbol correspondence. The programme also develops multisensory strategies in teaching and learning. Repetition is also built into this programme as the authors acknowledge the value of automaticity for dyslexic children.

The Teaching Reading Through Spelling Programme is essentially a psycholinguistic approach because, although it recognises the importance of phonic knowledge, particularly for dyslexic children who may not obtain full benefit from 'look and say' approaches, it also emphasises articulation and speech training. Linguistic competence, performance and linguistic concepts are therefore guiding principles of this programme.

The authors of the programme appreciate that spelling, being a recall skill (as opposed to reading which is a recognition skill), can present more serious difficulties for the child and therefore the programme attempts to develop an understanding of the spelling system as an aid to developing the processing skills necessary for reading.

The programme is structured in units aimed at different activities. For example there are units on the Foundations of the Programme, the early stages, later stages, spelling, activity for infants and beginners and a handwriting copy book.

Section one of the foundation programme begins with alphabet work and includes the use of a variety of strategies to help the child become familiar with and retain the letters of the alphabet. Games such as alphabet bingo, alphabet dominoes, mazes and crosswords introduce some variety and enjoyment in this section of the programme.

The early stages programme proceeds through sound-symbol relationship (auditory), sound-symbol relationship (visual), short vowels, voiced and unvoiced consonants, initial and final consonant blends, syllables, syllable division for reading and spelling, grammatical rules and suggested lesson plans for teaching letters and sounds.

The later stages programme develops the work of the early stages and in addition, looks at word families and elaborates on the use of the reading and spelling pack.

The Teaching Reading Through Spelling Programme is very detailed and thorough in its approach to phonic and linguistic aspects of teaching reading and spelling. Such a structured approach may easily lend itself to monotony and dullness, particularly since it incorporates the essential aspects of over-learning and automaticity. The programme authors, however, have attempted to overcome this by introducing a variety of stimulating games and strategies which help to provide enjoyment to children, as well as reinforcing the central aspects of the programme (see Fig. 36).

In general the programme provides a good, clear structure and can be readily utilised by the class teacher.

Fig. 35

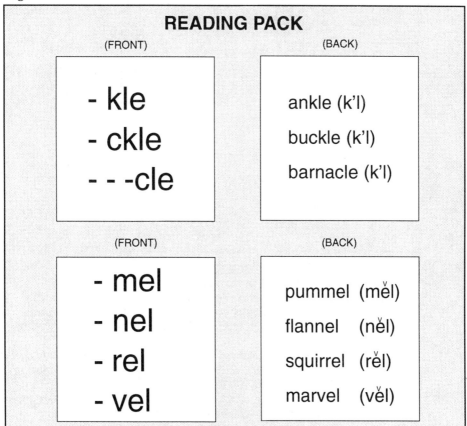

READING PACK

(FRONT)	(BACK)
- kle - ckle - - -cle	ankle (k'l) buckle (k'l) barnacle (k'l)

(FRONT)	(BACK)
- mel - nel - rel - vel	pummel (mĕl) flannel (nĕl) squirrel (rĕl) marvel (vĕl)

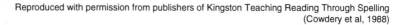

Reproduced with permission from publishers of Kingston Teaching Reading Through Spelling (Cowdery et al, 1988)

Fig.36: Teaching Reading Through Spelling

THE (i) GAME

A reading game that reinforces the different spellings of the sound (ī). Suitable for all pupils that have covered the programme to <u>igh</u> and had <u>buy</u> and <u>height</u> pointed out as exceptions, should the teacher wish to include them. This game can be adapted to teach the choice of <u>l</u> and <u>ll</u>; <u>ble</u> and <u>bble, ble</u> and <u>nel</u>.

Aim: To consolidate the use of the (ī) spelling card.

Materials: A pack of cards. On each card write the beginning or end of a word with the sound (ī) in it. About 32 cards will be required to make the game playable.

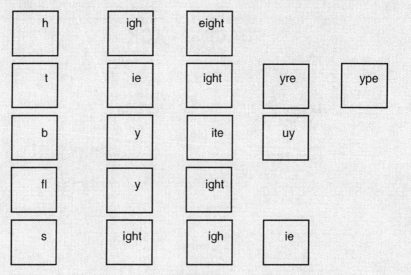

METHOD

1. Shuffle the cards and deal 7 cards to each player.
2. The players then look to see if they can make any words with their cards.
3. They put the completed word/s on the table and read them.
4. The remaining pack is put face down in the middle of the table and one card is turned face up.
5. The player on the left of the dealer has a choice of taking the exposed card that has been turned face up or the top card of the remaining pack, to see if s/he can make a word with the cards in his/her hand.
6. If the first player can make a word s/he puts it on the table and reads it clearly, then throws out a card and the second player has a turn.
7. The winner is the first player to use all the cards in his/her hand.

Conclusion

The range of individualised programmes for children with dyslexia is impressive and this chapter has provided summaries of some of the main approaches.

Some of the principles of the programmes and the methods advocated by their authors, such as 'multisensory', 'structured' and 'cumulative' approaches can provide useful pointers in the development of support materials for dyslexic children. Ideally, for a programme to be of maximum benefit to teachers, it should not only be easily understood and implemented, but also flexible and adaptable to different contexts and types of dyslexic difficulties. The following chapter on Support Approaches emphasises the benefits of such flexibility and adaptability.

Chapter 8

Support approaches and strategies

Introduction

IN ADDITION to the impressive number of individualised programmes available for children with dyslexia, there is also an abundance of support materials which can be utilised by teachers to complement teaching programmes and curriculum approaches. Conceptually most of the individualised programmes have much in common, emphasising aspects such as structure, multi-sensory aspects, over-learning and automaticity. Support materials, however, do not necessarily provide an individual programme, but rather can be used by the teacher to help the child develop some competencies to allow access to the full range of curriculum activities.

Some of these support materials and approaches are discussed below.

Phonological awareness approaches

There is strong evidence to suggest that phonological factors are of considerable importance in reading (Ellis and Large, 1988; Stanovich, 1991). Children with decoding problems appear to be considerably hampered in reading because they are unable to generalise from one word to another. Studies have shown that dyslexic children display difficulty with phonologically regular non-words when matched with controls of an equivalent literacy level (Frith and Snowling, 1983; Seymour, 1987; Halligan and Johnston, 1988). This means that every word they read is unique, indicating that there is a difficulty in learning and applying phonological rules in reading. It therefore emphasises the importance of teaching sounds/phonemes and ensuring that the child has an awareness of the sound/letter correspondence. Learning words by sight can enable some children to reach a certain standard in reading, but prevents them from adequately tackling new words and extending their vocabulary.

If children have a phonological awareness difficulty they are more likely to guess the word from the first letter cue and not the first **sound**, i.e. the word 'KITE' will be tackled from the starting point of the letter 'K' and not the sound 'ki' so the dyslexic reader may well read something like 'KEPT'. It is important, therefore, that beginning readers receive some structured training in the grapheme/phoneme correspondence; this is particularly necessary for dyslexic children who would not automatically, or readily, appreciate the importance of phonic rules in reading.

Phonological awareness relates to factors such as syllabic awareness and segmentation skills, rhyme awareness and rhyme production, and awareness of alliteration. The awareness of alliteration has been shown to be a reliable predictor of phoneme segmentation skills and of reading and spelling ability. Bryant and Goswami (1990) and Bradley and Bryant (1991) have shown that the prediction and awareness of rhyme from three years of age relates to subsequent literacy development. The implication of this is that structured programmes focusing on phonological awareness of rhyming for pre-school children may help to prevent, or minimise, subsequent literacy problems.

Exercises and programmes on phonological awareness usually involve some of the following: sound to word matching; word to sound matching; word to word pairing (see Fig. 37); sound recognition (see Fig. 38); identifying missing phonemes (see Fig. 39); phoneme substitution (see Fig. 40); segmentation of phonemes.

Fig. 37

WORD TO WORD PAIRING

This involves matching words with other words sharing the same sounds.

Thus from the list below, which two words start with the same sound?

NIP	DIP
LAST	DARE
LOOK	HAM

The task can be extended by asking which words from the same list end with the same sound. Again this requires both the use of visual and auditory stimuli and analysis within the context of the word.

These exercises on matching can help the child become aware of sounds, the importance of sounds in words and the different sounds in words beginning with the same letter.

Figures 38, 39 and 40 extend this further by distinguishing between sounds which are fairly similar. These exercises focus particularly on sounds at the beginning of words. Similar exercises can, of course, be constructed for sound endings.

Fig. 38

SOUND RECOGNITION

This method concentrates on the actual sounds in words and encourages the child to recognise and discriminate these actual sounds. Lewkowicz (1980), after reviewing research on phonological awareness found isolation of the initial phoneme to be the most useful method in teaching children with decoding problems.

Thus, the child is asked to say the initial sounds in words. This encourages both the visual recognition and the auditory discrimination of the sounds.

For example: what are the first sounds in the following words?

FISH	SOME
FARE	LAST

Fig 39

IDENTIFYING MISSING PHONEME

This involves comparing two words, one with a single initial sound, the other with a blend. Therefore one phoneme is omitted.

For example: the word 'TRAIN' can be compared with 'RAIN' and the child will be asked which sound is missing.

Fig. 40

PHONEME SUBSTITUTION

This focuses on the prefixes of words.

For example: saying a word with a different sounding initial letter.

Thus the child would be asked to say the word 'LIGHT' and then asked to say the word using different initial letters e.g. 'F', 'M', 'N'.

Rhyming and analogous reading

Bradley's research has given considerable focus to the use of rhyme and to the importance of rhyming awareness and rhyming skills in reading development.

Figure 41 provides examples of analogous reading which use rhyming as a method of attacking new words. This has been the subject of considerable research (Ehri and Robbins, 1992; Bruck and Treiman, 1992; Goswami, 1988, 1993, 1994; Goswami and Bryant, 1990). Analogous reading involves decoding new words, not by phonemic segmentation (see below), but by using 'onset' and rhyme strategies. Thus in the example in Figure 41 the beginning reader will break the word 'fish' into the onset 'f' and the rhyme 'ish' and match it to the word 'wish'.

Interestingly, Bruck and Treiman (1992) found that it was more difficult for children who were learning new words by analogy to transfer the new learning to other contexts. Such children still needed to rely, to a large extent, on correspondences between individual phonemes and graphemes in the decoding of new words.

Fig. 41

ANALOGOUS READING

This involves children being able to recognise words which rhyme. Bradley (1990) argues this is important for phonological awareness.

For example: which two words from the list below rhyme?

NEAR	WISH
SEA	WILL
FISH	WAIT

Bradley, in her experimental work, found significant correlations between children at nursery school who had difficulty in recognising and reciting rhymes and those who had subsequent reading difficulties. Teaching rhyming skills may well be a useful exercise, particularly if multisensory aspects are involved such as saying, listening, looking and moving to the rhyme.

Segmentation of phonemes

This focuses on the need for beginning readers to be aware of the segments in words. Such awareness is made quite difficult for some beginning readers because units of speech – syllables – are represented by even smaller units in the alphabetic script. Children with reading difficulties therefore can segment speech into syllables, but they may not understand that syllables can be analysed into shorter segments, e.g. the word 'caravan' contains three syllables, but is represented by seven letters in the printed word.

Some exercises which can help deal with problems of phoneme segmentation are outlined below.

Practice at using rhyming words

Bradley (1990) puts forward a strong argument that the use of rhymes, jingles and alliteration in the classroom can help children categorise words according to their sounds. Practice therefore at using rhyme would seem to be an important element in the acquisition of phoneme segmentation.

Phoneme awareness

Phoneme awareness may be developed by teaching the child to tap out the rhythms of words, i.e. the child identifies the phonemes in a word and also

---

rhythmically acknowledges these sounds by tapping on the desk – each tap represents a phoneme.

Liberman (1990) and Shankweiler (1985) present a number of different principles in phoneme awareness exercises.

- Phoneme analysis requires a very slow 'stretched' pronunciation of the word to be segmented.
- All the tasks are first auditorily presented only after these tasks are mastered are letters and words visually presented.
- In auditory tasks, children learn first to analyse short words into phonemes blending phonemes into syllables; words are introduced later.
- Analysis of words with two phoneme segments is mastered before segmental analysis of three phonemes is presented.
- Vowel/consonant syllables such as 'is' and 'am' should be introduced before consonant/vowel syllables such as 'no' and 'he' are introduced.
- Decoding of simple words is introduced after these skills are mastered.

Aaron (1989) argues that dyslexic children over-learn the letter-name association to such a degree that they are not able to remove themselves from this bond which prevents them from learning other phonemes associated with that letter.

Irregular words

Many children have problems remembering 'chunks', such as 'igh' in 'sight', and 'fight'. If children cannot do this, then every word will be unique. Irregular words can also be learnt using the multisensory techniques indicated in Fig. 42.

Fig.42

SIMULTANEOUS ORAL SPELLING

1. Have the word written correctly, or made with the letters.

2. Say the word.

3. Write the word, spelling out each letter as it is written, using cursive script.

4. The child needs to – see each letter
   – hear its name
   – receive kinesthetic feedback through the movement of the arm and throat muscles.

5. Check to see if the word is correct.

6. Cover up the word and repeat the process.

   Continue to practise the word in this way, three times a day, for one week. By this time the word should be committed to memory. However, only one word will have been learned.

7. This step involves the categorisation of the word with other words which sound and look alike. So if the word that has been learned is 'round' the student is then shown that s/he can also spell 'ground' 'pound' 'found' 'mound' 'sound' 'around' 'bound' 'grounded' 'pounding' etc. That is s/he has learned six, eight, or more words for the effort of one.

Reproduced by kind permission of Lynette Bradley
(Personal Communication, 1994)

In relation to spelling, Liberman and Shankweiler (1985) have shown that a clear difference exists in the performance in phonological tasks between good and poor spellers. This implies that successful spelling is related to children's awareness of the underlying phonological structure of words. This is supported by Rohl and Tunmer (1988) who found that good spellers were better at phonemic segmentation tasks than older children matched for spelling age.

Furthermore Bradley and Bryant (1991) showed that measures of rhyme judgment and letter knowledge in pre-school children were a good predictor of subsequent performance in spelling. Thus children who can recognise words which sound and look alike would tend to have a good memory for spelling patterns. Indeed Bradley and Huxford (1994) show that sound categorisation in particular plays an important role in developing memory patterns for spelling. Bradley (1989, 1990) has shown that rhyming is a particularly useful form of categorisation for developing spelling skills and that practice in sound categorisation through nursery rhymes and rhyming word games in early language play helps spelling.

Clearly phonological aspects are important in the development of reading and spelling skills. This seems to have considerable importance, particularly for dyslexic children who do not automatically relate the sounds to the visual images of print. Exercises in phonological awareness are therefore of great importance, not just to assist with reading but also to help with spelling, by allowing children to learn and understand sound patterns and to recognise how these are transposed into print.

It must also be borne in mind that other interactive factors are important in the acquisition of reading skills, that language experiences enhance the processes of reading and that children develop competencies in literacy skills through reading (Clay, 1989).

Phonic Code Cracker

This set of materials is sub-divided into twelve units, each unit covering a different aspect of teaching literacy, e.g. Unit 3 deals with initial and final consonant blends, Level 5 deals with common word endings (see Fig. 43) and Unit 9 deals with common silent letters.

Phonic Code Cracker (Russell, 1993) is a very comprehensive and teacher friendly set of materials. The scheme has been devised to provide intensive phonic practice for children who have been having difficulty acquiring basic literacy skills. It has been successfully used with children with specific reading difficulties in mainstream primary and secondary schools.

Essentially the scheme consists of support material and can be successfully used in combination with other schemes. Precision teaching methods are used, but no timescale is recommended as the author acknowledges that each child will have a different rate of learning. Assessment of the pupil's progress is measured through the use of pupil record skills. There are also fluency tests, time targets, accompanying computer software and – very important for building self-esteem – a mastery certificate which the child can retain as a record of his/her achievement.

Fig. 43

---- s and ---- es

Plural means more than one. We add s or es.

1 cat	2 cats	1 box	2 boxes

1 peg	4 pegs	1 fox	3 foxes
1 tin	6 tins	1 bus	4 buses
1 crab	3 crabs	1 kiss	8 kisses
1 bed	2 beds	1 glass	5 glasses
1 van	5 vans	1 cross	2 crosses
1 stamp	8 stamps	1 dress	7 dresses

FLUENCY TEST – TIME TARGET 20 SECONDS

vans	buses	legs	foxes
tins	crosses	glasses	pigs
boxes	stamps	kisses	tops

	sec.	sec.	sec.	sec.	sec.

Level 5 4

Reproduced by kind permission of Sylvia Russell
(Russell, 1993)

Quest – Screening, Diagnostic and Remediation Kit

These materials, designed for children around seven to eight years of age, contain suggestions and materials which teachers can use to prepare further specific programmes or to supplement existing programmes. The kit also includes screening and diagnostic tests in both reading and number work.

The reading test assesses basic word identification skills as well as reading comprehension and the number test focuses on basic number concepts. There are also tests for word attack and pre-reading skills.

A profile sheet for both reading and number links individual skills and concepts to particular sections of the handbook and the prepared workbooks. This helps the teacher prepare individual programmes for the child.

Quest offers a good example of materials which can directly link assessment and teaching; the diagnostic element of the assessment provides the teacher with valuable information to help prepare and monitor teaching programmes and materials.

Reason and Boote

Reason and Boote (1991) provide a step-by-step approach to teaching phonics. Their sequence begins with auditory recognition of initial letter sounds through games and activities, and progresses to syllable blending such as 'car-pet' and 'hos-pit-al'; then the child is helped to recognise sounds which rhyme and those which do not. Such discrimination between rhymes and non-rhymes is important, not just for the development of phonics but also for spelling skills. The programme outlined by Reason and Boote suggests teaching single letter sounds using an illustrated alphabet before introducing the child to word building skills.

When teaching word-building skills, it is suggested that the use of context is encouraged as is the use of known sight words as a basis for word building. The programme also suggests the development of phonic checklists which illustrate initial consonant blends, final consonant blends, consonant digraphs, vowel digraphs and silent 'e'. A useful aspect of the programme is that of record keeping and monitoring of progress. This is done in a structured manner using headings such as **learning target and standard** (e.g. reads fluently at least three times in any order). In this way teachers can decide the learning targets and indeed the standard so this type of 'checklist' is useful and flexible (see Fig. 44).

Fig. 44

A RECORD OF CONSONANT - VOWEL - CONSONANT WORD BUILDING

LEARNING TARGETS simple sentences from	STANDARD	COMMENTS	WORKING ON	MASTERED	CHECKED
pat, can, map, man, sat, pan, cat, fan, fat	Reads fluently at least 3 times, in any order.				
pen, net, red, leg, pet, hen, set, men, let	As above.				
pat, dog, top, fog, hot, got, job, not, hop	As above.				
pig, tin, big, fit, bin, sit, win, bit, bin	As above.				
bus, cup, run, sun, but, hug, bun, but, hut	As above.				
The 'sound dictionary'	At least 5 words for each vowel located correctly.				
Words from the above targets read in any order.	All words correct and fluent (but in some cases allowing some errors.				
The pupil can write simple sentences from dictation, e.g. 'It is fun to sit in the sun'.	Usually all correct.				
At Stage III further targets can be introduced for initial and final consonant blends and diagraphs.					

Extract from *Learning Difficulties in Reading and Writing* reproduced by kind permission of the Publishers
(Reason R., Boote R., 1991)

Aston Portfolio

The Aston Portfolio consists of teaching strategies which provide some framework and direction for the teacher. The Portfolio can be used in conjunction with the Aston Index (see Chapter 4) an assessment which highlights areas of strengths and difficulties. Once such information has been obtained, the teacher can then locate the appropriate teaching technique card in the Portfolio box. Each card provides specific remediation exercises and areas on which the teacher should focus.

The teaching technique cards in the Portfolio include: reading–visual skills; reading–auditory skills; spelling; handwriting; comprehension and written expression. The reading–visual skills section, for example, contains cards relating to teaching, sequence, discrimination, reversals, memory, sight vocabulary and word structure. It also contains lists of materials which can be used by the teacher to help the child develop visual reading skills. The Portfolio box also contains a handwriting checklist.

Although the Aston Portfolio can be useful in helping to direct the teacher to appropriate teaching areas and can also be used selectively by the teacher, it does possess some drawbacks. Clearly the size of the cards, by necessity, restrict the amount of information which can be provided; therefore the information is presented more as a collation of helpful 'tips' than as a structured programme of teaching. Yet the cards do have a tendency to be prescriptive and, because of the nature of the Portfolio, overlook the individuality of children. Perhaps a closer link between the Index and the Portfolio could have helped to overcome this.

Although the handbook indicates that the teaching technique cards can be used to help to construct an individual programme for the child, this may in fact be rather difficult without extensive reference to other appropriate resources and strategies. If the teacher is to use the Portfolio, it can only be to provide some 'ignition' to help identify other appropriate resources.

Counselling approaches

Impressive data (Hales, 1990; Biggar and Barr, 1993) support the view that teachers need to appreciate the emotional needs of children with specific learning difficulties. In a number of studies, Hales showed that even very young children are adversely affected by the realisation of their difficulty with literacy. Indeed Hales also provided evidence for the persistence of personality traits of inadequacy among dyslexic people. His study of a group of adult male dyslexics showed they

Specific Learning Difficulties (Dyslexia)

had a preference to be 'people who were unconventional, individualist and more likely to be rejected in group activities'.

Hales therefore suggests that considerable scope exists for personal counselling of the dyslexic individual. This would allow people with dyslexia the opportunity of talking through their fears, and some attempts could be made to help to match 'self image' with reality since often dyslexic children have a self-image which presents a distorted and unrealistic picture of themselves. Although Hales points out that while there is no specific personality disorder which affects dyslexic children independently of other factors, there is still a strong case for considering closely the individual and personal aspects of children and adults with dyslexia. Indeed he argues that it may be important to consider counselling and social support of the 'dyslexic person' before dealing with the 'dyslexic difficulty'.

This is reinforced by Biggar and Barr (1993) who reported how children with specific learning difficulties seemed acutely aware of their failure to develop literacy skills in a similar fashion to their peers, and how they would attempt to deal with this by concealing or denying their difficulty. The research conducted by Biggar and Barr indicated that factors such as inappropriate attributions, disagreement between adults, and teasing and verbal abuse hindered emotional development. They suggested the following strategies to help facilitate the emotional development of the child:

- ensure that the child's difficulties are accurately described in order to remove doubts, anxieties or prejudices;
- ensure agreement between the significant adults in the child's life, such as parents and teachers;
- ensure the child has a voice, is understood and has a trusting relationship with those adults.

This research places some emphasis on the adult and teacher to attempt to appreciate how it may **feel** for the child to have this type of difficulty.

There is also considerable evidence which shows the positive correlation between self-esteem and scholastic achievement (Burns, 1979; Bar-Tal, 1984). Clearly, therefore, it is particularly important to recognise the value of counselling, sensitivity and success for children with specific learning difficulties.

Furthermore research has shown (Lawrence, 1985) that counselling, in addition to specific teaching programmes, can not only enhance the self-esteem of children, but also enhance their reading attainments to a level in excess of children who received only the teaching programme. In his study, the teaching programme used was DISTAR (see Chapter 7) and counselling continued for twenty weeks, once a week, and was conducted by non-professionals.

Lawrence suggests certain curriculum subjects have the potential to be particularly enhancing in terms of self-esteem. These include music, art, drama and creative writing. Clearly, therefore, this offers scope for the teacher to optimise the confidence of children with specific learning difficulties since art and drama have less of a reliance on literacy. Music and creative writing may well be skills which are well developed among children with specific learning difficulties, but the degree of literacy difficulties which they possess may well prevent them from gaining full access and full success from those areas. This, however, should not be the case! Supporting and encouraging the creative writing and musical ability of children with specific learning difficulties is of great importance, just as is for example the development of phonological awareness.

The case for a dual approach to the teaching of reading, incorporating counselling, seems in the case of children with specific learning difficulties very strong. Lawrence draws the distinction between the teacher's view of children with severe reading difficulties as 'potentially improving readers' and that of the children who may continue to see **themselves** as 'permanently retarded readers'. It seems therefore that some children have internalised their reading failure, so that irrespective of the benefits of an approach or programme, success will be either superficial or minimal.

Counselling itself, therefore, can perform a dual role – it can be utilised as a mode of interaction with children to create the correct therapeutic environment and state of mind to aid the fostering of skills in learning, in order to maximise the child's potential; it can also be seen as integral to the implementation of a teaching programme and conducted simultaneously with teaching. This may be seen as a counselling approach and conducted more informally than planned and progressive individual counselling.

Visual aspects

It may be useful for the teacher to consider the influence of visual aspects in the development of literacy skills. Although the research appears to lean towards phonological and linguistic areas as the principal difficulty relating to dyslexia (Stanovich, 1990; Snowling, 1989), there is a body of opinion which highlights the visual areas and recommends strategies to help deal with such difficulties (Stein, 1991; Wilkins, 1992; Irlen, 1983,1989).

Research has been conducted on eye dominance and binocular control (Stein and Fowler, 1993) and eye tracking has also been the subject of some research (Blau and Loveless, 1982). Pavlidis (1990) suggests that children with dyslexia have less efficient control over eye movements.

Stein and Fowler (1993) argue that a number of children with dyslexia have binocular instability and suggest that this can be remedied through short-term use of monocular occlusion.

Bishop (1989) argues that practice in reading can develop binocular stability, but Stein and Fowler (1993) suggest this is **not** the case and that short-term use of monocular occlusion will result in binocular stability and should thus help promote significant gains in reading.

Furthermore, Cornelissen, Bradley, Fowler and Stein (1994) found that children who experienced visual confusion of text during reading, because of unstable binocular control, were less likely to incorporate visual memories for letter strings into their spelling strategies, relying instead on sound-letter conversion rules, thus spelling words phonologically. This supports the view, therefore, that unstable binocular control not only affects how children read, but also how they spell.

Irlen (1990) has made claims for a scotopic sensitivity syndrome which can affect the child in terms of light sensitivity, the ability to see print clearly without distortions, the ability to perceive groups of words at the same time, and the ability to sustain focus for a period of time.

Irlen recommends the use of coloured perspex overlays or tinted lens treatment to help overcome these difficulties. The research to support this is, however, fairly patchy. Rosner and Rosner, 1987) reviewed the majority of studies of the tinted lens treatment and found significant problems in experimental design and Mosely (1990) found that any significant effect of coloured overlays was due to the reduction in light rather than due to any specific colour. Studies, however, by Richardson (1988), and Wilkins (1990 and 1992) have shown some significant improvement in children using overlays and lenses, particularly in visual activity and muscle balance – and subsequent reading attainments.

Kyd, Sutherland and McGettrick (1992) used the Irlen overlays for children with specific learning difficulties and found significant improvements in reading rate. They are currently involved in follow-up studies examining the effect of the overlays on reading comprehension and accuracy. The results of this study are consistent with the preliminary findings from a project in Norfolk (Wright, 1993) which also provides impressive data for reading rate progress. Wilkins (1993), following extensive research, has developed a set of materials called Intuitive Overlays which can be used both in assessment and learning situations.

Research evidence relating to the visual magno-cellular system, which consists of large cells used for depth perception, indicates that these cells appear to be more disorganised and smaller among dyslexics (Galaburda, 1993). This would mean that stimuli would need to be delivered more slowly in order to be accurately processed.

The Structure of Words

The Structure of Words (Rule 1984) is a compact approach which aims to give the secondary school student some awareness and insight into the structure of words to help with reading, pronunciation and spelling. This approach appreciates the duality of language – it has spoken and written forms – and Rule argues that the spoken form alone is insufficient because the learner needs to see the written form in order to visualise the spelling. This learning of spoken and written forms together greatly strengthens the learning process of each form, with each acting as a reinforcer to the other. This, of course, is further strengthened by kinesthetic activity, the writing of the word with the hand at the same time as it is seen and spoken.

Rule suggests the following procedure for learning and consolidating new words:

Fig. 45

1.	Listen carefully when the word is dictated and see it in detail when it is written (registering sound and sight).
2.	Form a visual picture of the word in your mind, syllable by syllable, and then as a whole (sight).
3.	Retain the picture: spell the word, preferably aloud or sub-vocally, with lip motions (sound and movement linked to sight).
4.	Write the word syllable by syllable, saying the letters as you write (movement, sight and 'naming' sounds).
5.	Read and say aloud the word you have written (sight translation into sound).

(Rule, 1984)

The Structure of Words programme is sequential and designed to teach basic pre-requisite reading skills such as knowledge of the alphabet, consonants, vowels and syllables. It, however, eventually progresses to compound words,

words often confused and rules. It also has a number of exercises in a separate section on prefixes, suffixes and word use, together with a useful answer book for the teacher.

This type of programme is essentially supplementary material which can be used selectively by the teacher with students who have reached, or are progressing, to a reasonable level of reading skill. Clearly, it would need to be supplemented by imaginative and meaningful material in order to maximise the positive effects of the approach.

Facilitating the learning process

Although considerable evidence indicates auditory and linguistic areas as those of prime concern in relation to teaching programmes for dyslexic children, other aspects which facilitate the learning process should not be ignored. Attention will be given to study and thinking skills in later chapters since these are important considerations. Also of some importance is the facilitation of skills utilising imagery.

The use of imagery

It has been argued (Bell, 1991) that although programmes directed at enhancing alphabetic and phonological skills are essential, one has to be wary of the 'cognitive cost' of such programmes – a cost which is reflected in a weakening of the gestalt, right hemispheric skills. The gestalt hemisphere is usually associated with imagery, creativity and comprehension.

The stress and effort which is necessary for children with dyslexia to fully engage their cognitive resources and to develop phonological skills is so great, according to Bell, that a weakening of the gestalt hemisphere results as resources are diverted from the right hemispheric functions to concentrate on the left hemispheric skills of decoding and phonological processing. Not only does this result in a restriction in the use of imagery but also in a stifling of the development of skills in comprehension and perhaps in creativity.

Bell has developed a programme 'Visualizing and Verbalizing for Language Comprehension and Thinking, (see Fig. 46). This programme provides a comprehensive procedure for the use of visualising to promote and enhance reading and comprehension. The stages outlined by Bell include picture imagery, word imagery, single sentence, multiple sentence, whole paragraph and whole page. Additionally, the programme provides an understanding of the functions of the gestalt hemisphere and useful strategies for classroom teaching.

Fig. 46

SUMMARY OF WORD IMAGING

Step 3.

Objective: The student will be able to visualize and verbalize, with *detail*, a single word.

1. **Object Imaging** (optional)
    a. Object imaging is for students who have difficulty understanding what it is to image.
    b. The student looks at an object, closes eyes, recalls and describes image.

2. **Personal Imaging** (not optional but only do one or two)
    a. The student recalls images, and describes something personal but simple such as a pet, room, toy etc.
    b. The teacher questions with choice and contrast.
    c. The structure words are checked through for details and reverbalization.
    d. The teacher gives a verbal summary using the phrase: '*Your words made me picture . . .*'

3. **Known Noun Imaging** (not optional)
    a. The student visualizes and verbalizes a noun. The word should be familiar as well as high in imagery.
    b. The teacher questions specifically with choice and contrast to develop detailed imagery.
    c. The structure words are checked through for details and reverbalization.
    d. If student has been given a choice, have the student describe the image to be sure not restating or paraphrasing.
    e. Request gesturing.
    f. Conclude session with a verbal summary using the phrase: '*Your words made me picture . . .*'
    g. Practise this step until very confident.

4. **Fantasy Imaging** (optional)
    a. Begin with a 'known noun' image and interact to create fanciful, humorous images.
    b. Encourage student to create own fantasy images.

5. **Group Instruction:**
    Apply this step to small groups of 3 to 5 students. Give one word to be described by all individuals in the group. Set the task as: *All students will help create one composite image, not separate images.* Each student will take a turn visualizing and verbalizing different aspects of the word to the group. The teacher will question, choose individuals to go through 3 or 4 structure words at a time, visualize, and summarize the composite image.

---

from *Visualizing and Verbalizing for Language Comprehension and Thinking.*
(Bell, 1991). Reproduced with kind permission

Specific Learning Difficulties (Dyslexia)

A parallel argument, using a different rationale from Bell, has been put forward in an interesting piece of research (Niklasson, 1993) looking at the effects of residual primitive reflexes in children. Niklasson identifies three aspects of young children's development:

- expression
- experience
- cognition.

He claims that each of the above builds a foundation for the other, but in our education system the first two, expression and experience, appear to be given a lower priority than cognition. In terms of attainments and performances in school it is the cognition aspect which is the principal determinant of school success, except perhaps in an alternative system, which can take a more holistic view and focus on expression and experience as important fundamental skills worthy of high status in the curriculum.

The conclusion which can be drawn from the work of Niklasson is that insufficient focus on expression and experience will result in the child failing to maximise his cognitive abilities, and hence there are strong reasons for ensuring that children with dyslexia obtain maximum exposure to expression and experience in order to facilitate the right hemispheric cognitive functions such as comprehension and imagery.

The inhibition of primitive reflexes

Blyth (1992) found that 85% of those children who have specific learning difficulties that do not respond to various classroom intervention strategies have a cluster of aberrant reflexes. He argues that as long as these reflexes remain undetected and uncorrected the educational problems will persist.

These reflexes should only be present in the very young baby and would become redundant after about six months of life. But if these reflexes continued to be present after that time, Blyth argued, the development of the mature postural reflexes is restricted and this will adversely affect writing, reading, spelling, copying, maths, attention and concentration.

Blyth and colleagues have developed a programme for assessing the presence of these reflexes, with a Reflex-Inhibition movement programme to control the primitive reflexes and release the postural reflexes. This view regarding the affect of uninhibited primitive reflexes on learning has been supported by other studies (Bender, 1976; Ayres, 1979 and 82; Mitchell, 1985; Retief 1990).

Blyth (1992) reports on 26 children selected randomly from the files at the treatment centre of the Institute for Neuro-Physiological Psychology in Chester. The average age was 12-17 years; all had been on the programme for 14 months. From the sample all had evidence of an asymmetrical tonic neck reflex; 20 had evidence of a symmetrical tonic neck reflex; 18 had a spinal galott reflex; 11 had not developed a full amphibian reflex; 23 had failed to develop a full segmental rolling reflex; more than 20 had evidence of a retained moro reflex; others showed lack of a fully developed oculo head righting reflex and labyrinth head righting reflex. Additionally, 23 of the sample had difficulty in getting their eyes to track smoothly backwards and forwards along a line and had problems with Visual-Motor Integration. After treatment using the programme developed at the Institute significant improvements in reading were found following a treatment period of on average 14 months.

These findings are indeed extremely interesting and must raise questions about motor-coordination programmes which set out to improve coordination but ignore the whole issue of the presence of primitive reflexes. Dobie (1993) reported on a programme she and colleagues developed, which was based on improving motor and physical coordination but took into account the presence of primitive reflexes, and which she argued was more effective than a coordination programme which does not take this into account.

Alternative approaches

Educational kinesiology (EK)

There has been a recent increase in the number of practitioners using kinesiology to help children with specific learning difficulties. This area is still very much in its infancy and few large scale research studies are available. Nevertheless, it may be worthy of consideration since the exponents of kinesiology claim that it helps to achieve hemispheric integration and improves children's self-esteem.

Educational kinesiology is a combination of applied kinesiology and traditional learning theory, although some aspects of yoga and acupressure are also evident in the recommended programme.

Kinesiology is the study of muscles and their functions and particular attention is paid to the patterns of reflex activity that link effective integration between sensory and motor responses. It has been argued (Mathews, 1993) that often children develop inappropriate patterns of responses to particular situations and that these can lock the child into inappropriate habits.

The practice of kinesiology therefore aims to unlock the child from the inappropriate pattern of reflexes, to help the child develop new connections, and to facilitate access to their information processing systems.

Reading is certainly an integrated activity and in theory if educational kinesiology helps to achieve integration between the cerebral hemispheres then it should aid progress in reading.

The assessment is achieved through a process of muscle testing and aims to provide information on how the body is coping with a particular activity. This is claimed to be a very sophisticated process for which specialist training is necessary.

Dennison (1986) has produced a series of exercises (Brain Gym) from which an individual programme can be devised for the child relating to the assessment. Many of these exercises include activities which involve crossing the mid line, such as writing a figure eight in the air or cross crawling and skip-a-cross, in which hands and legs sway from side to side. The aim is to achieve some form of body balance so that information can flow freely and be processed readily.

Experimental studies are few and usually small scale, although in these some positive results have ensued (Mathews and Thomas, 1993; Brydon, Carson and Reid, 1989).

Kinesiology and educational kinesiology illustrate the importance of integration of the human body and the brain in relation to learning. They also suggest how some other factors associated with learning might influence the process of reading.

Neuro-linguistic programming (NLP)

NLP appears to be essentially a behaviour-modelling therapy, gathered together from many different strands and sciences, modified and applied generically to accommodate different therapy settings and purposes. It was developed by Bandler and Grinder (1990) who attempted to look for patterns in the most effective therapy and from this developed NLP, a synthesis of many different fields. The name NLP arose from this synthesis: neuro – relating to how the brain processes the messages from the five senses; linguistic – the relationship between thinking and language structures and programming – looking at how all behaviour can be structured and shaped to facilitate learning.

Although not specifically developed for educational settings, it has been used with varying degrees of success in the teaching of dyslexic children (Monteiro, 1992; McLean, 1993).

The educational basis for NLP rests on the following.

- It acknowledges that individuals perceive the world in a different way depending on the development of their auditory, visual and kinesthetic senses. Thus an attempt is made to identify preferred modalities.
- It focuses on rapport matching. The practitioner attempts to match non-verbal aspects of the client such as posture, vocabulary, breathing and eye movements. This can help to achieve some form of congruence with the client or pupil which may facilitate more effective learning.
- Some of the NLP techniques emphasise visual processing and the need to develop visual skills. These visual skills are then used to learn and recall new learning.
- By acknowledging modality preferences in children and modality styles in teaching, it is possible for teachers to become more aware of both their own style and the student's style and thus to match the two styles in the learning situation.

NLP is a difficult concept to grasp, but basically it seems to offer a simple message in complex language. That is, it attempts to help children and adults become resourceful learners, taking responsibility for learning and gaining confidence from self-knowledge and success.

It does, however, require extremely specialist training and few research studies have evaluated the long-term effects of using NLP techniques, although it is currently being used successfully by teachers at the Helen Arkell Dyslexia Centre (McLean, 1993).

Conclusion

The support approaches and strategies discussed here illustrate the range of materials available, the different theoretical opinions, and the range of needs within the population of children with specific learning difficulties. Clearly such diversity underlines the importance of informal assessment and of acknowledging the individuality of the learner. Many approaches do share similarities. Some can be regarded as alternative or fringe approaches and some may not lend themselves readily to the practicalities of the classroom situation. It is important to examine new approaches, materials and programmes which may be portrayed as the answer for dyslexic children thoroughly and critically. Some techniques may seem successful by virtue of the 'novelty value', or because of some other factor such as the child being provided with extra attention. This, however, should not mean that any particular strategy should be discounted. It is important to have at least an awareness, and indeed some practical experience of a wide range of strategies, in order to deal effectively with the broad range of difficulties evident among the population of children and young people with specific learning difficulties.

Chapter 9

Assisted learning

Assisted learning

ASSISTED learning approaches are essentially teaching approaches which require considerable interaction between the learner and others. This interaction may take the form of some kind of participant modelling. There may be an element of repetition and even simplicity in these approaches but, based on the principles of modelling and of facilitating the learning process, they can be successfully utilised with reading, writing and spelling.

Paired reading, peer tutoring, cued spelling and the apprenticeship approach to reading will be discussed here in relation to the concept of assisted learning and consideration will be given to the degree of effectiveness these approaches may have in helping children with specific learning difficulties.

Paired reading

Paired reading was originally devised to meet the need for a reading approach which could be both applied generally and utilised by non-professionals with a minimum of training (Morgan, 1976).

Studies have shown (Neville, 1975; Wilkinson, 1980; Bell, 1991) that releasing children from the burden of decoding can facilitate or enhance comprehension. This is highlighted in a study examining the decoding processes of slow readers (Curtis, 1980) which found that the cognitive applications to decoding reduced the amount of attention available for other reading processes. This resulted in deficits in comprehension of text. Emphasis, therefore, can be placed on the use of context rather than the skill of decoding, but the question remains whether poor readers are able to utilise context as successfully as proficient readers.

Clark (1988) observed an inefficient use of context among dyslexic children, although she noted that dyslexic children utilised a wide variation of strategies and preferences in an attempt to use context to aid comprehension.

Lees (1986), however, in an examination of the data from four different studies concluded that poor readers had similar capabilities to good readers in the utilisation of context to aid word recognition. Evans (1984) reported on two studies using paired reading for dyslexic children, both of which showed significant gains in reading comprehension and vocabulary.

Topping and Lindsey (1992), therefore, argue that the evidence suggests that poor readers have an over-dependence on decoding strategies at the expense of developing skills in comprehension, using contextual cues. This is a practice reinforced by many teaching programmes which over-emphasise analytical decoding approaches, resulting in sequential decoding processes which can inhibit full use of comprehension skills. This is indeed consistent with the literature on learning styles (Carbo, 1987) which suggests that young children tend to have a preference for processing information globally rather than analytically. Yet one must be cautious of fostering global processing methods such as whole-word, at the expense of analytical methods such as phonics, since the teaching approaches which combine both these approaches are arguably more effective (Vellutino and Scanlon, 1986; Reason et al, 1988).

Paired reading may be particularly useful for children with specific learning difficulties since it provides both visual and auditory input simultaneously. It is a simple technique which focuses on the following:

- parent and child reading together
- programme to be carried out consistently
- child selects reading material
- as few distractions as possible
- use of praise as re-inforcement
- discussion of the story and pictures (see Fig. 47).

Fig. 47: Paired reading

The two principal stages of paired reading are: reading together and reading alone.

- **Reading together** is when the parent/teacher and child read all the words aloud, with the adult adjusting the speed so that the pair are reading in harmony. The adult does not allow the child to become stuck at a word and if this happens will simply say the word to the child. This process, together with discussion, can help the child obtain meaning from the text and therefore enjoy the experience of language and of reading.
- **Reading alone** occurs when the child becomes more confident at reading aloud. The adult can either read more softly, thus allowing the child to take the lead, or remain quiet. This can be done gradually to allow the child's confidence to build up (Topping, 1993). When the child stumbles at this stage, the adult immediately offers the word and then continues reading with the child again, until he/she gains enough confidence to read unaided.

Topping and Lindsey (1992) report on a number of other programmes, mostly from North America, which show similarities to paired reading. One such programme is the Neurological Impress Method (NIM) (see Page 228). This method involves the student and the instructor reading aloud together in unison. The instructor sits a little behind the student and speaks directly into the right ear of the learner. No corrections are made during or after the reading session. The method is intended for use by professionals.

There are few evaluation studies of this particular technique but an interesting comment can be made on the strategy of speaking directly into the right ear. Presumably the purpose of this is to engage the left language hemisphere, yet a study looking at sensory deprivation, and particularly auditory perception (Johansen, 1992), suggests that children with reading problems have a better left ear than right in relation to auditory discrimination.

Evaluation of paired reading as a strategy

Although it is not yet clear why exactly paired reading is an effective method of teaching reading, it has been generally well evaluated (Topping and Lindsey, 1991).

Paired reading may well help children with specific learning difficulties develop a desire to read. Clearly an adult model, either parent or teacher, can act as a good reinforcer.

Other factors have also been attributed to the success of paired reading. These include the pacing of the text which helps to regulate the child's reading flow and may help to overcome the segmentation and syllabification problems outlined by many researchers (Bradley, 1990; Snowling, 1993). The fact that it is multisensory, particularly utilising the combination of visual and auditory modalities may also be significant. It may also help to provide weaker readers with a global strategy through the practice of non-interruption of the reading flow. The value of paired reading in enhancing self-image should also not be ignored. The importance of this for children with reading problems (Lawrence, 1986) is well documented in the literature.

Some other advantages of paired reading are:

- failure is not an evident factor because if the child 'sticks' at a word the adult says the word almost immediately;

- the experience of gaining enjoyment from the language of the text helps reading become pleasurable and increases the desire to read;

- children are provided with an example of how to pronounce difficult words and can simultaneously relate the auditory sound of the word with the visual appearance of that word;

- children can derive understanding from the text because words are given expression and meaning by the adult and discussion about the text follows at periodic intervals.

Thus paired reading can be useful as:

- a strategy to develop motivation and confidence in reading;

- an aid to the development of fluency and expression in reading;

- a technique which could also enhance comprehension on the part of the reader.

Paired reading, however, is seen as complementary to other strategies such as structured language teaching and phonics skills and does not attempt to replicate or replace this dimension of learning to read. However, it utilises the participation of parents and this is clearly a great advantage, both for the child and the school.

Topping (1993) sees paired reading as a strategy which can reduce the anxieties of reading for dyslexic children, reduce their all-consuming fear of failure and encourage reading practice.

The approach is essentially one which can effectively combine the psycho-linguistic aspects of the use of context with the phonic skills associated with word attack. This coupled with parent or peer support and appraisal may well account for its success.

Parents, children and teachers (PACT)

Although the PACT project was established in Inner London in 1979 and educational developments and curriculum innovation have moved on since then, the project showed clearly that parents can and should be successfully employed as effective partners in helping in children's reading, irrespective of the acknowledged or anticipated difficulty the child may exhibit. Griffiths and Hamilton (1984) provide an approach to the key aspects of developing and utilising parental skills at all stages of education.

Three methodological features discussed by Griffiths and Hamilton are the meeting of parents and teachers to set up the partnership, the sharing of professional knowledge with parents and of parental understanding with teachers, and the establishment of reliable structures to maintain the new dialogue.

Home reading

Drummond, Godfrey and Sattin (1990) argue that there are a number of methods for enlisting parental support with children's reading and that it is not necessary, nor wise, for a school to 'buy into' a specific scheme. They propose the view that whatever method of parental involvement in reading is used, enhancement in learning and reading ensues and in some cases the success can be quite dramatic. They outline some key features of an effective home reading programme.

- a well ordered series of books/pre-reading;
- genuine welcome and seeking out of parents;
- alternative dates and personal invitations to meetings;
- good method for parent and child reading together;
- good demonstration of method to parents;
- two-way record cards;
- routines for daily/weekly operation;
- routines for trouble shooting and encouragement;
- monitoring and feedback.

The implications of the work carried out by Drummond, Godfrey and Sattin is that parent/child reading programmes can be flexible and adapted to local requirements, although the principles governing such programmes may be similar.

Cued spelling

The cued spelling technique shares the same principles as paired reading and other peer tutoring developments (Croft and Topping, 1992).

The technique comprises ten steps for learning and spelling, four points to remember and two reviews (see Fig. 48). The points to remember help to consolidate the learning and the two reviews involve a daily and a weekly review. In the daily review the speller writes all the words for the day and checks them – the wrong words are then noted and the learner goes through the ten steps again for these words.

The speller adopts the same procedure for the weekly review and identifies the wrong words. Discussion would then take place on the best approach for the learner to tackle the wrongly spelt words.

If the learner writes a word inaccurately he/she is encouraged to delete the word from memory by erasing it or boldly scoring it out. This can be particularly useful if the learner has a strong visual memory and the image of the incorrect word may remain and be recalled at some future point.

The cued spelling technique is highly interactive but aims to encourage 'self-managed' learning. The technique attempts to eliminate the fear of failure through the use of prompt correction procedures. As in paired reading, modelling and praise are integral to the application of cued spelling. According to Topping and Watt (1993) seven year old children have been successfully trained in its use in about one hour, substantial progress can be made on norm-referenced spelling tests, and improvements have been found in error rate and qualitative indicators in continuous free writing.

A number of studies support Topping and Watt's assertion regarding the merits of the technique (Emerson, 1988; Scoble, 1989; Harrison, 1989).

Scoble (1988) describes how the technique is also used with adult literacy and provides some examples of the application of Cued Spelling in the home with spouses, parents and friends as tutors.

Fig. 48: Cued spelling: the ten steps

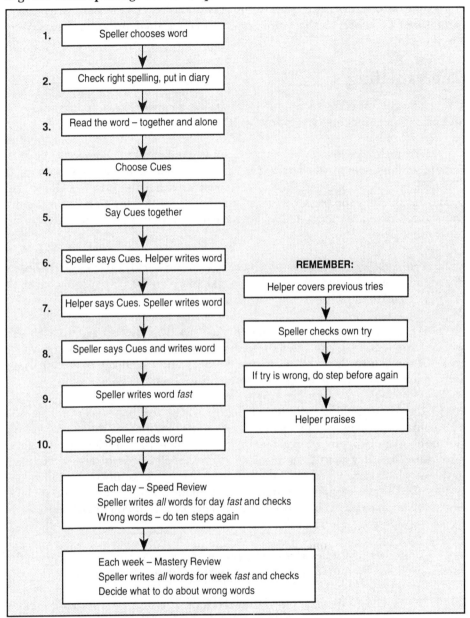

1. Speller chooses word
2. Check right spelling, put in diary
3. Read the word – together and alone
4. Choose Cues
5. Say Cues together
6. Speller says Cues. Helper writes word
7. Helper says Cues. Speller writes word
8. Speller says Cues and writes word
9. Speller writes word *fast*
10. Speller reads word

Each day – Speed Review
Speller writes *all* words for day *fast* and checks
Wrong words – do ten steps again

Each week – Mastery Review
Speller writes *all* words for week *fast* and checks
Decide what to do about wrong words

REMEMBER:

Helper covers previous tries

Speller checks own try

If try is wrong, do step before again

Helper praises

Reproduced by kind permission of Keith Topping, Centre for Paired Learning, University of Dundee
(Topping, 1992)

Oxley and Topping (1990) report on a peer-tutoring project using Cued Spelling in which eight seven and eight-year old pupils were tutored by eight nine-year-olds. The self concept as a speller of both tutees and tutors showed a significant positive shift compared to a control group.

France, Topping and Revell (1993) demonstrate the effectiveness of Cued Spelling, particularly in the short-term, although they accept that further research on its longer-term effects is still required.

The Cued Spelling technique is relatively simple to apply and the pack includes a demonstration video.

An Apprenticeship Approach

In discussing the rationale for this approach, Liz Waterland (1986) questions traditional assumptions about the hierarchical taxonomy of reading skills and the need to build these skills into a reading scheme in a sequential and cumulative manner. She suggests that reading should be viewed as more than decoding print and should include aspects such as:

- readers' language experience;
- previous knowledge and level of understanding;
- decoding strategies;
- relevance of text
- visual cues;
- use of context;
- interest level of child.

She argues that:

- the acquisition of written language is comparable with that of spoken language;
- reading cannot effectively be taught in a formal sequenced manner;
- reading is not a series of small interconnecting skills;
- reading is a process of obtaining meaning;
- the actual text is of crucial importance;
- the adult has an important role to play in assisting the child's acquisition of literacy skills.

The role of the adult is in fact of considerable importance in this approach, not only in helping in the selection of appropriate texts for the child, but in reading with the child in an enjoyable experience sharing manner. It is important when using this approach, that reading should be meaningful for the child. If the child, therefore, does not possess the prior knowledge to understand the text, then the text needs to be read to him/her in order that he/she can build and develop a schema to aid reading and understanding of the text. This type of approach has been the subject of considerable criticism (Turner, 1991) since it assumes that children can benefit from reading, even though they may not have acquired the reading vocabulary.

One of the strengths of the Apprenticeship Approach, however, is the role of the parents in facilitating and engaging the child to perceive books and reading as a meaningful and pleasurable activity. The approach, by its very nature, can also develop good home/school links through promotion of language experience and experience based projects. Clearly from that perspective the Apprenticeship Approach should not be described as necessarily unsuitable for dyslexic children because it can help to fulfil one of the major objectives of reading – to gain meaning and pleasure from books.

While the Apprenticeship Approach clearly encourages enjoyment of books – a very worthwhile objective – it might be argued that the approach is insufficient on its own to provide dyslexic children with the knowledge they require to learn to read. The approach does rely to a certain extent on 'incidental learning', which is within the grasp of many readers, but may not be so readily accessible to dyslexic readers. For example, phonic rules which most readers learn spontaneously usually have to be taught in a structured manner, with continual over-learning with dyslexic learners.

Conclusion

Assisted learning implies that learning, quite rightly, is an interactive process and the role of peers and adults is of great importance. This form of learning in many ways minimises the adverse effects of failure, because if the child cannot respond to a particular text or situation then assistance is provided. The important point is, however, that assistance is not necessarily provided because the child is not succeeding, but because it is inbuilt into the reading or learning strategy. The learner, therefore, is not necessarily obtaining the sense of failing but rather of working cooperatively with another person.

The interaction with other peers or adults is certainly a major factor in the success of assisted learning techniques. Not only does it promote active learning, it also increases the pleasure of learning and is often accompanied by an awareness of progress and success. At the same time, however, it is important to be aware of potential pitfalls of such approaches with dyslexic children, particularly those who have yet to acquire a basic knowledge of word attack skills, and clearly such approaches may need to be supplemented with some more traditional approaches, such as those outlined in previous chapters.

Chapter 10

Whole-school approaches

Introduction

THE KEY questions in relation to support for children with specific learning difficulties are how can their specific needs be most effectively met within the school and the curriculum; and how can specialist teaching be most efficiently directed to help meet those needs?

The issue of specialist teaching interfacing with the mainstream curriculum is one which has been a source of concern and controversy for some time. Of particular concern is the question of the effectiveness of specialist teaching if it is divorced from the normal class curriculum, and the extent to which the gains that are made in any period of specialist teaching will be transferred to other areas of learning, thus enhancing the learner's performance in the mainstream curriculum.

Since the Warnock Report (1978), the focus has shifted from highlighting individual pupils' needs to attempting to view educational needs from the perspective of the 'community of learners'. The dilemma and the conflict arise if there is a mismatch between individual children's needs and those of the 'community of learners'. Not surprisingly with the focus on meeting the needs of all pupils, some traditional individual approaches have been difficult to implement. This, according to Bradshaw (1990), has led to a loss of the benefits of these approaches to pupils with specific learning difficulties.

This chapter will examine these conflicts and tensions and present a model to minimise these difficulties to the advantage of both teacher and child.

Whole-school policy

What is meant by whole-school dimensions or whole-school policies? Clearly they embrace an acceptance of the needs of all children within the school and furthermore an acceptance that the responsibility for certain pupils does not reside exclusively with some trained specialists, but rather responsibility for all pupils rests with all staff under the direction of a school management team.

The implications of this are two-fold. Firstly, identification and assessment procedures need to be established and monitored to ensure that children who may present specific learning difficulties, even in a mild form, are identified at an early stage. Secondly, the school needs to be resourced in terms of teaching materials and training of staff to ensure the educational needs of children with specific learning difficulties are effectively met. As children with specific learning difficulties progress through the school it is important that each new teacher they meet has at least some training and understanding of specific learning difficulties. Additionally, the school will need to possess a teacher with a high degree of specialist training to complement the class teacher input and to provide consultancy and training to staff and management.

Roles and perceptions

Responsibility for pupils with learning difficulties lies ultimately with the class teacher. Deep-seated difficulties deriving from the structure and vocabulary of the language employed in teaching or of a conceptual nature, require to be dealt with in the class or subject context in which they arise. Class and subject teachers cannot escape their responsibility for dealing with them.

(HMG, 1978)

The issues of 'appropriate intervention' are reflected in the competing ideologies of 'remedial' and 'support services'.

'Remedial' services can be seen as an attempt to remedy some area of failure within the child, thus adopting a negative and reactive standpoint, while support services can be seen as focusing on the positive and perceived as pro-active and preventative.

The concept of 'support' services clearly fits in with the philosophy of mainstream and whole-school policies in dealing with all children. The concept has much to commend it – it should ensure consultancy and discussion and therefore promote school procedures and policies in identification, assessment and teaching of children with dyslexic difficulties. The concept is also multi-disciplinary in nature and should involve the participation of other support agencies such as educational psychologists, speech therapists and occupational therapists. It is important to note that the word 'other' rather than 'external' was used in the previous sentence to describe support services. Support services should not be seen as 'external' but rather as an integral part of the school team.

It can be argued that current role perceptions and attitudes result in an integrated, team approach being some distance from reality and that some teachers may have difficulties relating to their roles. These difficulties include:

- **role demands** – these are the behaviours expected of people because of their position in the organisation;
- **role ambiguity** – when expectations about a teacher's role are unclear;
- **role overload** – when expectations are excessive;
- **role conflict** – when meeting one set of expectations means that meeting another set is difficult.

Reid (1991a and 1991b) found that of the different populations of teachers within school, learning support teachers were the most vulnerable to perceive work stress in relation to the role factors outlined above.

It has also been recognised that misconceptions may occur over the perception of roles (Allen, Brown and Munn, 1991). In this study there was evidence of a mismatch between the perceptions of classteachers and learning support teachers in relation to their views of their roles. For example, the factors below in relation to class teachers' perceptions of learning support staff can be noted.

- They have **specialised knowledge and skills** which are necessary in order to help meet the needs of pupils with learning difficulties.
- They **possess** considerable knowledge about the pupils learning difficulties and what constitutes appropriate curricula for them.
- They are **skilled** at adapting tasks to an appropriate level for pupils with learning difficulties.
- They are particularly **adept** at modifying the design and language used in curriculum materials.
- They **support** mainstream staff in responding to the diverse learning needs, activities and interests of their pupils.

These perceptions differ from those of learning support teachers' views of their own role as outlined below.

- They **facilitate** the professional development of mainstream teachers.

- They **help** mainstream teachers **differentiate** more effectively among all pupils.

- They need to **educate,** rather than support, staff to meet the needs of pupils.

- They can **provide** additional pupil support when necessary.

Fig. 49

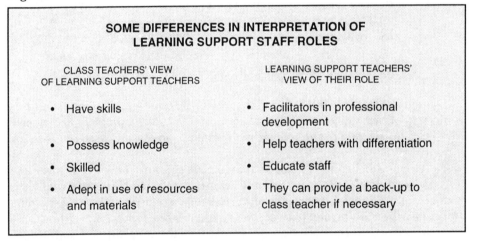

**SOME DIFFERENCES IN INTERPRETATION OF
LEARNING SUPPORT STAFF ROLES**

CLASS TEACHERS' VIEW OF LEARNING SUPPORT TEACHERS	LEARNING SUPPORT TEACHERS' VIEW OF THEIR ROLE
• Have skills	• Facilitators in professional development
• Possess knowledge	• Help teachers with differentiation
• Skilled	• Educate staff
• Adept in use of resources and materials	• They can provide a back-up to class teacher if necessary

Models and processes

Two possible models of intervention within the school are highlighted on pages 86 and 87 in Chapter 5. Fig. 24 focuses on the needs of the children, while Fig. 25 predominantly focuses on the curriculum. It might also be argued that the stage process model (Fig.24) is a reactive one since the assessment and intervention develops throughout a period of stages – beginning with the class teachers' observations and progressing to regular multi-disciplinary meetings to monitor progress.

The whole school interactive model (Fig. 25) focuses on training, the curriculum and consultancy. The rationale behind this model is one of early identification through training class teachers, and indeed student teachers undergoing teacher training courses, matching the curriculum with the learner in order to maximise the learner's potential for success, and regular consultancy arising not out of a need to discuss problems but out of a desire to share professional expertise for the benefit of the school as a whole and in order to help produce a productive and efficient school system within an atmosphere of collaboration and empathy.

Clearly, there is scope for both models to operate simultaneously within schools, but professionals must be flexible and open to operating in ways which can accommodate both a whole-school interactive model as well as a stage process model. Ideally both these models can be combined because identification and assessment will follow some progression, as in the example outlined below.

Initial early warning signs

- The class teacher may identify coordination difficulties, difficulties with pencil grip, immature use of language, sequencing or organisational difficulties **prior** to the teaching of reading skills. These difficulties can be highlighted through classroom observation, discussions with parents and diagnostic assessment.

Assessment/consultancy with management team

- to discuss the difficulties and possible materials and resources which can be used. This is an important aspect and time should be specifically allocated for this.

Close monitoring of progress when reading skills are taught, looking for:

- difficulties with **phonological awareness,** e.g. awareness of rhyme, syllabification, natural breaks in speech and written language;
- **auditory discrimination** recognising and repeating sounds;
- **visual difficulties** such as failure to recognise letters, comparison between visually similar letters, missing lines when reading confusing picture cues;
- **sequencing difficulties** such as confusing order of letter or words or digits;
- **organisational difficulties** such as directional confusion, laterality problems and sequencing difficulties;
- **memory** – inability to follow instructions, particularly when more than one item is to be remembered;

- **motor difficulties** – for example, poor pencil grip, awkward gait, poor coordination, difficulty doing two simple tasks simultaneously.

Monitoring/review meeting

- This would probably be with school management and nursery staff to discuss the necessity of a fuller assessment and how this should proceed. Some suggestions for teaching to support the teacher needs to be made at this stage. Discussions with parents are also important here.
- Suggested revisions to teaching may be carried out, during which time teacher records progress and difficulties.
- School management review with parents to discuss progress and further action if necessary, for instance the involvement of other professionals such as educational psychologists and speech therapists.

This is essentially a stage process model, but it can be viewed as one which is interactive and involves the whole school, because it also emphasises the need for staff training, awareness of the curriculum and teaching implications, and regular consultancy.

The curriculum

Curricular aspects can promote whole-school involvement and interaction. There are a number of examples of teaching and learning programmes which involve every child in the school. Examples of this include self-esteem programmes, such as the Circle Time Programme (White, 1991) which can be undertaken by every teacher and every child in the school, at the same time. The content, aims and outcomes of this are, therefore, the same for all.

Thinking skills programmes provide another example of a piece of work which can be undertaken by all, irrespective of a child's particular skills or abilities (De Bono, 1986; Somerset Thinking Skills, 1988). In Scotland the 5-14 Curriculum provides a common, structured curriculum which has the potential to meet the needs of all children, including those with specific learning difficulties (Crombie and Reid, 1994).

The curriculum, therefore, can provide a unifying facet to the school, help to identify and monitor progress of all children, and provide a common vehicle for whole-school liaison and consultancy between staff.

Secondary school dimensions

Consultancy

The secondary school is usually considerably larger than the primary school, and pupils are seen by many different teachers throughout the school day. In some cases because of the sheer numbers of pupils, teachers may take some time to become familiar with the abilities and difficulties presented by their pupils. Learning support staff, however, are usually in a better position to identify and recognise the pupils' strengths and weaknesses and it is, therefore, of considerable importance that sufficient time is allocated to consultation, not only between learning support staff and subject teachers, but between teachers in different subjects. In this way teachers can obtain a more complete picture of the pupil.

Cooperative teaching

Cooperative teaching has much to offer since it can have extremely beneficial effects for all concerned – the subject teacher, learning support teacher and the pupil. The learning support teacher, in cooperative teaching, is allowed the opportunity to observe and work with the pupil within the context of the classroom. Thus information can be obtained on how the pupil deals with the actual curriculum, and indeed how he/she relates to others in the class within the learning situation. Irrespective of the merits of individual tuition (Reid, Carson and Bryden, 1989), such information is invaluable.

Cooperative teaching, however, does not 'happen'. It requires considerable planning, cooperation, understanding and motivation on the part of those involved. It is important, therefore, to recognise this and allow for such planning within the school timetable.

Preparation for examinations

Examinations and the examination system do not naturally favour the dyslexic student. Factors such as writing within a time limit, reading under pressure and recalling information almost instantly, are usually those the dyslexic child finds difficult. The help which can be provided, such as a 'reader' to read the script, or a scribe, can be useful, but requires considerable preparation and practice. Such forms of aid should not be provided only at examination time. The student would need to become familiar with this form of help if it were to be seriously considered. This emphasises that preparation for examinations and special concessions should begin virtually as soon as the pupil enters secondary school.

It is important, therefore, that dyslexic students are known, not only to learning support teachers but to all subject teachers, since the type of examination help required will vary from subject to subject. Identifying students for examination concessions, and helping to maximise the benefits of these concessions should, therefore, be seen as a whole-school issue. Administrative structures, therefore, need to be in place to monitor these arrangements. This may include a school sub-group, preferably involving the school psychologist, guidance teacher, management, learning support and some subject teachers. The function of such a group would be to discuss students who may need special arrangements, and how these could be effectively implemented within the school system. It is important that dyslexic students are not unduly restricted because of the nature of the school examination system, and that **all** their abilities are assessed **equally** and not only their performances in the area of literacy.

The key features of this hybrid model areshown in Fig. 50 below.

Fig. 50

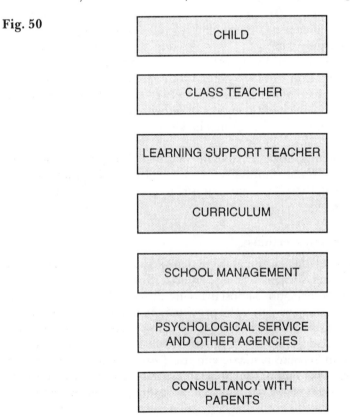

Specific Learning Difficulties (Dyslexia)

Primary/secondary liaison

This is an extremely important aspect. Primary-secondary transfer is by its very nature a period which can affect pupil's self-esteem and general confidence (Reid, 1986). Dyslexic pupils can be extremely vulnerable at this point. It is, therefore, extremely important that early and effective liaison between primary and secondary schools takes place.

It is acknowledged that there are some practical constraints in relation to this, but time-tabling and school policy should recognise the need to allow key members of staff sufficient flexibility to allow for effective liaison. Such liaison should commence as early as possible during the school year prior to transfer. This would allow, for example, learning support staff from the secondary school an opportunity to monitor the progress of the dyslexic pupil throughout the final year at primary. This is clearly preferable to being handed a report, even a comprehensive one, just before transfer takes place. Early liaison allows the secondary staff to build up a picture of the pupil; begin to plan and prepare subject teachers in the secondary school to deal with the kinds of difficulties presented; and to report on the progress and strategies employed during the final year at primary school.

If possible class teachers should also be involved in this type of liaison.

Support and resources

What kind of support and support structures can be implemented to assist learners and professionals and help to make the education of dyslexic children a whole-school responsibility?

Dyer (1988) provided an analysis of school 'supports' which included:

*   support at a systems level in organising teaching groups;
*   planning curricula;
*   counselling and pastoral care;
*   adaptation and differentiation of teaching materials.

This analysis indeed covers the main aspects of whole-school support utilising curriculum analysis, counselling and training. It is therefore important for schools to ensure that these supports are in place in order fully to utilise the skills of staff and to ensure early and accurate identification and assessment of dyslexic children (Brown, 1993).

Pumfrey and Reason (1991) suggest the following types of intervention might be provided for pupils with specific learning difficulties:

- specially prepared or highlighted work sheets;
- teaching the technical vocabulary prior to a lesson;
- providing a tape recording of literature being studied;
- providing a photocopy of notes to save note-taking at speed;
- facility to tape-record notes or 'written work';
- teacher time to transcribe or to help the pupil transcribe the above tape recording for extended pieces of written work;
- tuition to help the pupil learn to use the wordprocessor effectively;
- tuition to help pupils organise their work more effectively;
- an individual programme for specific areas of skills weakness.

Clearly, these interventions depend on skilled teachers who can:

- assess the needs of the pupils;
- examine those needs in relation to the curriculum;
- consult with colleagues, parents and other professionals.

It is expected, therefore, that the skills which the pupil develops assisted by such intervention can be transferred to the mainstream curriculum and assist in cross-curricular activities.

Some of the above suggestions can be very time-consuming and teacher time needs to be allocated if these are to be effectively carried out.

Other strategies which can be utilised within a whole school approach include:

- **peer tutoring and paired reading** – this has been shown to be a successful type of intervention (Topping, 1991);
- **reciprocal teaching and 'scaffolding'** – These have been described as being particularly successful in developing reading comprehension (Moore, 1988). They involve considerable interaction between child and teacher and can provide a good basis for team teaching. Reciprocal teaching involves the child and the teacher together building up ideas through question and answer techniques (to do this the teacher initially may have to feed in more information than is received back from the child). These ideas develop into concepts and schema, thus the technique facilitates a deeper understanding and can provide the child with a framework of knowledge on the topic which is being

discussed. Scaffolding is essentially a framework for building up ideas and concepts (Cudd and Roberts, 1994).

It can be argued that these methods can be highly successful with children with specific learning difficulties because they will less likely be subjected to 'critical comment and more likely to become incorporated into the social fabric of the class'. They can also be readily incorporated into a whole-school philosophy of support teaching.

However, such is the severity of difficulty of children with specific learning difficulties that it is not certain that such approaches alone can help some children significantly to improve reading attainments (Pumfrey and Reason, 1991). Although such approaches combined with other strategies should help:

- to enhance self-esteem;
- to maintain social cohesion of all pupils within the school;
- to allow children access to the appropriate level of language.

These are worthwhile objectives for which all schools should strive.

Conclusion

In the case of specific learning difficulties a whole-school approach utilising a systems model can be an effective strategy but only if:

- the needs of the pupils are accurately assessed;
- effective liaison exists within school, between schools and with out-side agencies;
- specialist teaching and programmes are available when necessary
- differentiation of the curriculum is in terms of mode of delivery so that it is essentially access to the curriculum which is being differen-tiated;
- sufficient supports are available for all professionals within the school to help deal with the demands of teaching pupils with specific learning difficulties within a system-initiated approach.

One should also be aware, of course, that in addition to building supports into schools and school systems every school, and indeed every teacher, has their own set of demands. These need to be offset if the inbuilt supports are to have some constructive effect on the school system and the staff. Fig. 51 on page 176 highlights, perhaps in a rather general way, the delicate balancing act which may have to be performed between supports and demands.

Fig. 51

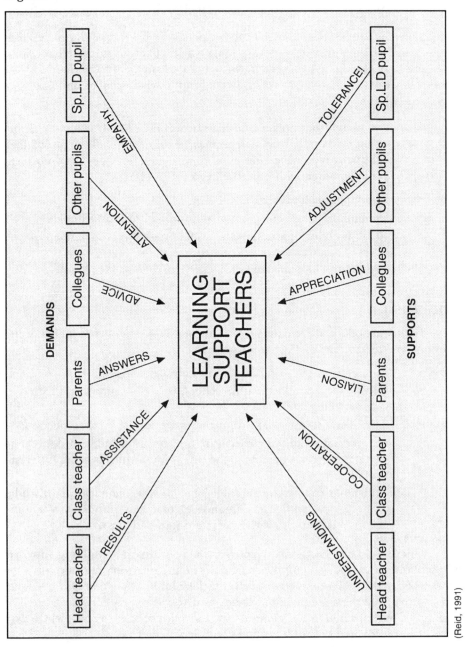

(Reid, 1991)

Specific Learning Difficulties (Dyslexia)

Section 4 –

The learning process

Chapter 11

Learning styles

Introduction

THE ACQUISITION of a successful learning style and of appropriate processes for learning is an important determinant of success at school, in further education and indeed in relation to all learning tasks encountered in adulthood.

It is, therefore, rather surprising that the actual processes involved in learning have not been afforded a higher profile within the curriculum and in the education system in general. Certainly, educational thinking has moved considerably away from advocating a content-driven curriculum with its aim of filling the student with knowledge, and from the presupposition that if the student had the ability the content would be retained, and if not it would need to be recycled into a simpler 'watered down' form. Although educational reforms have helped to steer a course away from such a dilution of the curriculum, there arguably and unfortunately remains a tendency, or at least a risk, that this may still be offered to dyslexic learners.

The reasons for this are twofold. Firstly, the difficulties of dyslexic learners may be undiagnosed or mis-diagnosed and consequently their skills and abilities may be overlooked. Secondly, the pressures inherent in teaching children with severe literacy problems may prevent teachers from focusing on the learning process as, perhaps understandably, they will harbour a preoccupation with improving attainments. As a result it is more likely that teachers will look for a solution to a severe literacy difficulty through curriculum and resources approaches rather than a detailed analysis of the learning processes and learning style of the child. That is not to say that these points are overlooked entirely – they are most certainly not, and may in some cases determine the teacher's decision to use a particular programme or approach.

Models of learning

Bloom's 'Model of School Learning' (1976) provides an interesting framework which encompasses student learning within the cognitive and affective domains and asserts that learning outcomes are influenced by the quality of instruction. Keefe (1987) describes this model as one which essentially looks at school learning from the instructional perspective, dealing with the nature of the learning tasks and learning effectiveness. It overlooks, however, the importance of the learning environment, and the stylistic variations in learning. It is these factors which for dyslexic children are of crucial importance. Their optimum learning environment may be, and will very likely be, different from other learners and this stylistic variation in learning needs to be diagnosed, analysed and considered in both the learning and teaching processes.

It is the aim of this chapter to examine those factors which relate to studying and learning and to suggest that these aspects need to be emphasised both in assessment and teaching, in order that dyslexic children can achieve optimum potential in learning and simultaneously acquire self-knowledge and success.

The process of learning

What does one mean when using the term 'process of learning'? There are three principal elements to learning: the input, the cognition and the output. The input can be absorbed in various forms, for example: by hearing or speaking; seeing events, print or illustrations; writing or experiencing through whole-body activities. The cognition is when the material is undergoing some form of change as the learner attempts to make sense of it; and the output indicates the level of understanding which the learner has achieved with the new material. Consideration needs to be given to the learner and the learning style at all stages of these processes. This is particularly important for dyslexic learners as they can display particular difficulty in the input and output stages and this can influence the 'cognition' process, thus preventing the learner from obtaining a full understanding of the learning task.

Fig. 52

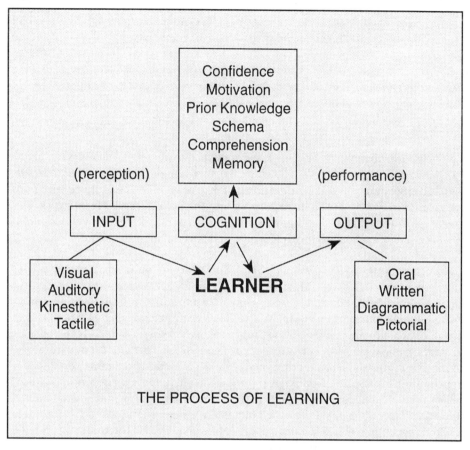

THE PROCESS OF LEARNING

In order that the dyslexic child functions effectively in the classroom it is important that these three dimensions are matched to the learner – a mismatch would obviously result in increased stress being placed on the learner with an accompanying degree of demotivation and possible task failure. There is no one single recipe for success. All of the modes of input of information are important in learning, although very young children are inclined to respond best to input of a tactile or kinesthetic nature, and not necessarily of a visual or auditory nature, indeed very few students prefer learning by listening. It is necessary, therefore, to consider each child individually in relation to the components of the learning process; individual preferences may be evident and these will influence the success or otherwise of both teaching and learning.

The concept of learning style

Learning style is a broad term to describe those factors which influence all aspects of learning. This is summarised in the extract below:

Learning styles are characteristic, cognitive, affective and physiological behaviours that serve as relatively stable indicators of how learners perceive, interact with, and respond to the learning environment.

(NASSP, 1979 from Keefe, 1987)

According to this definition, learning style encompasses a broad perspective incorporating cognitive style as well as the physiological/environmental factors and affective/emotional considerations of learning. Thus the three elements considered in Fig. 52 are all incorporated into the learning styles framework. It is therefore crucial that in dealing with dyslexic learners, both in assessment and in teaching, factors associated with learning style are taken into consideration.

Keefe (1987) proposes a three dimensional view of learning styles incorporating cognitive, affective and physiological aspects. The cognitive dimension includes modality preferences, attention, automisation, memory processes and concept development; the affective dimension includes personality variables which can influence learning such as persistence and perseverance, frustration and tolerance, curiosity, locus of control, achievement motivation, risk taking, cautiousness, competition, cooperation, reaction to reinforcement and personal interests; the physiological dimension includes sex related behaviour, health-related behaviour, time of day rhythms, need for mobility and environmental elements. These dimensions and elements have been the focus of considerable research and applied models have been developed. One of the most widely used and well researched models, developed by Rita and Kenneth Dunn, is illustrated in Fig. 53.

Fig. 53

Learning Styles Model
Designed by Dr Rita Dunn and Dr Kenneth Dunn

(Dunn and Dunn, 1993)

This model is one of the most popular and widely accepted models of learning styles. It has been the subject of extensive research (Dunn and Dunn, 1992).

Given (1993) skilfully merged several approaches to personality and learning styles into one comprehensive model for teaching and learning. Her model used Dunn and Dunn's (1993) five learning style domains for the structural framework. Within this structure she includes personality types as first articulated by Carl Jung and later organised by David Kolb (1984) and Susan Dellinger (1989). The five major personality types Given developed (Figure 54) define the predominant ways individuals react to the world – by intuition, empathy, analysis, ambition, or inquiry. Intuition falls in the emotional domain, empathy in the sociological domain, analysis is representative of the psychological domain, ambition which suggests movement and action falls in the physiological domain, and enquiry, because it is conducted within an environment, represents the environmental domain.

Given calls the merged styles 'areas of influence' because each area is interdependent with and influences all other areas. When individual personality types and learning styles are accepted, habit formation for life-long learning is nurtured such as the habits of self-determined learning, collaborative learning, intentional learning, self-managed learning and reflective learning. When they are ignored or left to chance, individuals learn in a trial and error, hit and miss fashion which tends to result in low self-esteem, intolerance and negativism, limited achievement, lethargy and depressed interest in learning. Given states that a learning environment that honours individual personality and learning styles and one that fosters corresponding learning habits allows each person to reach his or her fullest potential in all five interconnected areas.

Fig. 54

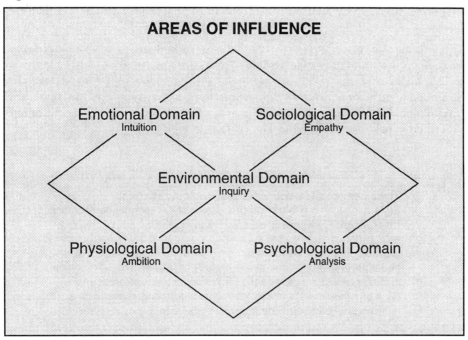

AREAS OF INFLUENCE

Emotional Domain
Intuition

Sociological Domain
Empathy

Environmental Domain
Inquiry

Physiological Domain
Ambition

Psychological Domain
Analysis

Reproduced by kind permission Barbara Given
(Personal Correspondence, 1993)

Learning styles research – theory and application

Keefe (1991) reports on three strands of learning styles research – early cognitive models, applied models and personality theory.

The cognitive models developed initially from a narrow perspective focusing on aspects of perception, particularly in relation to learning and intelligence. These models were broadened to include 'psychological differentiation' (which looked at more general modes of perception, retention and learning), the role of bipolar cognitive styles such as analytic and non-analytic and reflective and impulsive, and learning strategies such as memory and retention styles.

The second strand highlights applied models (see Fig. 53) which have been developed following extensive piloting and research. These models utilise self-report techniques such as interviews or questionnaires for obtaining information about student preferences. This strand is more readily applicable to the classroom situation.

The third strand relates to personality theory, principally based on psychological types emanating from Jungian theory (Myers and Myers, 1980).

Keefe also reports on the work of a distinguished task force which examined forty elements of learning style leading to a new instrument for assessing learning style. This instrument, the Learning Styles Profile, viewed learning styles as an 'umbrella term' which included dimensions in relation to cognitive, affective and physiological dimensions. Four higher order factors in learning styles were also identified. These are outlined in Fig. 55 (Keefe 1991).

Fig. 55

1. Three perceptual responses (visual, auditory, emotive)
2. Eight cognitive or information processing styles (sequential processing, simultaneous processing, discrimination, analytic, spatial, memory, categorization, and verbal-spatial)
3. Six study preferences (persistence, posture, mobility, sound, lighting, and afternoon study time; evening study time preference did not load in this analysis, but may be thought of as a study preference)
4. Six instructional preferences (verbal risk, grouping, manipulative, temperature, early and late morning study time).

From Keefe J. (1991) *Learning Style: Cognitive and Thinking Skills*

The learning styles research suggests that consideration of learning styles within teaching programmes and the curriculum can help students 'learn how to learn' and that 'at risk' students such as those weak in analytic and discrimination skills can learn to control their learning and thus process information more efficiently and effectively.

Keefe (1991) suggests that teachers planning learning styles based on instruction should follow the steps outlined in Fig. 56 below:

Fig. 56

Planning learning style-based instruction involves several steps:
1. Diagnosing individual learning styles
2. Profiling class or group tendencies and preferences
3. Determining significant group strengths and weaknesses
4. Examining subject content for areas that may create problems for learners with weak skills.

Fig. 56 (cont.)

<table>
<tr><td>5.</td><td>Analysing student prior achievement scores and other products (curriculum-referenced tests, skill tests, portfolios, etc.) for patterns of weakness that may reflect cognitive skill deficiencies</td></tr>
<tr><td>6.</td><td>Augmenting (remediating weak cognitive skills)</td></tr>
<tr><td>7.</td><td>Assessing current instructional methods to determine whether they are adequate or require more flexibility</td></tr>
<tr><td>8.</td><td>Modifying the learning environment and developing personalized learning experiences.</td></tr>
</table>

From Keefe J. (1991) *Learning Style: Cognitive and Thinking Skills*

Learning styles and dyslexia

Multisensory strategies are used widely in the teaching of dyslexic children. The evidence suggests that the effectiveness of these strategies is based largely on the provision of at least one mode of learning with which the learner feels comfortable. Thus, if the learner has a difficulty dealing with information by way of the auditory channel, this could perhaps be compensated for through the use of the visual channel. The use of such compensatory strategies is well documented in the literature and is a feature of teaching programmes for dyslexic children. It is logical therefore that consideration of the learner as an individual should be extended to a holistic appreciation of the learner's individual style. Factors such as affective and physiological characteristics will have some bearing on how the dyslexic child responds to the learning situation, and a holistic perspective should therefore be applied both in assessment and teaching of dyslexic children.

Looking at, for example, the Dunn and Dunn learning styles model, one can recognise how the elements identified can influence the performances of dyslexic learners. It must be appreciated that dyslexic learners are first and foremost learners, and like any other learners will be influenced by different conditions. Some dyslexic students therefore, will prefer a 'silent' environment for concentration while others may need some auditory stimuli, perhaps even music, in order to maximise concentration and performance. Similarly, with 'light' – individual preferences such as dim light and bright light should be recognised.

In relation to emotional variables, two of the elements, responsibility and structure, should certainly be addressed. It has been well documented that dyslexic learners benefit from imposed structure – most of the teaching programmes recognise this and follow a highly structured formula. At the same time, however, taking responsibility for one's own learning can be highly motivating and generate success – dyslexic learners therefore should not be deprived of the opportunity to take responsibility as some may possess a natural preference for responsibility and structure.

Programmed Learning Sequences (PLS) is a highly structured approach to learning (Dunn, 1992) and is directed towards students who tend to extract meaning visually, either in reading or in pictorial or graphic form. There is also a considerable degree of tactile learning in this type of approach, since visual learners tend to learn new information using visual resources followed by tactile or kinesthetic reinforcement (Dunn, 1992).

Many programmed software activities tend to be analytic, thus building up ideas and concepts on a step-by-step basis. This formula, however, may not hold the interest of global learners so PLS begins with a short attention capturing anecdote or story. PLS lists objectives that indicate exactly what must be learned; the text teaches the subject matter and the back of each frame in the sequence gives an answer to questions posed on its front. The back of each frame often also includes jokes and humour about the content – thus making it appealing to global learners.

In relation to global and analytic preferences dyslexic students, like other learners, will display differences. Carbo, Dunn and Dunn (1986) showed how most primary aged children are more global than analytic, but much of the teaching, including reading programmes, has a tendency to be analytic. It is thus important that if an analytic reading scheme such as a phonic, structured and sequential approach is used it must be balanced by global activities such as creative work, language experience and visual imagery.

Dunn (1993) reports on a number of research studies which show that when children were introduced to new and difficult reading material through their learning preferences, higher achievement was evident. She therefore suggests that teachers identify which young children are auditory, visual, tactile, kinesthetic, non-preferenced or multi-preferenced and also whether they are global or analytic. It is suggested that, for example, children with auditory preferences and at least three of the following, also have analytic inclinations:

- a preference for quiet;
- a preference for bright light;
- a preference for formal design;
- persistence.

On the other hand, auditory children who have global preferences will also display at least three of the following:

- a preference for sound;
- a preference for low light;
- a preference for informal design;
- lack of persistence;
- a preference for learning with peers.

Dunn suggests for auditory analytics, teaching should begin with phonics, emphasising alphabetic letters and their sounds to provide opportunity for the children to read back to the adult. For auditory global learners, she suggests that teaching should begin by reading stories – often and dramatically, emphasising comprehension – reinforced by games, dramatisations, discussions and role-playing.

Similar considerations can also be directed to other types of learners. For example, kinesthetic global learners do not cope well with multiple directions; they do not follow sequential steps well and tasks and activities should be demonstrated to them. Tactile global learners may prefer to create their own stories emphasising ideas. It is important for this group that reading should be meaningful and enjoyable and not tedious or threatening. Such children may prefer to play, and have a short attention span when faced with a reading text. It is necessary, therefore, to supplement the reading lesson with play-type activities which may be preferred by children with a tactile global preference.

It is also suggested that global learners need to begin with a story that includes the new words to be learnt, whereas analytic learners should start with the words and review with the story.

It is widely accepted that dyslexic children have a primary difficulty in phonics and phonological awareness (Stanovich, 1990) and the teaching of at least a basic knowledge of phonics is important (Reason and Boote, 1991) to foster the use of contextual cues. At the same time the teaching of phonics can itself be adapted to suit the child's learning preferences (see Fig. 57). In this plan, Organizing for Phonics, a variety of methods can be noted in the teaching procedures and the accessing of resources.

Fig. 57

ORGANIZING FOR PHONICS		
Introduction: Step One	**Reinforcement: Step Two**	**Reinforcement: Step Three**
Auditory Analytics	Hear and see words first; accent on letters in sequence	Then hear story which includes words; then make Task cards* with words and practise. +
Visual Analytics	See and hear words first; accent on visual formation	Then hear story which includes words; then make Task Cards* with words and practise. +
Tactual Analytics	Use Task Cards first, matching pictures and words	Then hear story which includes words while seeing storybook or page transparency. +
Kinesthetic Analytics	Stand (or walk) while they follow the procedures for children with their same secondary perceptual strength	Stand (or walk) while they follow the procedures for children with their same tertiary perceptual strength. +
Auditory Globals	Hear story first, but look at storybook pages or transparencies of them during listening to story	Then use Task Cards * and practise. +
Visual Globals	See storybook pages or transparencies of them while listening to story	Then use Task Cards * and practise. +
Tactual Globals	Handle Task Cards of pictured story sequence combined with words first; then see and hear story	Then use Task Cards * and practise. +
Kinesthetic Globals	Stand (or walk) while they follow the procedures for children with their same secondary perceptual strength	Stand (or walk) while they follow the procedures for children with their same tertiary perceptual strength. +

* Electroboards, Pic-A-Holes, or Flip Chutes can and should be substituted on an alternate basis.
+ Practice should be based on each child's preference – alone, in a pair, or in a small group.

Reproduced by kind permission of Rita Dunn
(Dunn, 1993)

Dunn and Dunn's model identifies five principal characteristics and twenty-one elements, all of which affect student learning (see Fig. 53). It is hypothesised that all these elements have to be considered during the assessment process and in subsequent planning of teaching.

Deschler and Schumaker (1987) discuss the creation of a 'strategic environment' in the classroom. This involves the teacher performing classroom tasks such as giving directions, reviewing assignments, giving feedback, classroom organisation and classroom management in a 'strategic' fashion. The creation of such an environment is helped by, for example, the teacher thinking aloud when discussing problems, so that students can understand some of the processes and strategies which a good learner uses in solving problems.

For example, Deschler and Schumaker describe how the use of such metacognitive strategies may be achieved. They suggest the teacher may start by analysing the problem, then a specific cognitive strategy might be selected to deal with the problem; perhaps referring to previous knowledge, but this may then be rejected when the teacher realises that it is inadequate to solve the problem, another strategy would then be selected; its effectiveness would be monitored and finally a self-coping statement would be generated regarding the teacher's ability to deal with the problem. This complete process would be a public one with the teacher thinking aloud. This would enable students to cue in to the teacher's strategies and encourage, not necessarily the replication of the teacher's strategies, but the student's own metacognitive thinking.

This example helps to highlight the link between metacognition (learning how to learn) and (learning styles) one's learning preferences. Clearly, it begs the question of whether one should be manipulating students' learning preferences to suit an appropriate learning situation. Nevertheless the teacher has a responsibility to help identify both preferred and appropriate learning styles and encourage and develop these in students. This is particularly the case for dyslexic learners who may become so 'hooked' into the learning aspects which cause them to fail, such as the difficulty with decoding, that they fail to develop or utilise other avenues of learning. The decoding difficulty effectively blocks the development and awareness of their learning skills and this requires recognition and consideration by the teacher so that s/he can help the student recognise and develop a learning style and learning skill. This is particularly important as it should be recognised that it is just as appropriate to learn to read by **decoding**, as it is by **recognising** words that have become familiar, as it is to learn new words through a **kinesthetic** floor game, as it is to learn through **tactile** resources.

The important point is that all children can learn to read **initially** through their learning style which can subsequently be reinforced by the deployment of other strategies, thus allowing other skills to be developed. Competence in decoding, therefore, may be one of the **additional** skills rather than the **initial** one, since it would be difficult for dyslexic children to acquire this skill in the beginning stages of reading. In support of this viewpoint Dunn (1992) contends that the strategy of decoding appears to be the best for analytic auditory learners; linguistics is most successful with analytic visuals, and whole language is most successful with global auditory and visual learners. It is important to match the method and the child's strong preferences (Sullivan, 1993).

Learning styles assessment

Students' learning styles can be assessed using questionnaires (Dunn, Dunn and Price, 1975,1989) and through observational strategies (Reid, 1992). In relation to the former, several instruments have been developed to identify individual students' learning styles (Canfield, 1976; Dunn and Dunn, 1977; Dunn, Dunn and Price, 1975; Gregorc, 1985; Hill, 1964; Keefe, Monk, Languis, Letteri and Dunn, 1986). Most of these measure one or two elements on a bipolar continuum. Three instruments – the Learning Style Profile (Keefe, Monk, Languis, Letteri and Dunn, 1986), Cognitive Style Mapping (Hill, 1964), the Learning Style Inventory (LSI) (Dunn, Dunn and Price, 1975, 1979, 1985, 1987, 1989), and its Primary Version (Perrin, 1983) are considered comprehensive in nature; that is, they assess multiple elements in combination with each other. The LSI (Dunn, Dunn and Price, 1977-1989) is a comprehensive and widely used assessment instrument in elementary and secondary schools.

The Learning Styles Inventory directs students to '. . . answer the questions as if you are describing how you concentrate when you are studying difficult academic material'. The instrument can be completed in approximately 30 to 40 minutes by elementary and secondary students. After answering all the questions on the LSI answer form (the test itself), each student's answer sheet is optically read and processed individually. Each student then receives his/her own LSI individual printout – a graphic representation of the conditions in which each learns most efficiently.

Dunn, Dunn and Price (1989) defined learning style in terms of each person's:
- immediate environment (sound level, temperature, light, and seating design);
- emotionality (motivation, persistence, responsibility, and structure);

- social preferences (learning alone, learning with peers, learning with adults present, learning in varied ways versus in patterns or routines, being motivated by a teacher; and being motivated by a parent);
- physiological inclinations (perceptual memory preferences, intake, energy highs and lows, and mobility); and
- physiological preferences (global/analytic).

In cases where youngsters do not read fluently, or where they have experienced learning difficulties, it is valuable to administer the instrument through a personal interview. The one-to-one relationship that develops as the teacher questions the youngster about his/her preferences often provides new insights into the individual's thinking that may not be afforded otherwise.

When observation is used to identify learning style research suggests that less elements appear identifiable (Beaty, 1986; Dunn, Dunn and Price, 1977) but useful and informative data can nevertheless be obtained. In observation it is important to note that one is observing the process and not testing the product of learning. In learning styles assessment there is no success or failure – instead one is examining areas of learning preferences. These preferences help to highlight the students' most effective mode of, and conditions for, learning.

Observational assessment

Observational assessment can be utilised by trained teachers who wish to develop an appreciation and understanding of the students and their strategies for learning (Reid, 1993,1994). This does not involve examining or predicting the students' potential, but looking at the student preferences and actual behaviour in relation to learning.

Criteria

A number of factors are necessary for effective learning. Some of the important, perhaps crucial criteria are listed below:

- interaction;
- communication;
- movement;
- organisation;
- attention;
- understanding;
- success.

An observation schedule can be compiled looking at these factors and developed in such a way that it can be used flexibly and adapted to different contexts.

For example looking at the criterion 'interaction' one can identify different responses which the student can exhibit in different situations (see Fig. 58).

Fig. 58: Interaction

ONE-WAY INTERACTION

This occurs when the teacher talks to the student, the student apparently absorbs the information, but there is no evidence from this that the student is understanding.

TWO-WAY SIMPLE INTERACTION

The tutor/teacher talks to the student and the student responds in a predictable manner, thus acknowledging but not necessarily understanding what has been spoken.

TWO-WAY COMPLEX INTERACTION

The student responds in a manner which indicates that he has understood what has been said.

MULTI-FACET INTERACTION (MEDIATED/UNMEDIATED)

This form of interaction can be observed when the student is involved in interaction with more than one person simultaneously and shows the ability to absorb and reflect on information. A mediated form of such an interaction would occur when the tutor or some other person controls and helps to elicit responses from the student.

This can provide information on the quality and degree of the student's interaction and will almost certainly provide information which will be useful in the development of the student's learning profile.

Similar frameworks can be developed for other criteria (see Fig. 59).

Fig. 59: Communication

(i)   Listening Skills
Communication and listening skills can be sub-divided into verbal and non-verbal aspects, and statements can be developed describing different types of behaviour:

Verbal

(a)   listening with minimal response
(b)   listening with some verbal response
(c)   listening with relevant questions
(d)   extended enquiry
(e)   clear understanding.

Non-verbal

(a)   no non-verbal interest displayed
(b)   displays some interest, e.g. eye contact
(c)   clear non-verbal engagement,

General Communication

(a)   initiates communication undivided/group
(b)   prefers one-to-one conversation
(c)   prefers group discussion.

These criteria can have considerable applications to children with specific learning difficulties.

Movement

This can provide some important data in relation to the difficulties experienced by dyslexic children. Some children need to touch and to move around in order to gain maximum benefit from the learning process. It is important, therefore, to assess the student's preference in this area by examining general movement while engaged on a task.

The following could therefore be examined in relation to length of time and duration of on and off task behaviour.

Fig. 60

•   posture on task
•   posture off task
•   body movements
•   locational movements.

Taken together they provide some indication of the student's preferred learning style in relation to seating arrangements and classroom setting.

Organisation

In relation to organisation, an enormous amount of useful information can be obtained from observing the student's organisational strategies.

Organisation can be divided into:

Organisation of materials for learning

- Does the student need to refer to a lot of materials at the same time, or only one reference or resource at a time?
- Is there any method in the way the student consults the materials?
- How does the student locate the materials and resources for learning in relation to accessibility? For example, does the student insist on order and precision, or is the preference for a more random approach to accessing materials.

Organisation of method of learning

- Does the student start with small detail, then advance to more general concepts?
- Is there a linear, sequential method to learning?
- Does the student consistently/seldom refer to other materials or to the teacher for information?

Cognitive organisation.

- What type of stimulus does he/she prefer   – visual?
        – auditory?
        – other?
- What kind of memory strategy does the student use when learning?
- To what extent does the student refer to over-learning? Is there any attempt to consolidate new knowledge ?

One should also observe the student's cognitive organisation by looking at aspects relating to:

- memory strategies;
- preferred mode of handling information, i.e. visual, auditory or tactile;
- preferred mode of expression, i.e. drawings, writing, movement.

It is now well established that success, particularly if reinforced through significant praise and highlighted by positive thinking on the part of the student, can provide the conditions for effective learning. The extent of students' success in most tasks can be readily observed. It may, however, be more beneficial to examine this not in relation to the level of success achieved by the student but in terms of the pupil's expectations. The teacher must therefore acknowledge the student's own expectations of his potential and actual performance on a task as a measure of whether the student feels that success has been achieved. It is important to obtain some acknowledgment from the student as to how realistic or otherwise their expectations are in terms of their performance.

Context for learning

The importance of the learning environment has already been acknowledged (Given, 1993; Dunn and Dunn, 1992; Keefe, 1991) and the context for learning needs therefore to be highlighted. The factors influencing the context include:

- the classroom
- the tutor/teacher
- the task
- the materials
- the targets.

Contextual variables will affect performance, but too often these variables are overlooked. For example the classroom is arranged essentially, though not always, from the teacher's perspective, but certainly for the benefit of the majority of the students. Yet the setting may not be particularly appropriate for all students and one should attempt to note the response of students to different classroom and learning settings.

Though it is very difficult in a mixed learning situation to cater for the diverse needs of all students simultaneously, it is important at least to be aware of these differences and of how they affect the learning and performance of individual students.

Conclusion

Buzan (1990) argues that not only do we, as humans, under-utilise our capacities for learning, but we are also unaware of how we learn; 'the reason for our "failures" is not that we are "only human" but that at this very early stage in our evolution we are still taking our first, babyish and tentative steps towards an understanding of the outstanding bio-computer we all possess'.

It is important to recognise learning styles not only as a means from which the teacher can shape the optimum curriculum and learning environment for students, but also to encourage students themselves to be more aware of how they learn and to help them develop effective strategies for coping with their own learning.

John Holt in his renowned text *How Children Fail* states:
Part of being a good student is learning to be aware of one's own mind and the degree of one's own understanding.

It is important to be aware of this. Careful observation and awareness of learning styles can help to build up a positive profile of the student, and it is essential that this positive profile is passed on to the learner to enhance and foster his/her responsibility for their own learning.

Chapter 12

Study skills

Introduction

STUDENTS, on their own initiative, usually develop a preferred method of tackling new material. Despite this, study skill techniques should be taught, encouraged and developed in all learners.

Children with specific learning difficulties may display additional difficulties in managing and organising their work and therefore would benefit from a structured 'study skills' programme.

Such programmes will vary with the age and stage of the learner. A study skills programme for primary children would be different from that which may help students cope with examinations at secondary level. Well developed study skills habits at the primary stage can provide a sound foundation for tackling new material in secondary school and help equip the student for examinations. Some of the principal factors in a study skills programme which will be discussed in this chapter include the following:

- communication skills
- transfer of knowledge and skills
- mapping and visual skills
- memory.

Communication skills

Communication skills is a fairly general term and relates to those aspects of study skills governing oral and written communication. Some of the factors which influence such skills include:

- organisation
- sequencing
- context
- schema development
- confidence and motivation.

Organisation

Children with specific learning difficulties may require help to organise their thoughts. A structure should therefore be developed to help encourage this. It may not be enough to ask children, for example, on completion of a story, 'What was the story about?' They need to be provided with a structure in order to elicit correct responses. This helps with the organisation of responses (output) which in turn can help to organise learning through comprehension (input). A structure which the teacher might use to elicit organised responses may include:

Fig. 61

- What was the title?
- Who were the main characters?
- Describe the main characters.
- What did the main characters try to do?
- Who were the other characters in the story?
- What was the story about?
- What was the main part of the story?
- How did the story end?

In this way a structure is provided for the learner to retell the story. Moreover, the learner will be organising the information into a number of components such as 'characters', 'story', 'conclusion'. This will not only make it easier for the learner to retell orally, but will help to give him/her an organisational framework which will facilitate the retention of detail. The learner will also be using a strategy which can be used in other contexts. This will help with the new learning and the retention of new material.

Sequencing

Children with specific learning difficulties may have some difficulty in re-telling a story or giving information orally in the correct sequence. It is important that sequencing of information should be encouraged and exercises which help facilitate this skill can be developed. Thus, in the re-telling of a story, children should be provided with a framework which can take account of sequence of events. Such a framework could include:

- How did the story start?
- What happened after that?
- What was the main part?
- How did it end?

Various exercises, such as the use of games, can be developed to help facilitate sequencing skills.

An example is shown below:

Fig. 62: Passage 1

> One thing about Mum, she was never fussed about anything, she took everything in her stride. Bossy, the cat I brought home one night, Patch the dog and Donny from Canada, who stayed about three years. Some people collect stamps, Mum collected stray cats and dogs . . . Being embraced by Mum was like tangling with a gorilla . . . Mum had a big heart, she was a real lady.
>
> (Adapted from *Mister God This is Anna*, Fynn 1974)

Use of visual strategies for sequencing

The passage above (Fig. 62) can be used as an example of how a mnemonic device such as a golf course can be helpful in remembering information (see Fig. 63). For example, on the golf course Mum can be shown striding on to the first hole, and Bossy the cat sitting beside flag number two shaded by the sun – to help remember that Bossy the cat was brought home one night. Patch the dog could be kicking the sand out of the bunker of hole number three. Donny from Canada is holding on to flag number four, having been in Canada for three years. Five people can be scattered around hole number five exchanging stamps while Mum with her stray cats and dogs is wandering through the trees which surround hole number six. Mum embracing a gorilla could feature somewhere beside hole number seven. A heart could symbolise number eight to show how big-hearted Mum was, while Mum can be dressed as a real lady being applauded by the onlookers as she sinks the final putt in hole number nine. This can help the learner retell the story in the correct sequence using the particular features at each hole to help remember the events in the text in the correct sequence. It can be particularly useful in enhancing visual skills and helpful in retention of information for those children who have good visual skills. The principle can be used for children of all ages.

Fig. 63

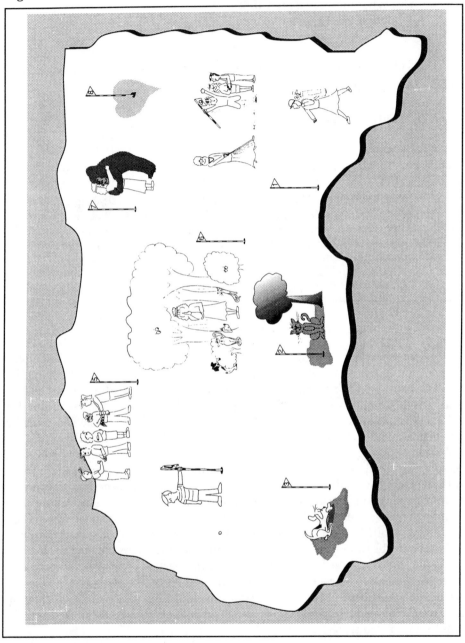

Another example of this strategy is provided in Figs. 64 and 65.

Fig. 64

> *Silence bothered her around him, so she talked. Told him about her growing years, the private school, the nuns, her parents – housewife, bank manager. About standing along the sea wall as a teenager and watching ships from all over the world. About the American soldiers that came later. About meeting Richard in a cafe where she and some girlfriends were drinking coffee. The war had disrupted lives, and they wondered if they would ever get married. She was silent about Niccolo.*
>
> From *The Bridges of Madison County* Waller, 1992)

The example in Fig. 65 is again of a golf course but the visual images which Fig. 65 conveys are the important elements which help the student remember the passage and the sequence of events.

Beside flag number one the woman featured in the passage is standing with arms folded representing the silence. The illustration at flag number two represents the growing years, number three the private school, number four, the nun, number five, her parents, number six, housewife and number seven the bank manager. Flag number eight shows the sea wall and a 'teenager' standing watching ships 'from all over the world'. Flag number nine is linked to the two American soldiers and number ten shows Richard drinking coffee in a cafe. Number eleven highlights the war and number twelve the question of marriage.

Clearly each student would develop their own images linked to the passage content, but the principal of using some form of visual representation is the important aspect.

Fig. 65

Context

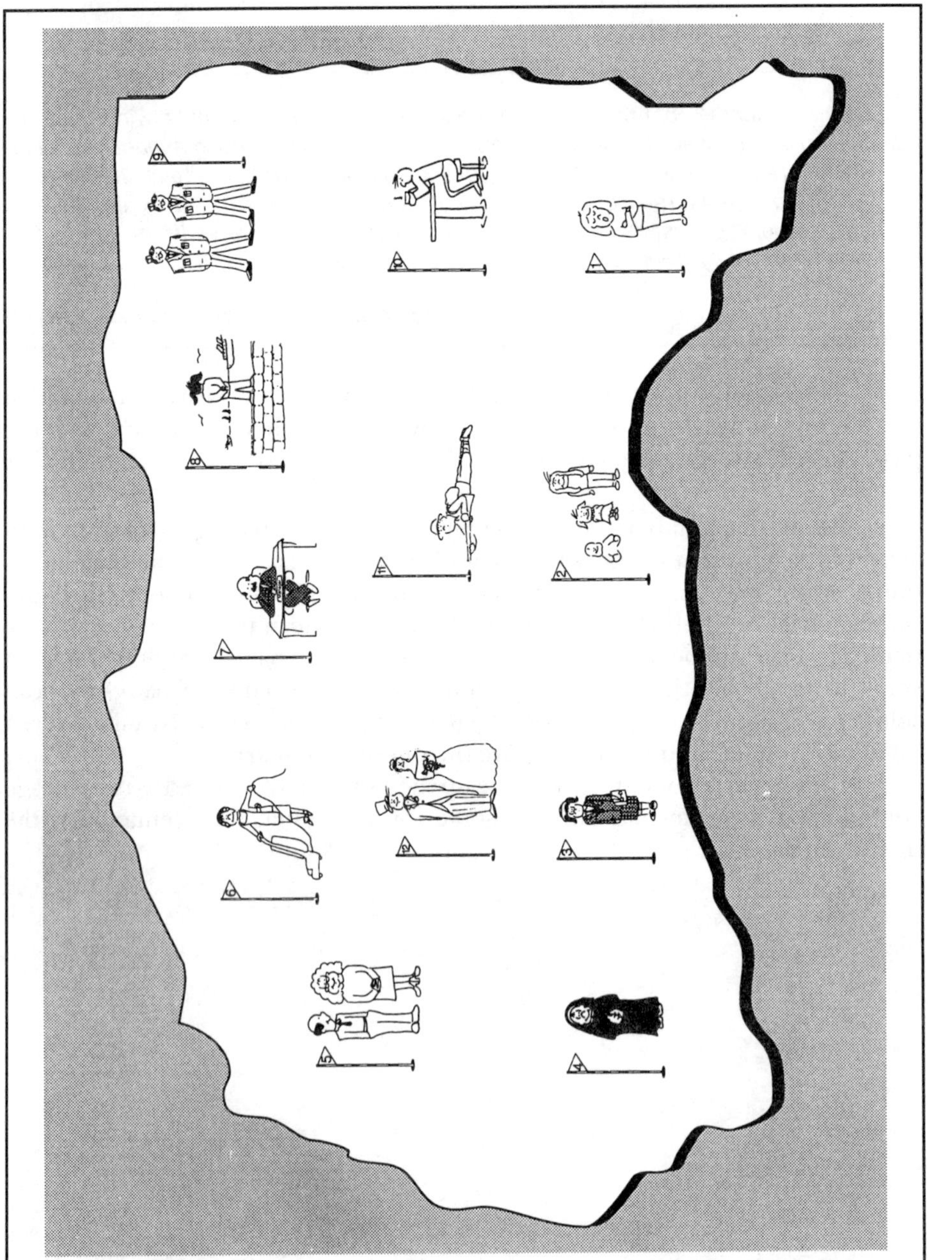

Contextual aspects are important elements in acquiring study skills techniques. Context can be used to help the learner in both the sequencing and organisation of materials as well as in providing an aid to comprehension.

Context can be in the form of syntactic and semantic context (see Chapter 2). In Study Skills, semantic context can be particularly valuable as a learning and memory aid. If the learner is using or relying on semantic context, this provides some indication that the material is being read and learnt with some understanding.

The content can therefore help to:

- retain information and aid recall;
- enhance comprehension;
- transfer learning to other situations.

Schema development

The development of schema helps the learner organise and categorise information. It also ensures the utilisation of background knowledge. This can aid comprehension and recall.

When children read a story or a passage, they need to relate this to their existing framework of knowledge – i.e. their own schema. So when coming across new knowledge, learners try to fit it into their existing framework of knowledge based on previous learning, which is the schema they possess for that topic or piece of information. It is important for the teacher to find out how developed a child's schema is on a particular topic, before providing more and new information. Being aware of this will help the teacher ensure the child develops appropriate understanding of the new information. Thus some key points about the passage could help the reader understand the information more readily and provide a framework into which the reader can slot ideas and meaning from the passage.

Schema, therefore, can help the learner:

- attend to the incoming information;
- provide a scaffolding for memory;
- make inferences from the passage which also aid comprehension and recall;
- utilise his/her previous knowledge.

There are a number of strategies which can help in the development of schema. An example of this can be seen in an examination of a framework for a story. In such a framework two principal aspects can be discerned.

- The structure of the story.
- The details related to the components of the structure.

The **structure** of a story can be seen in the following components:
- background
- context
- characters
- beginning
- main part
- events
- conclusion.

The **details** which may relate to these components can be recalled by asking appropriate questions. Taking the background as an example, one can see how appropriate questioning can help the learner build up a schema to facilitate understanding of the rest of the story.

- What was the weather like?
- Where did the story take place?
- Describe the scene.
- What were the main colours?

Previous learning

Schema depend to a great extent on the learner's previous knowledge. It can, therefore, be useful to provide the learner with cues or information relating to the story, before it has been read. In this way the learner is able to select and modify schema of his own which will help to predict the material to be read and so help it become meaningful. The example below illustrates this point:

Fig. 66

LUNCH AT THE SCHOOL HOLIDAY CAMP

Everyone was rushing around. Time was running out fast. The servers were looking around but most people were looking at the board. It seemed to be a repeat of yesterday and naturally Tom and Jane were disappointed.

The passage above can be read with the existing schema one may possess in relation to 'lunch', 'school' and 'holiday camp'. The words servers and board would refer to the people serving the food and the menu board.

If, however, the title was different and read 'Rain stops play again in mixed doubles' the meaning would be entirely different because the reader would use a different set of schema (see Fig. 67).

Fig. 67

RAIN STOPS PLAY AGAIN IN MIXED DOUBLES

Everyone was rushing around. Time was running out fast. The servers were looking around but most people were looking at the board. It seemed to be a repeat of yesterday and naturally Tom and Jane were disappointed.

In this case the servers would be the tennis players whose turn it was to serve and the board would refer to the scoreboard.

If the passage was given **without** a title this could lead to confusion and misconception regarding the text. It is important therefore to provide the learner with a set of cues, such as the title and some key ideas about the text **before** the reading is tackled.

Background knowledge

Background knowledge is an important aid to comprehension. It is postulated that background knowledge in itself is insufficient to facilitate new learning, but must be skilfully interwoven with the new material which is being learnt. It is important that the learner is able to use the new information in different and unfamiliar situations. Hence the connections between the reader's background knowledge and the new information must be highlighted in order for the learner to incorporate the new knowledge in a meaningful manner.

The ideas contained in a text therefore must be linked in some way to the reader's background knowledge and that the ideas need to be presented in a coherent and sequential manner. Such coherence and sequencing of ideas at the learning stage not only allows the material to be retained and recalled, but also facilitates effective comprehension. Being aware of the learner's prior knowledge therefore of a lesson is of fundamental importance. Before embarking on new material prior knowledge can be linked with the new ideas, in order to pave the way for effective study techniques and strategies to enhance comprehension and recall.

Confidence and motivation

Confidence and motivation are important for effective studying. Study skills programmes can help achieve this by:

- Enabling the student to succeed.

  It is important that the learner meets with some initial success – success builds on success and early and significant success is an important factor when new material is being learnt.

- Provision of tasks unrelated to the learning which is taking place.

  Through the provision of tasks, even simple ones such as 'fetching a ruler', the learner can feel more at ease and prepared to tackle the new material with more confidence and motivation.

- Encouraging independent thinking.

  It is important to help promote independent thinking. Being able to make decisions and come to conclusions without too much direction from the teacher can instil confidence in a learner, and help to motivate the learner to tackle new material.

Some thinking skills' programmes such as Somerset Thinking Skills and the CORT programme devised by Edward De Bono can not only help to achieve enhancement in thinking skills, but can also help students to use these skills by helping them to structure their own studying. This can help to develop appropriate study habits and maximise retention and transfer.

Transfer of knowledge and skills

A key aspect of effective study skills training is the transfer of skills to other curriculum areas. A number of studies support the view that to achieve this great importance must be given to the context in which learning takes place (Nisbet and Shucksmith, 1986). Study skills, therefore, should be integrated into day-to-day teaching in a meaningful context, and not as a separate area of the curriculum. Nisbet and Shucksmith criticise the study skills movement for being too general, too removed from context, and in many cases merely consisting of a collection of 'tips' for coping with specific difficulties. To overcome these pitfalls it is necessary to teach study skills within some theoretical or thematic perspective such as schema theory or reciprocal teaching, in order that applicability to the wider curriculum and transfer of skills can be achieved (Brown, 1993).

Reciprocal teaching refers to a procedure which both monitors and enhances comprehension by focusing on processes relating to questioning, clarifying, summarising and predicting (Palincsar and Brown, 1984). It is an interactive process. Brown (1993) describes the procedure for reciprocal teaching in the following way:

The teacher leads discussion by asking questions . . . this generates additional questions from participants, the questions are then clarified by teacher and participants together. The discussion is then summarised by teacher or participants, then a new 'teacher' is selected by the participants to lead the discussion on the next section of the text.

This procedure can be referred to as scaffolding, in which a 'scaffold' or supports are built to develop the understanding of text. This may be in the form of the teacher either providing the information or generating appropriate responses through questioning and clarifying. The supports are then withdrawn gradually, when the learner has achieved the necessary understanding to continue with less support.

Cudd and Roberts(1994) observed that poor readers were not automatically making the transfer from book language to their own writing. As a result the students' writing lacked the precise vocabulary and varied syntax which was evident during reading. To overcome this difficulty Cudd and Roberts introduced a scaffolding technique to develop both sentence sense and vocabulary. They focused on sentence expansion by using vocabulary from the children's readers, and using these as sentence stems encouraged sentence expansion.

Thus the procedure used involved:
- selection of vocabulary from basal reader;
- embedding this vocabulary into sentence stems;
- selecting particular syntactic structures to introduce the stem (see Fig. 68);
- embedding the targeted vocabulary into sentence stems to produce complex sentences;
- discussing the sentence stems, including the concepts involved;
- completing a sentence using the stems;
- repeating the completed sentence providing oral reinforcement of both the vocabulary and the sentence structure;
- encouraging the illustration of some of their sentences, helping to give the sentence a specific meaning.

Cudd and Roberts have found that this sentence expansion technique provides a 'scaffold' for children to help develop their sentence structure and vocabulary. Preliminary examination of writing samples of the students has revealed growth in vocabulary choice and sentence variety. The children, including those with reading and writing difficulties, were seen to gain better control over the writing process and gained confidence from using their own ideas and personal experiences.

Fig. 68

EXAMPLES OF CLAUSES AND PHRASES USED AS STEMS FOR SENTENCE EXPANSION

While on our daily journey to the cafeteria, _____

Behind the huge wooden door _____

Although Lauren is petite, _____

Ahead of the herd of stampeding elephants _____

After Rodney discovered the huge dinosaur bone, _____

Before appearing on Hidden Oak News, _____

Besides collecting baseball cards, Tyrone _____

On top of the swaying flagpole _____

During Alberto's perilous journey across the Sahara Desert, _____

In addition to lifting weights, football players _____

As a result of the unexpected snowstorm, _____

Takeshia is so strong that _____

_____ is a teacher who _____

Note: Each stem is composed of vocabulary and syntactical structures the children have encountered in their basal reader, children's books, or content area material. Often the stem is a subordinate clause. As the primary school children (Grades 1 - 3) expand each stem they produce complex sentences of the type that appear in written language – a step toward their own writing of complex prose.

From 'A scaffolding technique to develop sentence sense and vocabulary'
Evelyn T. Cudd and Leslie L. Roberts, *The Reading Teacher*, December 1993/January 1994.
Reprinted with permission of Evelyn T. Cudd and the International Reading Association.

Transfer of skills can best be achieved when emphasis is firmly placed on the **process** of learning and not the product. This encourages children to reflect on learning and encourages the learner to interact with other learners and with the teacher. In this way effective study skills can help to activate learning and provide the student with a structured framework for effective learning.

Nisbet and Shucksmith describe one example of such a framework which focuses on preparation, planning and reflection.

Preparation looks at the goals of the current work and how these goals relate to previous work. Planning looks at the skills and information necessary in order to achieve these goals, and the reflection aspect assesses the quality of the final piece of work, asking such questions as, 'What did the children learn from the exercise and to what extent could the skills gained be transferred to other areas?'

This example displays a structure from which it is possible to plan and implement a studies skills programme, and at the same time evaluate its effectiveness in relation to the extent of transfer of knowledge and skills to other curricular areas.

Mapping and visual skills

Learners with specific difficulties usually have orientation problems which can be evident in directional confusion (Miles and Miles, 1991). This aspect, even though it may not directly affect every aspect of the curriculum, can lead to loss of confidence which **can** permeate work in other areas.

To what extent can the teacher help to promote and enhance visual and orientation skills in children with specific difficulties?

According to the principles of skill transfer (Nisbet and Shucksmith, 1986) it is important that such enhancement takes place within the curriculum and is contextualised within a meaningful task. Games or specific exercises in mapping and orientation can help to build up confidence in the learner but there is some uncertainty as to whether such exercises, in isolation, would have a significant skill enhancement effect, and so it is important to use directional and visual cues as much as possible within the context of the curriculum. It may be advantageous therefore to develop specific exercises from materials the learner is using and to focus particularly on visual cues and directional aspects.

For example, if the student is working on a thematic study of the Romans, exercises and questions can emphasise particular directional aspects such as:

- direction of travelling armies;
- location of walls, forts and camps;
- planning of towns, forts and camps.

These aspects are likely to be central to most studies on the Romans, but students with specific learning difficulties would benefit from the additional focus on directional aspects of the study. The use, and indeed the construction, of maps utilising the principles of multisensory learning (see Chapter 7) would also be helpful.

Memory skills

Children with specific learning difficulties may have difficulties in remembering, retaining and recalling information. This may be due to short term memory problems or naming difficulty, i.e.. difficulty in recalling the name or description of something without cues. It is important therefore to encourage the use of strategies which may facilitate remembering and recall. Such strategies can include repetition and over-learning, simple mnemonics and mind mapping.

Repetition and over-learning

Short-term memory difficulties can be overcome by repetition and rehearsal of materials. This form of over-learning can be achieved in a variety of ways and not necessarily through conventional, and often tedious, rote learning.

In order to maximise the effect of repetition of learning it is important that a Multisensory mode of learning is utilised. Repetition of the material to be learned can be accomplished through oral, visual, auditory and kinesthetic modes. The learner should be able to see, hear, say and touch the materials to be learned. This reinforces the input stimuli and helps to consolidate the information for use, meaning and transfer to other areas. There are implications here for multi-mode teaching, including the use of movement, perhaps drama, to enhance the kinesthetic mode of learning.

Simple mnemonics

Mnemonics can be auditory or visual, or both auditory and visual. Auditory mnemonics may take the form of rhyming or alliteration while visual mnemonics can be used by relating the material to be remembered to a familiar scene, such as the classroom.

The 'golf course' strategy discussed earlier in this chapter can be used as a mnemonic device. The scene can be elaborated by including particular pieces of shrubbery, trees and bunkers which can represent specific points which need to be remembered. Clearly, this kind of skill calls for a well developed visual capacity, yet it is not outwith the scope of most learners. Indeed, this can be quite valuable training for children with specific learning difficulties. They should be able to develop advanced visual skills, but often these skills are restricted due to the teaching focus being directed to 'left' hemispheric verbal decoding and structured learning (Bell, 1991).

Mind mapping

Mind mapping is now widely used (Buzan, 1993). It can be a simple or a sophisticated strategy depending on how it is developed. It is used to help the learner to remember a considerable amount of information and encourages students to think of, and develop, the main ideas of a passage or material to be learned. It adopts in many ways some of the principles already discussed in relation to schema theory.

Essentially mind maps are individual learning tools and someone else's mind map may not be meaningful to you. It is important, therefore, that children should create their own, in order to help with both understanding of key concepts and in the retention and recall of associated facts.

Fig. 69 on the next page illustrates a framework for a fairly basic mind map. This mind map framework on dyslexia begins with some fundamental aspects (these are shaded) and from these other points have been developed. Other aspects can in turn be developed from these. Mind mapping can help not only to remember information, but also to help organise that information and this exercise in itself can aid understanding. Elaborate versions of mind maps can be constructed using pictorial images, symbols and different colours (Buzan, 1993).

Fig. 69

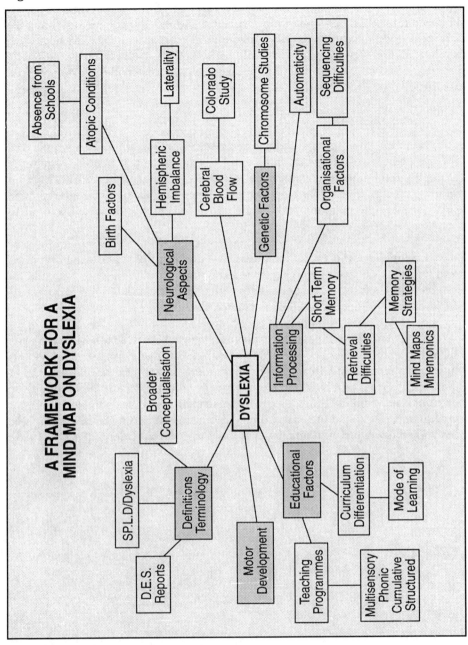

A FRAMEWORK FOR A
MIND MAP ON DYSLEXIA

Specific Learning Difficulties (Dyslexia)

PEP strategies

'PEP' in this case refers to 'People', 'Events' and 'Places'. Information which has to be recalled can be categorised using this 'PEP' strategy.

The following passage contains a considerable amount of information, particularly names and descriptions of places. This passage is used to illustrate how 'PEP' strategies may help the student categorise the information for ease and accuracy of recall.

Fig. 70

'JUST A SUNDAY'

It was bitterly cold. Tony was anxiously waiting for the others to arrive – he had been waiting for some hours now – calming his anxieties by reflecting on the high spirits of the earlier part of the day. All in all it had been an eventful day for the leader and still it was far from over. As he stood there, hunched beside the overhanging, jagged rock, which formed a shelter from the biting wind, Tony thought back on how the day had started.

The group had met at the usual place and the bus had soon taken them to the remote starting point for the day's walk. They were greeted by a scene of swirling heather, trees rustling, branches bending and creaking by the force of the gusting wind, the path ahead silhouetted by a bleak horizon of peaks and valleys.

Fig. 70 (cont.)

> The day's outing had started in the usual way. Rosemary and Priscilla chatted happily, Veronica and Shona purposefully stepped out at a striking pace, Wilson and Andy engrossed in exchanging stories, unaware they had begun to deviate from the general direction of the group. Neville hastily collected money from the group for future events, and Cyril and Mandy reviewing the latest in music and the arts, leisurely took up the rear.
>
> Soon the leader took over and began to establish a fast pace, passing the old twisting burn, crossing the creaking, hardly used bridge over the deep part of the burn, and heading purposefully towards the challenging peak in the distance.
>
> On reflection the day had started quite uneventfully – no hint of the trauma which was to engulf the happy group could be detected, as the brightly clad walkers advanced to the gradual incline of the hill which presented a feature, of mystical splendour amidst the shrouding mist, forming a broken circle just below the protruding peak.

Using this passage, the following strategy may be adopted to assist with remembering the most important information.

People	Events/Situation	Places
Tony	bitterly cold, waiting	beside overhanging, jagged rock
Group	starting point for the day's walk, gusting wind, bleak horizon of peaks and valleys	swirling heather, trees
Rosemary and Priscilla	chatted happily	start of walk
Veronica and Shona	striking pace	start of walk
Wilson and Andy	stories	wrong direction
Neville	collected money	start of walk
Mandy and Cyril	review music and arts	leisurely, took up rear
Leader (Tony)	fast pace	twisting burn, creaky hardly used bridge, leading towards the peak in the distance
Happy group	brightly clad walkers	gradual incline of the hill, shrouding mist, protruding peak.

Using this formula, therefore, the student can usually remember more information, more accurately. Remembering one of the three aspects, i.e. either people, events or places can often trigger off the other two. This form of strategy – categorisation and grouping – can clearly be adopted using other headings, although the student may well find that the 'people, events and places' strategy can have widespread reference.

Summary

Study skills undoubtedly are important, and it is essential that the development of these skills is given a high priority for children with specific learning difficulties. The main aspects which have been discussed here (communication skills, which can be aided by organisation, sequencing, context, schema, confidence and motivation; the transfer of these skills to other areas of the curriculum; mapping and visual skills; and strategies in remembering and retention) are all important. These aspects can be developed with and by the learner. Although the teacher can help to facilitate these strategies and skills in the learner, it is still important that any skill or strategy which is developed must be personalised by the learner. This means that different learners will adopt different ways of learning and remembering materials, but the responsibility to allow the learner to do this and to understand the principles associated with study skills rests with the teacher.

Section 5 –

Sources and Resources

Chapter 13

Review of resources

THIS chapter will give consideration to a number of the resource materials which are currently available for use with students with specific learning difficulties.

Fig. 75

General texts

Specific Learning Difficulties (Dyslexia)
Challenges and Responses
Peter D. Pumfrey and Rea Reason
Routledge (1991).

This is an extremely useful text book for anyone wishing to further their knowledge within the field of specific learning difficulties.

The authors provide the reader with a sound, well researched background relating to concepts and definitions, cognitive, emotional and social factors, intervention and evaluation. There are also interesting sections on psychological issues and the responses from a national survey involving local education authorities, education psychologists, organisations and examination boards.

Children's Difficulties in Reading, Spelling and Writing
Edited by Peter D. Pumfrey and Colin D. Elliott
Falmer Press (1990).

This book consists of eighteen chapters from different contributors looking at the National Curriculum, assessment and sub-types of specific learning difficulties, phonological approaches, evaluation of teaching programmes and classroom applications. A very useful source book for the student and the teacher.

Dyslexia – Integrating Theory and Practice
Edited by Margaret Snowling and Michael Thomson
Whurr Publishers (1991).

The book presents a selection of the papers prepared for the Second International Conference on Specific Learning Difficulties held in 1991, and consists of twenty-eight chapters representing different aspects of specific learning difficulties. There is a chapter on 'biological bases' which focuses on neurological research; one on literacy which looks at recent research on phonological processing; and the other chapters provide some practical help in areas such as mathematics, study skills, communication, reading and writing.

A worthwhile reference book, useful for both researcher and teacher.

The Many Faces of Dyslexia
Margaret Byrd Rawson
Orton Dyslexia Society, Maryland (1988).

As the title suggests this excellent text examines the different dimensions of dyslexia. In many ways the book epitomises the Orton Society's four-way analysis of dyslexia:

- the differences are personal;
- the diagnoses is clinical;
- the treatment is educational;
- the understanding is scientific.

Like the Orton Society, the book portrays the 'united whole'. It looks at education, neurophysiological and social aspects of the dyslexic learner, the history and developments of the Orton Society, the 'interfaces and reflections' and the different facets of dyslexia.

A very useful book.

Dyslexia – Theory and Practice of Remedial Instruction
Diana Brewster Clark
York Press Inc., Maryland (1988).

This excellent text provides an understanding both of the nature of dyslexia and of the reading process as well as evaluative comment on a wide range of teaching programmes for dyslexic children.

It provides a superb overview of teaching for dyslexics including aspects such as phonological awareness training, reading comprehension, instruction, handwriting and composition instruction, spelling and the reading-writing relationship.

A very useful book.

Dyslexia or Illiteracy? Realising the Right to Read
P. Young and C. Tyre
Open University Press (1983).

An excellent book which analyses the problem of dyslexia in relation to the processes of reading. In addition, therefore, to discussing the concept of dyslexia and different models of reading, the authors present an overview of dyslexia research and pose some relevant questions associated with dyslexia such as: 'Is dyslexia a result of language deficiency?' and 'Do dyslexic children have persistent spelling difficulties?' There is also a comprehensive chapter on assessment and a useful glossary of terms.

Children with Literacy Difficulties
Edited by Pat Pinsent
David Fulton – published in association with the Roehampton Institute (1990).

The book consists of an interesting collection of eleven chapters from a range of contributors with expertise in various aspects of literacy.

The chapters include assessment, parental involvement in reading, peer tutoring, classroom management, writing, spelling and perceptuo-motor difficulties, micro-technology and the use of art in literacy. This book is essentially based on practice and contains useful information for class and specialist teachers.

Dyslexia – A Hundred Years On
T. R. Miles and Elaine Miles
Open University Press (1991).

An extremely useful and informative text which provides an excellent overview of causes and sub-types. It also provides an informative summary of teaching methods and programmes as well as some commentary on the debate regarding the concept of dyslexia.

The important area of brain research and genetics which is revealing much useful information to help explain the basis of dyslexic difficulties is discussed. The debate on the concept of dyslexia is commented on by way of thesis and antithesis, such as 'dyslexia is a medical matter – dyslexia is an educational matter' and 'dyslexia is a unity – dyslexia is a diversity'! The authors point out that these debates reflect a difference in emphasis rather than total disagreement.

Specific Learning Difficulties (Dyslexia) A Teacher's Guide
Margaret Crombie
Jordanhill Publications, Glasgow (1992).

This guide aims to meet the needs of teachers who must deal with the problems but who have not necessarily an in-depth knowledge of specific learning difficulties (dyslexia). The book considers various aspects of a child's difficulties, including the incidence and the nature of the problems. The assessment process is discussed and guidance is offered on how to interpret the results.

An eclectic approach is adopted in discussing the practicalities of teaching the dyslexic child in the classroom situation. Various areas of the curriculum are considered in relation to the child's learning. Ideas to help the teacher cope and meet the needs of dyslexic children in a mixed-ability classroom are of a practical nature. Further suggestions are offered in areas of curriculum support such as memory and motivation.

The book concentrates mainly on the primary school age-group of children, adopting the view that if needs are met at this stage, then later difficulties will be minimised.

The appendices at the end contain details of useful assessment and language teaching materials as well as addresses for obtaining these.

Your Child's Growing Mind
Jane M. Healy
Doubleday Dell Publishing Group, New York (1989).

This volume provides a comprehensive insight which helps the teacher and the parent understand the development of children and their learning potential. It examines the foundations of intelligence, and neurological development and provides guidelines for 'brain-building play'.

Jane Healy successfully combines brain development, learning style and educational, social and cultural aspects to illustrate how the potential of learning-disabled children may remain unfulfilled. She discusses how educators need to get to the heart of learning and appreciate how children learn, and hence discusses factors which can seriously discourage and undermine learning.

She provides numerous examples of how to motivate children to learn. For example to encourage children to write she suggests 'Read aloud on a regular basis, even with older children. Delve into poetry, literature, essays and good journalism. Don't be afraid to broaden your own tastes . . . Do not waste time on watered-down versions of classics with 'pop' language. You'll be surprised how much children can understand and enjoy (even Shakespeare!) if it is read to them dramatically in a pleasurable atmosphere.'

The author's closing paragraph epitomises the essence and flavour of the book when she asserts that 'learning is something that children do, not something that is done to them. You have the wisdom to guide the process but not the power to control it'.

A very useful and informative book.

Endangered Minds
Jane M. Healy
Touchstone, Simon and Schuster (1991).

In this useful, interesting and insightful text Jane Healy explains, complemented by research from several disciplines, how changing lifestyles may be altering children's brains in critical ways. She questions many aspects and assumptions about current educational trends through analysing children's performances and attainments. She also discusses how 'technological and social changes' have propelled us into an uncertain world – of video, computers, the 'global village'. She does not criticise parents or teachers, but rather describes the helplessness of the adult to keep in touch with children and their developmental needs, in the face of 'contemporary pressures.'

She describes how some dyslexic children who have been provided with language and literacy stimulation can compensate for their difficulties in reading with such success that they may altogether escape detection, often by displaying talents in predominantly right-hemisphere skills such as visual arts, mathematical reasoning, music and mechanical aptitude. She explains how neuro-scientists are finding out more about the dyslexic brain, particularly in relation to pre-natal cell migration which, if it goes wrong, can affect literacy development, but also discusses Galaburda's studies (1988) as showing the enormous capacity of the human brain to compensate for innate difficulties, given the right kind of support.

This book, therefore, discusses how society is coping with children's development and the changing brain and how support which children need should be provided by adults. The author argues that the quality of curiosity is one which needs to be preserved. Neglect of this and of the associated factors such as language, thought and imagination can truly endanger children's minds.

About Dyslexia – Unravelling the Myth
Priscilla L. Vail
Programs for Education/Modern Learning Press, USA (1990).

Throughout this book Priscilla Vail helps the reader become aware of dyslexic people's abilities and needs. She highlights the need to acknowledge and foster a positive self-concept among dyslexic students and illustrates the teacher's role in helping to foster this especially in the area of creativity – 'they need chances to pretend, to invent their own personal imagery and to keep imagination alive'. This short, well written book can be a useful motivator to both teacher and student.

Children's Learning Difficulties – A Cognitive Approach
Julie Dockrell and John McShane
Blackwell (1993).

This excellent reference book provides a thorough and well researched understanding of cognitive dimensions and of cognitive approaches to assessment in reading, language and number work. The authors classify learning difficulties, analyse tasks and discuss the interaction of the task, child and the environment. In relation to reading difficulties the publication examines reading components, word recognition, causes of decoding difficulties, perceptual deficits, phonological processing, memory deficits, sentence processing and metacognitive knowledge.

Perspectives on Dyslexia Vol. 1
Neurology, Neuro-psychology and Genetics
Edited by George Th. Pavlidis
John Wiley and Sons (1990).

This is an extremely well researched and useful reference book for students and teachers. This volume includes sections and chapters looking at sub-types of dyslexia, the role of genetics, cerebral asymmetries and different correlates of reading disability. Additionally there is an extensive section on the significance of eye movements in diagnosing dyslexia.

Pavlidis presents many fascinating insights into the importance of eye movements in reading and presents predictive evidence relating eye movements at the beginning of schooling to subsequent school performance. The issue of abnormal eye movements among dyslexic students also receives considerable attention.

This volume consists of contributions from international researchers.

Perspectives on Dyslexia Vol. 2
Cognition, Language and Treatment
Edited by George Th. Pavlidis
John Wiley and Sons (1990).

This second volume in the series examines issues relating to diagnostic criteria for dyslexia, cognitive deficits, phonological deficiencies, meta-linguistic aspects and perspectives on spelling.

There are also sections looking at dyslexia in adulthood, social factors and some alternative treatments. This latter aspect provides an interesting insight into hemispheric functions. Dirk Bakker discusses the 'balance model of reading acquisition' which describes initial reading as requiring visual-spatial skills while advanced reading requires semantic-syntactic analysis. Thus since visuo-spatial skills are primarily a right hemispheric function and semantic-syntactic analysis is a left hemispheric function, Bakker asserts that beginning readers would predominantly use the right hemisphere in reading while advanced readers use the left. This is followed up by a summary in the final chapter looking at the retraining of basic neurological functions.

The Neurological Impress Method (NIM) is discussed. This is a direct re-programming of the brain not unlike the 'look and listen' method in the Netherlands and treatment methods based on 'Living Language' such as 'look and say' and whole word methods. The assumption here is that training focusing on the strong functions is preferable and more effective as compared with training the weak function with the objective of strengthening it. This, however, is still a controversial issue. The authors of this chapter (Dumont, Oud, Van Mameren-Schoehuizen, Jacobs, Van Herpen and Van den Bekerom) discuss their own study of a treatment programme and highlight the importance of starting such a programme as early as possible and of sustaining it. They describe their treatment programme as meeting the principles for teaching dyslexics: structured, sequential, cumulative and separate learning tasks. Their programme included phonological training, preparatory reading to illustrate phoneme-grapheme correspondences, initial reading – grapheme by grapheme, the recognition and reading of polysyllabic words, sentence reading, texts and reading for memory. One can note from this the cumulative and sequential flow of the programme.

In general this volume contains interesting well researched chapters which can provide the basis for further study.

Neuro-psychological Correlates and Treatment Vol. 1 and Vol. 2
Edited by Dirk J. Bakker and Harry Van der Vlugt
Swets and Zeitlinger, Amsterdam (1989).

This is an excellent publication for those engaged in research. It contains discussion on a range of research studies on initial reading performance, motor precursors of learning disabilities, dyslexia sub-types, the neuro-anatomy of dyslexia and EEG studies. The second volume looks at cognitive processes, in particular auditory information processing and top down attention deficit; social aspects such as personality, adjustment problems and integration. There is also a section on remediation focusing on mathematics, audio support, strategies and verbal practice. A good source text for those engaged in research.

Other general texts include the following:

Augur J. (1992) *This Book Doesn't Make Sense*. Bath Educational Publishers.
Blight J. (1986) *A Practical Guide to Dyslexia*. Egon.
Chasty H. and Friel J. (1991) Children with special needs: *Assessment, Law and Practice. Caught in the Act.* London, Jessica Kingsley Publishers.
Ellis A. (1991) *Reading, Writing and Dyslexia: A cognitive analysis*. Open University.
Hales G. (ed.) (1990) *Meeting Points in Dyslexia*. British Dyslexia Association, London.
Hales G. (ed.) (1994) *Dyslexia Matters*. Whurr Publishers.
Heaton P. and Winterson P. (1986) *Dealing with Dyslexia*. Better Books.
Miles T. R. (1983) *Dyslexia: The Pattern of Difficulties*. Collins.
Miles T. R. and Miles E. (eds) (1992) *Dyslexia and Mathematics*. Routledge.
Miles T. R. and Gilroy D. (1986) *Dyslexia at College*. Methuen.
Miller R. and Klein C. (1986) *Making Sense of Spelling*. DCLD London.
Naidoo S. (ed.) (1988) *Assessment and Teaching of Dyslexic Children*. ICAN London.
Sharon H. (1987) *Changing Children's Minds*. Condor Press.
Snowling M. (1991) *Children's Written Language Difficulties*. NFER Nelson.
Snowling M. (1990) *Dyslexia: A Cognitive Developmental Perspective*. Blackwell.
Stoel Van Der (ed.) (1990) *Parents on Dyslexia*. Multilingual Matters, Clevedon.
Thomson M. (1989) *Developmental Dyslexia*. Whurr, London.
Tyre C. and Young P. (1994) *Specific Learning Difficulties* a staff development handbook. QED, Staffordshire.
Webster A. and McConnell C. (1987) *Children with Speech and Language Difficulties*. Cassell.
Welchman M. (1981) *Suggestions for Dyslexic Child at Home*. Better Books.
Welchman M. (1983) *Dyslexia – Your Questions Answered*. Better Books.

Reading

The Art of Reading
Edited by Morag Hunter-Carsch
Blackwell Education, Oxford (1989).

This volume represents a collection of thirty-two contributions from a wide range of experts focusing on pre-reading aspects, reading policy and practice, classroom communication and literacy difficulties, and complemented by contributions from the international arena.

The book contains a wealth of interesting ideas on reading, including enhancing reading comprehension through creating visual images, whole school language policy, linguistics, word processing, and adult basic literacy.

A useful reference book.

Reading Problems – Consultation and Remediation
P. G. Aaron and R. Malatesha Joshi
Guildford Press (1992).

This is a superb text on reading, particularly for those engaged in extended study. In addition to looking at the psychology of reading, including sensory encoding, word recognition, sentence and text comprehension and metacognition, the authors discuss differential diagnosis of reading disabilities and intervention strategies.

The book is an extremely well researched piece of work and with its emphasis on 'consultative approaches to educational intervention' should prove to be extremely useful to educational psychologists as well as teachers involved in further study.

Reading by the Colours:
Overcoming Dyslexia and other Reading Disabilities through the Irlen Method
Helen Irlen
Avery Publishing Group, New York (1991).

This extremely interesting and informative book discusses and describes Helen Irlen's work relating to Scotopic Sensitivity Syndrome and the use of colour filters to help students with reading problems.

The book provides an explanation of Scotopic Sensitivity Syndrome and how it affects reading. There is a chapter discussing how it particularly relates to dyslexia. The author acknowledges that if the dyslexic student has a phonological difficulty or a language problem then coloured filters will not totally remediate the difficulty. If, however, the difficulty is diagnosed as visual/perceptual then coloured filters can improve reading.

The book also contains an extremely useful section on screening and the importance of colour selection.

Phonological Skills and Learning to Read
Usha Goswami and Peter Bryant
Lawrence Erlbaum Associates Ltd (1990).

This book examines issues relating to phonological knowledge and analyses the role of phonological skills in early reading. A range of aspects such as the relationship between phonological awareness and reading, the development of phonological awareness in childhood, the role of rhyming and the use of onset and rhyme strategies in reading are discussed.

The authors refer to considerable research and provide an interesting argument that children, in learning to read, do not rely on letter-sound relationships but instead learn to read using a global strategy, thus recognising words as a pattern. This is contrasted in writing and spelling where children do depend heavily on letter-sound relationships. The authors, however, also argue that the relationship between phonological processing and early reading may be based on onset and rhyme strategies which form phonological units and strings of letters and not on grapheme-phoneme correspondence. This extremely well researched book provides a sound basic coverage of all aspects of phonological processing and literacy.

Games to Improve Reading Levels
Jim McNicholas and Joe McEntree
A NASEN Publication, NARE Publications, Stafford (1991).

This short text consists of seventy-four interesting games which can bring pleasure and motivation in helping the development of reading skills. The authors justify the use of games as an approach by asserting that children learn most of their concepts of self, orientation, size and number by playing games. They also argue that children will respond more readily without instructions and can be observed more naturally in a game playing 'mode'. The authors, however, do stress that there should be some check to ensure that learning is, in fact, taking place.

The vast number of games included in this slim volume are neatly categorised into those relating to body image, directional orientation, auditory factors, visual aspects, vocabulary, word attack and word building, reading for meaning and paper and pencil games to improve reading and writing. There is also a section on the use of games to develop phonic skills.

A very useful publication.

Phonics and Phonic Resources
Edited by Mike Hinson and Pete Smith
Nasen Publication (1993).

This useful volume examines the field of phonics teaching. It discusses the concept of phonics teaching, referring to reading schemes, other published materials and computer software and games.

The book provides some useful suggestions such as teaching phonics as a small group activity, particularly when sounds are being taught for the first time, to ensure that 'fine' pronunciation is acquired by the child.

A useful chapter discusses the direct teaching of phonics in terms of organisation, teaching initial letters, blending, recording and monitoring progress.

In relation to assessment the book discusses a number of strategies such as miscue analysis, running record (Clay 1985) and individual and group phonic tests.

A large part of the book comprises a list and some details of available resources appropriate to help with:

- visual discrimination
- auditory discrimination
- initial letter sounds
- final letter sounds
- short 'a', 'e', 'i', 'o' 'u' (vowel sounds)
- short vowel revision
- 'b', 'd', 'p' comparison
- double consonants at end
- final consonant blend revision
- consonant digraphs
- magic 'e'
- consonant blends
- vowel digraphs
- prefixes, suffixes
- silent and soft letter sounds
- compound words

This should prove to be a useful reference book on phonics for the class teacher.

Recipe for Reading
Nina Traub with Frances Bloom
Educators Publishing Service Inc., Cambridge MA (1993).

This revised and expanded edition provides a sequentially organised and well evaluated programme for teaching reading. The authors believe the technique to be effective for children with specific learning difficulties, and assert that a 'recipe for reading, like all good recipes, requires that you (i) know what ingredients are needed, (ii) understand how they are to be combined and (iii) are able to adapt the recipe to individual needs'.

The programme is based on exposure to a structured phonic base to help beginning readers develop an awareness of sounds and eventually word attack skills.

The sequence of introducing sounds is determined by auditory, visual and kinesthetic factors rather than alphabetic order. For example, of the first nine letters to be taught 'c', 'o', 'a', 'd' and 'g' have similar kinesthetic factors and these are highlighted. The other four letters which make up the first nine are 'm', 'l', 'h' and 't'.

The programme is clearly highly structured and utilises a range of phonic materials such as phonetic sound cards, phonetic word cards, phonetic phrase cards, phonetic storybooks, word games and sequence charts.

The teacher's manual provides an easy-to-follow guide to lesson procedure including how the letters and sounds are introduced, introduction of two syllable words, vowel digraphs and spelling rules. There is also a useful section on prefixes and suffixes.

Reading Recovery in New Zealand
A Report from the Office of Her Majesty's Chief Inspector of Schools.
HMSO London (1993).

This booklet provides an extremely interesting and informative account of an HMI's visit to New Zealand to study the application of the Reading Recovery Programme.

It provides a summary of a Reading Recovery Programme and highlights a lesson which the report suggests 'aims to make pupils into independent and autonomous readers'.

In relation to the effectiveness of the programme the report suggests that evidence of short- and long-term benefit is available although clearly because of other 'contaminating' factors it is more difficult to distinguish the effects of the Reading Recovery Programme from other intervening factors.

The report compares the New Zealand system of teaching reading in the early stages with that of the UK and notes many similarities in relation to philosophies and classroom organisation of materials. It is also noted, however, that New Zealand primary schools appear to give more time to language activity and early reading than is the case in the UK.

Although the report accepts that the limitations of the visit in terms of time and scale meant that a fully comprehensive and reliable survey was not possible,` it did acknowledge some key issues such as the importance of literacy in the New Zealand education system, supported by the free distribution of the national reading scheme (Ready to Read series), school journals containing collections of reading materials, and widely shared professional procedures in diagnosis.

The report concludes that although the Reading Recovery Programme is particularly well suited to the New Zealand context, 'there is no reason to suppose that it is not transferable to other education systems'.

All Language and the Creation of Literacy
Orton Dyslexia Society Inc. Baltimore (1991).

This useful publication includes the presentations at two separate symposia – 'Whole Language and Phonics' and 'Language and Literacy'.

The whole language and phonics section is represented by five expert contributors – Sylvia Richardson, Joanna Williams, Jeanne Chall, Diane de Ford and Marilyn Jager Adams.

Sylvia Richardson provides an historical perspective describing the evolution of approaches – looking at visual, auditory and kinesthetic approaches and the attempts to provide combined approaches. She also comments on the need to acknowledge diversity in education in order to help meet the needs of every child.

This is developed by Adams who asks the question – 'Why not phonics and whole language?' She provides an excellent exposition of the whole language approach, citing the lack of precise definition but agreeing that this should not prevent educators from enlisting some of the benefits of this approach such as child-centred instruction and integration of reading and writing. She argues that whole language should be a core component of 'a long overdue and highly constructive educational revolution'.

The section on Language and Literacy sees Sylvia Richardson discussing the roots of literacy and Margaret Snowling looking at speech processing and spelling. Snowling shows that dyslexic children's spelling is generally more impaired than their reading and that the phonological spelling system is an extension of the speech processing system.

A section on organising decoding instruction is presented by Marcia Henry in which she argues that the education system should be equipping students with strategies to understand and deal with the structure of words. Robert Calfee, Marlyn Chambliss and Melissa Beretz look at the aspect of comprehension and discuss a four component core model – connect, organise, reflect and extend. They also discuss the importance of prior experience in reading comprehension. They argue that teachers need to recognise that every student possesses some background knowledge relevant to any classroom topic and should attempt to help students share that knowledge. This can be done by developing a collective, coherent framework during the early stages of engaging in the topic. They argue that learning is more effective and efficient for every person 'when it connects with prior experience'.

A very useful and stimulating publication.

Other useful books on reading include:

Augur J. (1990) *This Book Doesn't Make Sense.* Bath Educational Pub.
Aaron P. G. (1988) *Dyslexia and Hyperlexia.* Kluwer Press.
Beard R. (1990) *Developing Reading 3-13.* Hodder & Stoughton.
Bryant P. and Bradley L. (1990) *Children's Reading Problems.* Blackwell.
Brady S. and Shankweiler D. (1992) *Phonological Processes in Literacy.* York Pub.
Clay M. (1992) *Reading–The Patterning of Complex Behaviour.* Heinemann Educational.
Conlan J. and Henley M. (1992) *Word Mastery.* Oxford University Press.
Harris Colin (1993) *Fuzzbuzz Books/Spell/Words/Letters.* Oxford University Press.
Hunt R. and Franks T. (1993) *Oxford Reading Tree Pack.* Oxford UniversityPress.
Kratoville B. L. (1989) *Word Tracking: Proverbs: High Frequency Words.* Ann Arbor Pub.

Lunzer E. and Gardner K. (1984) *Learning from the Written Word*. Oliver & Boyd.

Jones-Elgar R. (1989) *The Cloze Line*. Ann Arbor Pub.

Smith J. and Bloor M. (1985) *Simple Phonetics for Teachers*. Methuen.

Snowling M. and Hulme C. (1993) *Reading Development and Dyslexia*. Whurr Publishers.

Stevens M. (1992) *Into Print*. Scottish Consultative Council on the Curriculum, Edinburgh.

Stirling E. G. (1990) *Which is Witch*, checklist of homopohones. St David's College, Llandudno, North Wales.

Topping K. (1986) *Paired Reading Training Pack*. Centre for Paired Learning, Psychology Department, University of Dundee.

Topping K. J. (1987) *Peer Tutored Paired Reading: Outcome Data from Ten Projects*. Educational Psychology 7,2, pp.133-145.

Tyre C. and Young P. (1994) *Specific Learning Difficulties*, a staff development handbook. Q.Ed. Pub.

Wade B. and Moore M. (1993) *The Promise of Reading Recovery*. Educational Review Publications-Headline Series No. 1. University of Birmingham.

Wade B. and Moore M. (1994) *The Promise of Reading Recovery*. Educational Review Publications-Headline Series No. 1. University of Birmingham.

Waterland L. (1986) *Read with Me*. Thimble Press.

Wolfendale S. (1990) *Word Play*. NARE Pub.

Young P. and Tyre C. (1990) *Dyslexia or Illiteracy: Realising the Right to Read*. Open University.

Teaching programmes

Maths and Dyslexics
Anne Henderson
St David's College, Llandudno (1989).

This publication is an extremely readable short reference for teachers faced with helping dyslexics with mathematical difficulties. The author identifies some major difficulties such as fear, poor short-term memory and difficulties identifying symbols and directions, and discusses these with examples. The book also refers to some other problems with mathematics such as language, the use of equipment, decimals, percentages, proportions and time.

Each section has a 'how to help' section, which provides handy hints on aspects which need particular attention and the book is well equipped with examples.

Dyslexia Basic Numeracy
Vicki Burge
Helen Arkell Dyslexia Centre (1986).

A very easy to follow short publication on basic numeracy. It provides advice on spatial awareness, number formation, language and terminology in mathematics, error analyses and gives special consideration to aspects of maths such as multiplication tables, fractions, decimals and percentages.

Reading and Thinking
Arthur J. Evans
Learning Materials Ltd Wolverhampton (1987).

This pack consists of five booklets which provide graded exercises intended to facilitate reasoning and deductive thought. There is also an answer booklet, accompanying audio tapes for each of the five booklets, and two booklets containing picture cues with accompanying questions.

The questions are intended to make the child think before answering since the answers to some of the tasks are not obvious. An example of a question in book 1 is: *A man is in a bus. He is holding out some money to a man who is standing in front of him. What is he doing? (a) buying a book? (b) reading a paper? (c) paying his fare? Is he facing the front or the side of the bus?*

Many of the questions help the child use visual skills and aid directional orientation.

Book 5, the most advanced, contains eighteen comprehension passages accompanied by relevant questions. A useful resource.

Teaching Talking – Teaching Resources Handbook
Ann Locke and Maggie Beech
NFER-Nelson (1991).

This kit is an excellent reference set for teaching talking. Three packs are available: nursery pack; infant pack; junior pack.

The set contains a teaching procedures workbook, teaching resources handbook and comprehensive assessment record forms. The teaching talking programme is in three stages which are usually implemented over a period of a year. This first stage is based on classroom observations, the second on 'low key' instruction with a group of children and the third involves working with a small group who are not progressing well and need more intensive help.

Assessment
The pack includes detailed profile checklists from ages 0-1; 1-2 and 2-5, and further checklists for those children identified as having significant language learning difficulties. The assessment pack also contains specific charts on speaking and listening, listening and understanding, play and social development and record sheets on pre-language, emerging language and maturing language.

Resources
The resources handbook provides ideas on promoting listening skills, developing vocabulary, enquiring, planning and developing talking, reading and writing and encouraging independence in talking.

The suggestions include a variety of games, use of songs, poems and stories, encouraging the development of phonic skills and rhyming with clapping rhymes, music and movement as well as games such as 'I Spy', odd word out and construction of riddles.

Teaching procedures
The teaching procedures handbook provides an overview of the teaching process for children with significant language learning difficulties and outlines how to use the record sheets and screening procedures most effectively. It also provides some case studies.

A very useful and comprehensive resource pack

Graded Activities for Children with Motor Difficulties
James Russell
Cambridge Educational (1988).

Although motor learning and literacy are two distinct strands of development there is a growing awareness of the link between the two, and hence this programme of activities may be extremely useful in helping the teacher tackle the difficulties associated with dyslexia. The programme is aimed at both primary and secondary sectors and can be used by teachers with little or no specialist training. It provides a comprehensive and easy to follow series of lessons each aimed at different aspects of motor development. These include gross motor control; balancing, catching, throwing and jumping; body and spatial awareness, visual tracking and handwriting activities.

Each of the fourteen programmes has a clear set of objectives, illustrations and a number of complementary activities.

Mathematics for Dyslexics – A Teaching Handbook
S. J. Chinn and J. R. Ashcroft (1993).
Whurr Publishers, London.

This comprehensive text examines a broad range of aspects relating to mathematics and outlines strategies which can effectively be used by dyslexic students. The central message of the book is the need to understand the way each child learns as an individual and this is particularly underlined in the chapter on cognitive styles in mathematics. This very useful text also includes chapters on testing and diagnosis of number concepts and of computational procedures for addition, subtraction, multiplication and division. A very useful teaching handbook.

Attention without Tension
A Teacher's Handbook on Attention Disorders
Edna D. Copeland and Valerie L. Love.
3 C? of Childhood Inc. Atlanta, GA (1992).

This comprehensive volume provides the reader with a useful guide and understanding of the field of attention deficit disorders (ADD) and attention deficit disorders with hyperactivity (ADHD).

The book begins with some key facts which indicate that about 30-40% of all referrals to child psychologists, psychiatrists and mental health agencies are related to children with some form of attention disorder.

The chapter on causes of attention disorders provides the reader with a fairly clear focus for the suggestions which follow. The authors acknowledge five major factors as contributory causes of ADHD and ADD including heredity, organic factors, diet and allergies, environmental toxins and other medical problems. They also acknowledge that social, cultural, educational and stress factors can cause, or exacerbate, attentional problems in many children.

Interestingly, the authors also assert that while it is not always the case that ADD/ADHD children have a coexisting learning difficulty in a significant proportion, in 20-40% a co-existent learning disability is evident. In those cases such difficulties tend to be a combination of auditory/visual perception and processing; sequencing; fine motor; visual motor integration; eye/hand coordination, reading/spelling/maths disorders and written language problems. The whole field of ADD requires considerable attention because of the range of difficulties which can be exhibited.

The authors also describe in a very clear manner some of the characteristics of ADD in relation to distractibility – short attention span, difficulty completing tasks, day-dreaming, easily distracted, much activity but little accomplished, enthusiastic beginnings but poor endings. They also describe the characteristics of other factors associated with ADD/ADHD stemming from impulsiveness, over-activity and hyperactivity, immaturity and emotional difficulties.

The comprehensive section on treating attention disorders should be of considerable value to teachers. This section focuses on goal setting, classroom management and organisation and various forms of assessment schedules such as the Copeland Symptom Checklist for Attention Deficit Disorders. In general this volume can provide the teacher with many ideas which can be adapted to help dyslexic children who may also exhibit signs of attention disorders.

Alphabet Soup – A Recipe for Understanding and Treating Attention Deficit Hyperactivity Disorder
A Handbook for Parents and Teachers
James Javorsky
Minerva Press Inc. Clarkston, MI (1993).

This useful handbook provides a comprehensive and informative guide to both parents and teachers who are involved with children with ADD. It provides an outline of the characteristics of ADD as well as of some of the causes of diagnostic procedures.

It provides suggestions for dealing with ADD by altering the classroom environment, developing individual learning plans and giving medical treatment.

A useful appendix contains a parents' guide to test results and outlines of individual learning plans.

Action Rhymes and Games
Max de Boo
Scholastic Publications (1992).

This book for early years provides a wealth of ideas and activities to help young children develop language, motor skills, social skills and creativity. There are also activities relating to music, mathematics and science.

The book comprises short, easy-to-follow activities together with objectives and further follow-up activities. For example some of the activities contained in the section 'Language Skills and Understanding' include the encouragement of recall and summarising, developing listening skills, providing experience of action verbs, sounds and prepositions, encouraging pronunciation skills and rhyming and reinforcing the concept of 'in' and 'out'.

A very useful resource work.

Words – Integrated Decoding and Spelling Instruction based on Word Origin and Word Structure
Marcia K. Henry
Lex Press CA, USA (second edition 1993).

This approach to reading and spelling is intended to supplement mainstream classroom activities. The approach emphasises decoding and spelling instruction based on word origin and word structure. The programme follows the principles outlined in the Orton-Gillingham programme (Gillingham and Stillman, 1956) and Project Read (Calfee and Henry, 1985). The lessons focus on spelling patterns and rules and word features, and students learn about Latin root words, their orthographic features and how they generate additional words. There are follow-up activities which reinforce these patterns. A framework matrix is provided which illustrates word origins and structure as guides for decoding and spelling. Thus Anglo-Saxon, Latin and Greek word origins are categorised into letter-sound correspondences, syllable patterns and morpheme patterns.

Each lesson has a purpose and an objective with follow-up activities. The lessons contained in Unit 1 'Organising Letter-Sound Correspondences' include consonant blends, consonant digraphs, long and short vowels and vowel digraphs. There are reviews and a unit test at the end.

Other lesson units include 'Syllable Patterns', 'Layers of Language', 'Morpheme Patterns', 'Strategies for Decoding Long Words' and 'Strategies for Spelling Long Words'.

Tutor 1 – Structured, Sequential, Multi-sensory Lessons based on the Orton-Gillingham Approach
Marcia K. Henry and Nancy C. Redding
Lex Press CA USA (1990)

This book of forty-two lessons is intended for primary aged children who are having difficulty in reading, writing or spelling.

The techniques and the presentation are based on the Orton-Gillingham approach and utilises a multi-sensory approach in a structured and sequential manner. The lessons provide a framework which teachers will need to supplement with their own materials. The initial lessons present new consonants or vowels, blending and dictation and copying, tracing and writing on paper while saying letter names. There are also activities focusing on auditory, sequential memory and story reading. Some lessons highlight linguistic awareness such as asking students to say some words beginning with specific blends which the tutor provides.

The book contains a useful section on spelling rules based on silent 'e', plurals, soft 'c' and 'g', double letter rule, suffixes and polysyllabic words.

Reasoning and Reading – Level 1
Joanne Carlisle
Educators Publishers. Cambridge MA, USA (1993).

This is essentially a training programme focusing on reasoning, language and reading comprehension – areas which the author believes are intrinsically intertwined in the process of learning and understanding. Thus the programme ensures that word recognition is an important aspect in reading comprehension, that reading comprehension is related to general language comprehension and that reasoning is a crucial ability not only to develop ideas but as an approach to reading and comprehension.

It can readily fit into existing schemes and can be used as support material for a mainstream class. The programme is divided into four units – Word Meaning, Sentence Meaning, Paragraph Structure and Meaning, and Reasoning.

The section word meaning looks at word relationships, e.g. categorising and identifying words which have common characteristics but have quite different meanings. This unit also looks at similarities and differences, related words, analogies and using words in context.

The unit sentence meaning looks at what a sentence is, jumbled sentences and word order.

The paragraph structure and meaning unit looks at main ideas, writing structure and key words.

The reasoning unit looks at aspects such as fact or opinion, judging opinions, relevant information, use of inference and solving problems.

An excellent book with an accompanying teachers' guide which highlights some of the important aspects of reading in context to gain some real understanding from text.

Differentiation: Your Responsibility
An In-Service Training Pack for Staff Development
T. Barthorpe and J. Visser
Nasen Publication (1991).

This in-service training pack perceives differentiation in the same manner as envisaged in the Warnock Report (1978).

The purpose of education for all children is the same; the goals are the same. But the help that individual children need in progressing towards them will be different.

The authors of this pack therefore anticipate that teachers will require a clear understanding of the learning processes of children, a knowledge of task analysis, to collaborate with colleagues, and knowledge of curriculum design and implementation in order to successfully achieve effective differentiation.

The pack aims to help schools formulate policies and practices for themselves and to give all children access to the full curriculum. The pack contains a number of master overhead transparencies and practical hints for using the materials. The materials are arranged in three sections – 'Understanding of the Term Differentiation', 'Pupils and Learning' and 'Differentiation in the Classroom'. There are also suggestions for delivery of the in-service sessions with examples.

A very useful resource.

Dyslexia and Mathematics
Edited by T. R. Miles and E. Miles
Routledge, London and New York (1992).

This book contains a collection of very useful chapters on different aspects of mathematics. It provides a theoretical perspective to provide a platform for the chapters on diagnosis and cognitive styles, language, reading and writing aspects of mathematics and the needs of, and strategies for, secondary pupils.

A very useful book.

IT Support for Specific Learning Difficulties
Edited by Sally McKeown
NCET (1992).

This booklet provides the teacher with a useful catalogue of hardware and software which can be useful with children with specific learning difficulties. It discusses the nature of the problem, illustrates how word processing can help with literacy skills and exemplifies this by using case studies. Information on software packages is provided, in particular predictive word processing packages such as Mindreader and PAL (Predictive Adaptive Lexicon). The former is an American package (Brown Bay software) while the latter was produced by a team at the University of Dundee. The booklet has a useful appendix with addresses for software and useful contacts.

Computers and Dyslexia – Educational Applications of New Technology
Edited by C. Singleton

Dyslexia Computer Resource Centre, University of Hull (1994).
This text is the product of a conference organised by the Dyslexia Computer Resource Centre held at the University of Coventry. It contains informative chapters on reading and writing, keyboard skills, the Somerset Talking Computer Project, memory and mathematics, and assessment and screening. An excellent source book on this increasingly important area and its application in the classroom.

A Guide to Using Talking Computers – Helping Children to Read and Spell
V. Clifford and M. Miles
Talking Publications (1994).

This is a useful guide to talking computers with sections on theory, programme preparation and implementing the programme. An appendix containing record sheets of addresses makes this a valuable resource on talking computers.

Using Computers with Dyslexics
Ted Pottage
(3rd Edition, 1994).

This is an extremely useful booklet containing a wealth of information on points to consider when choosing hardware and software. There is also a useful section on the use of computers for dyslexics looking at keyboarding skills, building language skills and programmes for maths skills.

Other useful teaching programmes include:

Augur J. and Briggs S. (1992) *Hickey Multi-Sensory Language Course. 2nd ed.* Whurr Publishers.

Bell N. (1991) *Visualizing and Verbalizing for Language Comprehension and Thinking.* Academy of Reading Publishers. CA, USA

Cooke A. (1993) *Tackling Dyslexia: The Bangor Way.* Whurr Publishers.

Cowdery L., McMahon J., Montgomery D., Morse P. and Prince M. (1984-8) *Kingston Programme-Teaching Reading through Spelling.* Frondeg Hall Publishers.

Cox A. R. (1993) *Foundations for Literacy.* Educ. Pub. Service, USA.

Davies A. (1992) *Handwriting, Reading and Spelling System* (THRASS) Writetract.

Henry M. K. and Redding N. C. (1993) *Word Lists: Structured, Sequential, Multi-sensory.* Lex Press, USA.

Hornsby B. and Pool J. (1989 and 1993) *Alpha to Omega Activity Packs. Stage 1, 2 and 3.* Heinemann Educational Publishers.

Kimmell G. M. (1989) *Sound Out.* Academic Therapy Publishers.

Kratoville B. L. (1989) *Word Tracking: Proverbs /High Frequency Verbs.* Ann Arbor.

McNicholas J. and McEntree J. (1991) *Games to Develop and Improve Reading Levels.* NASEN Pub.

Miles E. (1992) *Bangor Dyslexia Teaching System* (2nd ed). Whurr Publishers, London.

Reason R. and Boote R. (1991) *Learning Difficulties in Reading and Writing.* NFER Nelson.

Russell S. (1993) *Phonic Code Cracker.* Jordanhill Publications.

Russell J. P. (1989) *Graded Activities for Children with Motor Difficulties.* Cambridge University.

Selman M. R. (1989) *Infant Teacher's Handbook.* Oliver & Boyd.

Singleton C. (1991) *Computers and Literacy Skills.* BDA University of Hull.

Slingerland B. H. (1993) *Specific Language Disability Children.* Educ. Pub. Service, USA.

Smith J. and Bloom M. (1985) *Simple Phonetics for Teachers.* Methuen.

Thomson M. and Watkins W. (1990) *Dyslexia: A Teaching Handbook.* Whurr Publishers

Topping K. (1992) *Promoting Cooperative Learning.* Kirklees Metropolitan Council.

Wendon Lyn (1992) *Letterland Teaching Programs.* Letterland, Cambs.

Wilkins A. (1993) *Intuitive Overlays.* IOO Marketing Ltd, 56-62 Newington Causeway, London.

Learning skills

Deveoping Your Child for Success
Kenneth A. Lane
Learning Potentials Publishers. JWC Louisville, Texas, USA (1991).

This comprehensive series of programmes provides activities to help develop children's perceptual and motor skills. The author provides a clear explanation of the role of visual perception in reading and asserts that basic perceptual skills are absolutely necessary for the young child to succeed in reading. The child needs to have an appreciation of feature identification, letter orientation and visual sequencing. The activities in this book aim to promote and develop such skills. They are divided into the following areas: visual; motor; occular motor; vision; laterality; sequential processing and simultaneous processing.

Some of the activities include one foot hop; heel and toe rock; creeping and crawling and laterality therapy procedures such as headroll; bodyroll; midline training and body awareness. There are also directional therapy procedures such as letter orientation; b, d, p, q sorting and vision therapy procedures such as static fixation and peripheral training.

This comprehensive programme also contains useful daily activity sheets to record and make observations from the activities.

Take Time:
Mary Nash-Wortham and Jean Hunt
The Robinswood Press, Stourbridge, England (second combined editions revised 1990).

There is a growing awareness of the link between language and movement, and this book highlights the connection with a series of movement exercises to help children with difficulties in speech and literacy.

It provides a useful section on pointers to areas of difficulty which include timing and rhythm, directional problems, spatial orientation and movement, fine motor centrality and laterality. This is followed by exercise sheets to help promote development in these areas. All the exercises are clearly set out and appropriately illustrated. The five motor control exercises for speech, writing and reading would be particularly useful for dyslexic children.

Analogical Reasoning in Children
Uswa Goswami
Laurence Erlbaum Associates (1992).

This interesting and useful book discusses the view that analogies are important in learning, problem solving and discovery. Piaget's theory of anological reasoning is initially examined and information processing models of analogical reasoning are discussed.

There are also chapters looking at analogies in babies and toddlers and in the real world of the classroom.

The book argues strongly for the importance of analogies in learning and development and relates this to classroom situations and classroom learning.

Word Play
Sheila Wolfendale and Trevor Bryans
NARE Publications. Stafford (1986).

This very useful booklet contains language activities for young children and their parents. It also provides a theoretical explanation for the programme, based on cooperation and partnership between parents and teachers. The introduction to the language activities section describes the procedure and the stages in implementing the programme: preparation; implementation; and measuring progress.

The activities are easy to follow and sure to be enjoyed by all involved in the programme. They provide some good ideas for conversational time with young children, story telling and story making as well as drama and games. The games and activities involve all the senses and provide a useful 'ideas' booklet for teachers and parents of young children.

Mapping Inner Space – Learning and Teaching Mind Mapping
Nancy Margulies
Zephyr Press (1991).

The use of mind mapping is becoming a valuable study tool and thinking skill for many students. In this text Nancy Margulies identifies mind mapping as a 'flexible, evolving system with unlimited potential'. The evolution of the practice of mind mapping is highlighted by the examples contained in this volume. Virtually every point made in the text is illustrated with a mind map and the easy-to-follow chapter headings make this a useful teacher manual in mind mapping. Essentially the text helps to prepare teachers to teach the skill of mind mapping to students.

The author suggests that to become a mind mapper it is initially useful to record your own ideas selected from topics such as plans for the day, the week, memories of a specific event, strategies for a new project, interests and hobbies, or a recent book. It may be essential to start with these meaningful and manageable topics since otherwise there is a risk of becoming daunted by the sophistication, elaboration and creativity of the ideas for mind maps illustrated later in this volume.

The author makes a useful distinction between the generation of ideas and the organisation of ideas, the two processes which together form the basis of a mind map. For those who are not naturally visually inclined a step-by-step symbol making guide is included. Following this manual, which is essentially an experiential volume, most readers should be able to develop and understand the concept and uses of mind maps.

Learning Styles
Priscilla L. Vail
Modern Learning Press, Rosemont, New Jersey (1992).

This volume explores various aspects of learning styles from kindergarten through to fourth grade and provides over 130 practical tips for teachers.

Priscilla Vail analyses how children process information – three dimensionally or two dimensionally, simultaneously or sequentially, visually, auditorily, kinesthetically or tactilely. Additionally, she focuses on how children make connections in relation to retrieving information already learned and consolidating that new information. She also addresses other types of personality and learning preferences such as utilising imagery, factual information and aesthetic stimuli.

The many suggested activities which follow on from this analysis provide the reader with easy-to-follow ideas on respecting and enhancing the individual learning styles of children. One of the suggested tips is for utilising kinesthetic and tactile learning skills.

Teach sound/symbol correspondence and letter formation by using the large muscles of the arm to 'sky write' The letters formed in the air should be as large as the arc of the child's swing.

*Teach a little verbal accompaniment such as 'd' starts the way 'b' starts, fills the 'house space',
closes the circle, goes all the way up through the attic and back down through the house!*

(from *Learning Styles,* Priscilla Vail).

A very useful book.

The Mind Map Book – Radiant Thinking
Tony Buzan
BBC Books (1993).

This book by Tony Buzan, the originator of mind maps, provides an excellent
detailed description of the concept and uses of the mind mapping strategy. The
book illustrates how mind maps can be developed from, for example, brain-
storming with words. There are plentiful exercises to help the reader practice the
strategy at different levels. The text also highlights the versatility of mind mapping
by describing its uses in personal, educational, business and professional areas.

Learn Playful Techniques to Accelerate Learning
Regina G. Richards
Zephyr Press (1993).

This comprehensive, easy-to-follow volume of interesting activities provides
useful strategies for learning for students of all ages. It is based on the set of
strategies which the author calls 'Learning – Learning Efficiently and Remembering
Mnemonics'. The foreword highlights important points which provide a scenario
and context for the chapters which follow, by reminding the reader that 'teachers
do not cause learning' but they can create conditions for enhancement of learning
where it is 'safe to try, possible to succeed and worth the effort'.

The book focuses on learning styles and highlights hemispheric specialisation
indicating how the left brain codes and processes messages in language, operating
in a linear, sequential and logical fashion while the right deals with non-verbal
material operating in a holistic, inventive, informal and symbolic mode. Reference
is made to Healy's use of the terms 'limpers and splitters' in relation to learning
styles – the 'splitter' organises information and plans tasks precisely, whereas the
'limper' uses predominantly right brain skills, processes information holistically
and simultaneously. Richards acknowledges that the brain prefers cooperation
rather than conflict and that most activities utilise both hemispheres.

The book provides an interesting chapter on the concept of visualisation in
learning. It looks initially at simple visual skills and proceeds to visualisation skills.

There is a useful chapter on memory foundations for multiplication which provides a step by step method for developing the strategy.

Spelling is also considered and suggestions are provided for creating mnemonic links in spelling. The author encourages the identification of patterns in words such as canoe and shoe and the use of this link mnemonically to facilitate remembering the pattern. Similar mnemonic techniques are encouraged for reading and this chapter provides exercises and visual help on the strategy known as 'COPS', i.e. categorisation, organisation, punctuation and spelling in relation to re-reading a piece of work.

There are also chapters on mind mapping, the use of music and rhythm in the classroom, and a development of the earlier theme of visual skills and visualisation.

Unicorns are Real
A Right-Brained Approach to Learning
Barbara Meister Vitale
Jalman Press, (1982).

This book begins with a clear introduction to hemispheric specialisation. It describes different modes of processing information such as linear and holistic, symbolic and concrete, sequential and random, logical and intuitive, verbal and non-verbal, and abstract and analogic.

This is followed by a useful section on modality and dominance screening looking at the characteristics of hemispheric dominance in relation to general factors, eye, hand and body.

The major part of the book is occupied by interesting and useful activities in relation to students' learning strategies. These include exercises on phonics, sequencing, mathematics, writing, organisation, and aspects of reading such as visual tracking. The exercises are easy to follow and can be particularly useful in enhancing right-brain skills and self-esteem in younger children.

Study Skills
Charles Cuff
Cambridge Educational (1989).

Study skills are extremely important to help provide dyslexic children with the opportunity of developing independent study habits.

This study skills programme for children aged 8 to 12 contains four volumes. The slim books consist of a range of varied activities in which the child has to complete a task. The exercises help to provide key skills such as organisation, selecting of main points, abbreviations, dictionary speed search and categorisation of information.

Useful activity books for this age group.

Somerset Thinking Skills Course
Nigel Blagg, Marj Ballinger, Richard Gardner, Mel Petty and Gareth Williams
Basil Blackwell in association with Somerset County Council (1988).

This series of books contains seven modules and a handbook designed to facilitate the development of learning skills. The modules include Foundations for Problem Solving, Analysing and Synthesising, Comparative Thinking, Positions in Time and Space, Understanding Analogies, Patterns in Time and Space, and Organising and Memorising.

Each module contains teacher guidelines and pupil materials and consists of illustrated materials which present the basis of the problem, including the background, strategies for proceeding with the task, resources and key vocabulary. Ideas on how the teacher may proceed to involve students in the task and how their responses can be transferred and generalised to other contexts are also highlighted in each exercise.

A very useful series of activities which cut across traditional subject boundaries and encourage the development of metacognitive and thinking skills.

Teaching Elementary Students Through Their Individual Learning Styles
Rita Dunn and Kenneth Dunn
Allyn and Bacon (1992).

The Dunn and Dunn learning styles model has been extensively researched. This book translates this accepted research into practical techniques and provides varied and relevant activities and instructional guidelines for teachers.

The authors discuss skills, styles and the learning context. They discuss the concept of learning styles, illustrate how to identify individual learning styles and discuss different approaches to teaching and classroom design based on the learning styles model developed by the authors.

This volume contains a wealth of information and resources on helping teachers develop an awareness of, and skills and provision to acknowledge and respond to, the individual needs and learning styles of children.

Learning and Teaching Style – In Theory and Practice
Kathleen A. Butler
Learners Dimension, PO Box 6, Columbia, Conn. (1987).

This useful volume is largely influenced by the 'Mindstyle' model of learning style developed by Anthony F. Gregorc. Butler provides an understanding of the model which highlights the qualitative differences among individuals and the 'four mind channels' of 'concrete sequential, abstract sequential, concrete random and abstract random'. Each channel has its own particular behaviour and characteristics, e.g. concrete sequential individuals display the practical, predictable, organised and structured aspects of behaviour while concrete random individuals show the original experimental, investigative and risk taking aspects of behaviour.

The abstract sequential individual displays intellectual, logical, conceptual, rational and studious characteristics while the abstract random person shows emotional, sensitive, holistic, interpretative and thematic preferences.

The volume describes this model in relation to teaching styles with many good examples; profiles children's learning styles showing criteria for identification; and discusses style application. The chapter on style application, teaching approaches and lesson design makes this useful for teachers, but the main purpose of the book is to help teachers to become aware of the importance of style and to use this awareness and understanding in the classroom.

Doing Your Research Project
A Guide for First-Time Researchers in Education and Social Science
Judith Bell
Open University Press (second edition, 1993).

This publication can help the student plan and implement a research project. There are chapters on planning, recording, negotiating access, interviews and questionnaire design. Chapters on reviewing the literature, interpreting and presenting the evidence and writing the report make this a useful reference book for students embarking on research projects.

Learning to Learn – A Study Skills Course Book
Pat Heaton and Gina Mitchell
Better Books Publishing Ltd (1987).

This study skills manual aimed at the older student should prove an excellent resource for both teacher and student.

It is divided into twenty-one units, each unit focusing on a different aspect of study skills. The units include 'notetaking', 'essay preparation and planning', 'references and bibliographies', 'interview techniques' and 'dealing with examinations'.

The units are clearly written and expressed in an experiential manner, actively involving the student throughout.

Other texts which may be useful include:

Baddeley A. (1987) *Working Memory.* Clarendon, Oxford.
Berry R. (1986) *How to Write a Research Paper* (2nd edition). Pergamon Press, Oxford.
Buzan T. (1988) *Make the Most of Your Mind.* Pan Books.
Caine R. N. and Caine G. (1991) *Making Connections.* Banta.
de Bono E. (1992) *CORT Thinking.* Pergamon Press.
Gardner H. (1985) *Frames of Mind.* Basic Books, USA.
Keefe J. W. (1993) *Learning Style: Theory: Practice: Cognitive Skills.* NASSP Pub. USA.
Levine M. D. (1993) *All Kinds of Minds.* Educ. Publisher.
Levine M. D. (1992) *Keeping A Head in School.* Educ. Publisher.
Lewis I. and Munn P. (1993) *So You Want to do Research.* SCRE, Edinburgh.
Macintyre C (1993) *Let's Find Why.* Moray House Publications.
McCarthy B. (1987) *The 4-Mat System.* Excel Inc.
Munn P. and Drever E. (1993) *Using Questionnaires in Small Scale Research.* SCRE, Edinburgh.
Nisbet J. and Shucksmith J. (1986) *Learning Strategies.* Routledge.
Pollock J. and Waller E. (1994) *Day to Day Dyslexia in the Classroom.* Routledge.
Selmes I. (1987) *Improving Study Skills.* Hodder & Stoughton.
Sharron H. (1987) *Changing Children's Minds.* Condor Press.
Springer S. P. (1989) *Left Brain, Right Brain.* Freeman.
Stirling E. G. (1991) *Help for the Dyslexic Adolescent.* Better Books.
Williams L. V. (1983) *Teaching for the Two-Sided Mind.* Simon & Schuster.

Assessment

Reading Assessment for Teachers (RAT Pack)
M. Cooper, R. Parker and S. Toombs
Wiltshire County Council (1991).

This is a very comprehensive and useful pack. Essentially a training course of six sessions, it provides a detailed analysis of reading errors and reading performance. The authors acknowledge the work of Marie Clay (1985) and Helen Arnold (1980) which has clearly influenced the development of the pack.

In addition to providing a clear guide to miscue analysis, the guide also offers some practical guidance on setting clear targets, avoiding unnecessary assessment, monitoring of progress and providing effective feedback. Indeed Session 2 'Further Assessment and Setting Aims' provides a very useful special needs file which allows the teacher to record detailed information on the pupil's progress on print concepts, text reading, word recognition, reading strategies and comprehension, and allows for a summary of diagnostic assessment, short-term aims and suggested changes to curriculum management of teaching arrangements.

Sessions 4 and 5 follow up the assessment by focusing on teaching. These sessions offer a summary of a range of strategies including paired reading, 'praise, prompt and praise', ideas for reading without the teacher, and a technique known as the Coventry technique which is a systematic approach to acquiring a basic sight vocabulary based on the child's own language. There are also suggestions for teaching print skills including grapho-phomemic skills, letter-sound correspondence, sounding out, principles of phonics, teaching and the multi-sensory approach.

A well balanced approach to assessment and teaching which has been positively evaluated (Cooper, Toombs and Parker, 1992).

Learning Inventory Manual – Tests and Remediation
Barbara Meister Vitale and Waneta B. Bullock
Ann Arbor Publishers, Northumberland (1989).

This set of materials helps the teacher determine the student's level of competence in a range of tasks and the student's difficulties and the reasons for those difficulties. The Level C materials aim to evaluate the students' skills in visual dissemination skills, visual motor coordination skills, sequential memory skills, aural skills, and comprehension skills.

The tests are aimed at students in the 10-14 age range. Each of the above dimensions of assessment has an accompanying explanation describing the classroom implications and some guidelines for remediation. It also provides some ideas for which of this publisher's other materials are most suited to help deal with the difficulty. For example, for visual discrimination difficulties the book suggests exercises in visual tracking, recognising visual cues and visual discrimination.

The materials are also available in different skill levels and include a student work book.

Assessment – A Framework for Teachers
Ruth Sutton
Routledge (1992).

This very readable book on assessment provides a useful overview of the field. It contains an informative glossary identifying key phrases (mainly in relation to the English National Curriculum) such as attainment targets and records of achievement. The author also discusses different types of assessment and the criteria for effective assessment, looking at validity, reliability, manageability, moderation and standardisation.

Other aspects of assessment such as planning assessment, objectives, record keeping and providing feedback to learners and parents are also discussed, as is the aspect of whole-school issues. Issues relating to the development of a whole-school policy, the use of performance indicators, cross curricular assessment and progression are examined.

Diagnosing Dyslexia – A Guide to the Assessment of Adults with Specific Learning Difficulties
Cynthia Klein
Adult Literacy and Basic Skills Unit, Kingsbourne House, London (1993).

This useful and well presented book provides a clear methodology for assessing adults, including the diagnostic interview, reading, writing and spelling assessment, and providing oral and written feedback.

The essence of the book centres round the need to provide a qualitative analysis of the students' or adults' difficulties and Klein suggests this can be achieved through an in–depth interview, a miscue analysis of reading, a reading comprehension test, spelling error analyses and an analysis of a piece of free writing.

This book provides a checklist to assist with the diagnostic interview, a marking system for miscue analysis with an indication of different types of errors such as visual or phonic, and some examples from passages highlighting error analysis.

There is also a summary of visual processing problems, auditory processing problems and motor processing problems, a section on the reading process, and an appendix containing examples of reading and spelling tests.

Bury Infant Check
L. E. A. Pearson and J. Quinn
NFER Nelson (1986).

This check is designed to identify those children who may display difficulties in language skills, number skills and perceptual motor skills such as copying shapes and visual discrimination. There is also a quick check procedure based on observation and responses from selected items.

Suffolk Reading Scale
Frank Hagley
NFER Nelson (1987).

This standardised test can be administered as a group test or on an individual basis. The results provide normative data on the reading level of an individual or a group and assist in selecting reading materials at appropriate levels for children. There is also an age equivalent and book titles page which is useful for the teacher.

The scale, although initially standardised in Suffolk, has now been standardised to match a nationally representative sample. It has three levels, each consisting of sentences or phrases with words missing and the pupil has to select the appropriate word from a multiple choice list. There are both computer and hand scoring sheets.

Test of Initial Literacy (TOIL)
Anne Kispal, Alison Tate, Tom Groman and Chris Whetton
NFER Nelson (1989).

This test is designed to provide information relating to the strengths and weaknesses of children in reading and writing.

It consists of nine separate scores based on tests of letter matching, word matching, copying, grammatical punctuation, orthographic punctuation, spelling of homophones, spelling, writing style and free writing. The tests are suitable for children aged between 7 and 12 years and the results provide acceptable score ranges for each of the tests.

Keele Pre-School Assessment Guide
Stephen Tyler
NFER Nelson (1980).

There are two sections to this assessment guide. In the first section the teacher records aspects of the child's behaviour and in the second section cognitive, social, physical and linguistic skills are itemised and arranged in ascending order of difficulty.

The cognition section includes items relating to space and time, properties of objects, sorting and classification skills, memory, number and problem solving. The language section includes language use, speech, vocabulary and comprehension.

This guide forms a useful short booklet for the pre-school or early years teacher.

Diagnostic Reading Record
Helen Arnold
Hodder and Stoughton (1992).

This assessment consists of a teacher's handbook and pupil profile sheets which aim to provide a means of assessing reading development through both observations using miscue analysis, and examination of oral reading through discussion, focusing on the level of understanding which the child has of the passage.

The author has also geared the assessment to the strands of the English National Curriculum which can help teachers make judgments about pupils' levels of achievement in relation to the National Curriculum. The teacher's manual contains informative case studies highlighting key aspects of the diagnostic reading record profile and examples of scoring the passage using miscue analysis.

The reading passages are in the form of photo-copiable masters.

An excellent assessment resource for the teacher.

Practitioner's Guide to Dynamic Assessment
Carol S. Lidz
Guildford Press (1991).

This publication represents a highly accomplished piece of work on dynamic Assessment. This form of assessment is described by the author as one which involves active participation by the learner, facilitates learning by focusing on the process not the product of learning, and provides information to help determine how change is best accomplished.

The book examines different dynamic assessment models, examines research, and looks at pre-school learning and curriculum based adaptation. There are also some case studies with sample reports and a useful appendix with examples of record forms.

Opening the Door – Guidance on Recognising and Helping the Dyslexic Child
Edited by A. Brereton and P. Cann
British Dyslexia Association, Reading (1993).

A very informative text on the crucial area of early recognition. The chapters reflect the perspectives of different professionals such as the teacher, doctor, speech therapist, psychologist and a physical education consultant. There is also an interesting chapter on hyperactivity and attention deficit, as well as an early recognition checklist which can be completed by both parents and teachers.

An Observational Survey of Early Literacy Achievement
Marie M. Clay
Heinemann Education (1993).

A text containing detailed descriptions of observation surveys in reading and writing. The class teacher will find this an extremely useful book – clearly presented, it provides examples and descriptions of observational strategies including how to take a running record of reading texts and other observation tasks such as letter identification, concepts about print, word tests, writing and dictation.

There is also a useful chapter on strategies to help with text, words and letters with examples of survey summaries.

Non-Reading Intelligence Tests
D. Young
Hodder & Stoughton (1989).

The Non-Reading Intelligence Test is primarily orally administered and can help the test administrator obtain an intelligence score for poor readers which may be a more accurate reflection of their ability.

There are three levels corresponding to chronological age, which ranges from six years four months to thirteen years eleven months. Each level contains a number of sub-tests and the author indicates that this test has been used to assist in the diagnosis of children with specific learning difficulties.

Other assessment materials include:

Ames E. (1991) *Teach Yourself to Diagnose Reading Problems.* Macmillan Educational.
Arnold H. (1992) *Diagnostic Reading Record.* Hodder & Stoughton.
Arnold H. (1984) *Making Sense of It: Miscue Analysis.* Hodder & Stoughton.
Aubrey C., Eaves J., Hicks C. and Newton M. (1982) *Aston Portfolio.* LDA.
Boder E. and Jarrico S. (1982) *Boder Test of Reading-Spelling Patterns.* Harcourt Brace Jovanovich.
Bradley L. (1980) *Assessing Reading Difficulties: Diagnostic, Remedial.* NFER Nelson.
Burt C. (1975) *Burt Word Reading Test.* Hodder & Stoughton for SCRE.
Clay M. (1985) *The Early Detection of Reading Difficulties.* Heinemann Educational.
Edwards P. (1992) *Edwards Reading Test.* Heinemann Educational.
Hagley F. (1987) *Suffolk Reading Scale.* NFER Nelson.
Jones-Elgar R. (1989) *The Cloze Line.* Ann Arbor Pub.
Kaufman A. A. (1992) *Intelligent Testing with WISC-R.* Psychological Corporation.
Klein C. (1993) *Diagnosing Dyslexia.* Albsu.
McCleod J. (1994) *GAP Reading Comprehension Test.* Heinemann Educational.
Miles T. R. (1983) *Bangor Dyslexia Test.* LDA Cambs.
Neale, M. (1989) *Neale Analysis* NFER Nelson.
Newton M. and Thompson M. (1982) *The Aston Index.* LDA Cambs.
Robertson A. H., Henderson A., Robertson A., Fisher J. and Gibson M. (1983) *Quest Reading and Number Screening Tests.* Thos. Nelson.
Raven J. C. (1988) *Mill Hill Manual and Vocabulary Scale.* NFER Nelson.
Raven J. C. (1992:1993) *Standard Progressive Matrices.* Oxford Psychologists Press, Oxford.
Slingerland B. H. (1985) *Screening Tests for Identifying Children with Specific Learning Disabilities.* Educators Pub.

Sutton R. (1992) *Assessment-Framework for Teachers*. Routledge.

Tyler S. (1980) *Keele Pre-school Assessment Guide*. NFER Nelson.

Vincent E. and de la Mare M. (1987) *New MacMillan Reading Analysis*. MacMillan Educational.

Vincent D. and Claydon J. (1982) *Diagnostic Spelling Test*. NFER Nelson.

Writing

Dysgraphia Why Johnny Can't Write
A Handbook for Teachers and Parents
Diane Walton Cavey
Pro-Ed Inc. Austin, Texas (Second edition, 1993).

This book focuses on dysgraphia by looking at explanations of dysgraphia, presenting this from the parents' and teachers 'perspective with suggestions for developing a teaching programme. It also looks at vocational training and a useful glossary is included.

For parents the book provides some early warning signs and some tasks which may be helpful. Examples of dysgraphic characteristics and ideas for teaching provide the teacher with useful guidelines for assessment and teaching. A very useful book.

Putting Pen to Paper
A New Approach to Handwriting
Melvyn Ramsden
Southgate, Devon (1992).

A very comprehensive and useful book on handwriting. The materials are well presented with plentiful examples. The book examines some misconceptions about handwriting, and some principles in relating handwriting to language, reading and spelling. The stages of teaching handwriting are addressed, supported by numerous graphics. There is also a separate chapter on the initial stages of handwriting.

Inspirations for Writing
Sue Ellis and Gill Friel
Scholastic Publications (1992).

This book provides the teacher with a vast collection of superb ideas to motivate children in joined writing tasks. The consistent relation of tasks to the curriculum context with the book is especially useful. It is well illustrated with chapters including functional, imaginative and collaborative writing. Each chapter has an activities section with indications of the age range most suited to the task. The ranges tend to be from five to nine years although there are some for children of up to twelve years.

The book also includes 30 pages of photo-copiable material related to some of the activities.

Joining the ABC
Charles Cripps and Robin Cox
LDA, Cambridge (1991).

This book focuses on why handwriting and spelling should be taught together. It provides both a theoretical and practical perspective on handwriting and spelling, and answers questions such as 'what kind of perceptual activities will help children differentiate between letters and joins in writing?' and 'do five year olds have the motor control for joining letters?'

The book discusses some issues relating to the teacher, such as the level of writing teachers should expect from each age group, implications for classroom organisation and the role of parents. There is also a simple guide for developing children's writing looking at handwriting, spelling and composing skills.

The chapter on resources and teaching techniques provide ideas for developing motor control and hand/eye coordination. An extremely useful reference book for teachers.

Some other useful publications in writing include:

Alston J. (1991) *Assessing and Promoting Writing Skills*. NASEN Pub.
Alston J. and Taylor J. (1992) *Handwriting Helpline*. Dextral Books.
Alston J. and Taylor J. (1992) *Writing Lefthanded*. Dextral Books.
Handwriting Reviews, published annually by *The Handwriting Interest Group*, provide useful guidance for teachers.

Harrison P. and Harrison S. (1989) *Writing for Different Purposes.* Folens.
McRoberts R. (1984) *Writing Workshop Teaching Materials.*
Ramsden M. (1992) *Putting Pen to Paper.* Southgate Pub.
Topping K. (1992) *Paired Writing Information.* Kirklees Metropolitan Council.

Spelling

Spelling; Caught or Taught – A New Look
Margaret L. Peters
Routledge (Revised edition, 1985).

This book highlights the generally agreed notion that reading is taught but spelling is caught – that it occurs incidentally. But as Margaret Peters points out – not all children catch it. This book therefore attempts to display how spelling can in fact be taught to those who for some reason do not 'catch it'.

The book looks at predictors of spelling ability such as verbal ability, visual perception of word form and perceptuo-motor ability. She discusses the skills used in spelling such as recall, learned behaviour, and letter relationships and sequences. She argues that spelling is different from reading, which is a more 'flexible' skill with performance variation depending on the purpose for which the child taps into his syntactic and semantic linguistic resources. There is also a more predictive element in reading than in spelling.

In relation to teaching children spelling Margaret Peters discusses the importance of attention and perception, visual skills, associative learning techniques (for example words within words and letter string), developing imagery and developing within children a firm strategy for learning new words.

There is also a chapter on the assessment of spelling, looking at normative spelling tests and positive assessment of spelling strategies.

A very useful book for the teacher.

Spelling in Context – Strategies for Teachers and Learners
Margaret L. Peters and Brigid Smith
NFER Nelson (1993).

This book includes a revision of Margaret Peter's well known *Diagnostic and Remedial Spelling Manual.* Divided into eight chapters, it discusses the role of spelling and writing within both the composing process and the secretarial process. Aided by an abundance of samples of children's work, the authors illustrate the process of writing and the teacher's role in guiding, monitoring and correcting.

There are also chapters on spelling development and classroom management. They include a suggested layout of a writing corner, a list of resources for the writing area, supporting the pupil, the use of the computer, presentation and display as well as aspects of spelling development such as phonological awareness. The assessment section, called 'Diagnosing Specific Spelling Difficulties', provides a very useful diagnostic grid of mis-spellings. It also contains detailed analysis of mis-spellings and strategies for spelling instruction and spelling recovery. The chapter which describes the diagnostic grid is well illustrated with examples supporting the look, cover, write, check routine. This is followed by a chapter containing ten case studies highlighting the diagnostic criteria for intervention, and support strategies from children aged from five to thirteen.

An extremely useful and very teacher-friendly volume.

Spelling Made Easy – Multi-sensory Structured Spelling
Violet Brand
Egon Publishers (1989).

This comprehensive spelling programme consists of four levels of work for different stages. Each stage comprises a teacher's book and copymaster worksheets. Level 1 aims to help the learner become familiar with the recognition and uses of word families within the context of a text. This is extended in Level 2, and Level 3 provides children with the opportunity to use their English skills in a variety of ways.

A very successful spelling programme which can be applied at both primary and secondary stages.

Remedial Spelling
Violet Brand
Egon Publishers (1985).

Part of the Spelling Made Easy series, this publication consists of a teacher's text and sixty proof-reading passages. The author contends that the teaching of spelling should be diagnostic and structured in such a way as to meet the needs of the student.

The text contains test passages and teaching points with extensive revision and reinforcement exercises. The proof-reading masters should prove to be a useful resource for the teacher with proof passages and teaching points.

Unscrambling Spelling
Cynthia Klein and Robin R. Miller
Hodder & Stoughton (1990).

This book examines the teaching of spelling by looking at a range of strategies and methods including analysis of errors, strategies for remembering spellings, look, cover, write and check method, the use of individualised spelling programmes within the classroom and programmes combining spelling and handwriting.

There are also useful resource sheets relating to a range of aspects such as identifying learning style, analysing errors, word building, editing and proof reading.

A very useful resource containing a range of materials which are easy for the class teacher to use.

The following may also be useful:

Brown G. D. and Ellis N. C. (1994) *Handbook of Normal and Disturbed Spelling Development, Theory, Processes and Interventions.* John Wiley & Sons.
Childs S. and Childs R. (1992) *The Childs' Spelling System – The Rules.* Better Books.
Cripps C. (1992) *A Hand for Spelling.* Cambridge Institute of Education.
Dykes B. and Thomas C. (1989) *Spelling Made Easy.* Hale & Iremonger, Sydneys.
Miller R. and Klein C. (1986) *Making Sense of Spelling.* DCLD London.
Sillars S. (1991) *Spelling Rules OK!* Chalkface Project, Milton Keynes.
Pollock J. (1990) *Signposts to Spelling.* Heinemann Education.
Pratley R. (1988) *Spelling it Out.* BBC Books.
Rudginsky L. T. and Haskell E. C. (1990) *How to Spell.* Educators Publishing Service.
Seymour P. H. K. (1986) *Cognitive Analysis of Dyslexia.* Routledge and Paul Kegan.
Topping K. (1992) *Cued Spelling Training Tape.* Kirklees Metropolitan Council.
Vincent D. and Claydon J. (1982) *Diagnostic Spelling Test.* NFER Nelson.

Parents

Parents on Dyslexia
Multilingual Matters
Editor Saskia Van de Stoel
Multilingual Matters. Clevedon, Avon (1990).

This book provides readable information in relation to a number of questions parents may raise relating to dyslexia. These include how the difficulties can be manifested at home and school, post-school and career aspects, social considerations, assessment, identification and provision. The book represents a comprehensive survey of the field, illustrated by a number of case studies with comments from specialists. Although the context for parents differs from area to area this text could still prove a valuable aid to parents requiring an account of dyslexia which is more advanced and detailed than simplistic pamphlets, but which is free from the academic and professional jargon often found in general texts.

Dyslexia – A Parents Survival Guide
Christine Ostler
Ammonite Books, Godalming (1991).

This well organised and comprehensive volume will be helpful to parents and professionals. It examines the problem of dyslexia and suggests how parents may deal with any anxieties, placing liaising with school as an essential step.

Christine Ostler also examines the difficulty from the child's perspective, highlighting her experiences as a parent of a dyslexic son, and as a trained teacher of dyslexic children.

The book contains particularly useful sections on study skills and looks at reading, spelling and maths from the perspective of helping the dyslexic child develop coping strategies through effective study habits.

This well written, easy-to-read book will provide parents with useful factual information in relation to support groups, and useful resources and addresses. The range of appropriate coping strategies interspersed throughout the book provides pointers for both parents and teachers and encourages effective liaison to help minimise the damaging effects of dyslexia.

The following may also be useful:

Cicci R. (1987) *Dyslexia: Especially for Parents*. Orton Dyslexia Society, USA.

Crisfield J. and Smythe I. (eds) (1993,1994) *The Dyslexia Handbook*. British Dyslexia Association, Reading.

Hornsby B. (1992) *Overcoming Dyslexia*. Optima.

Osmond J. (1993) *The Reality of Dyslexia*. Cassell.

Selikowitz M. (1993) *Dyslexia and Other Learning Difficulties*. Oxford University Press.

Chapter 14

Journals and articles

JOURNALS and articles provide a useful source of reading materials for the student and teacher. Journals are usually fairly readily available in libraries, if not the Librarian can usually obtain the journal article for you from another library.

Journal articles have an advantage in that they are usually very up-to-date, often have an abstract or summary and provide additional up-to-date references. Additionally, they are usually relatively short, which is invaluable for the busy teacher.

Journals

Below is a list of some of the journals in which useful articles may be found.

American Educational Research Journal
American Journal of Education
American Psychologist
Applied Linguistics
Applied Psycho-linguistics
Australian Journal of Education
British Journal of Curriculum and Assessment
British Journal of Development Psychology
British Journal of Educational Psychology
British Journal of Educational Studies
British Journal of Psychology
British Journal of Special Education
British Journal of Teacher Education
Centre for Specific Learning Difficulties Newsletter, Moray House, Edinburgh.
Child Development
Child Education

Child Language Teaching and Therapy
Childhood Education
Cospen News
Curriculum
Curriculum Journal
Dyslexia Contact – British Dyslexia Association
Early Childhood
Early Years
Education
Education USA
Education Canada
Education for Teaching
Educational and Child Psychology
Educational and Psychological Measurement
Educational Psychology
Educational Psychology in Practice
Educational Research
Educational Research Quarterly
Educational Review
Educational Studies
European Journal of Psychology of Education
European Journal of Special Needs Education
Exceptional Children
Handwriting Review
International Journal of Educational Research
International Review of Education
Journal of Child Language
Journal of Child Psychology and Psychiatry
Journal of Communication Disorders
Journal of Curriculum Studies
Journal of Education for Teaching
Journal of Educational Psychology
Journal of Educational Research
Journal of Learning Disabilities
Journal of Research and Development in Education
Journal of Research in Childhood Education
Journal of Research in Reading
Journal of Special Education
Language and Learning
Language and Speech
Language for Learning

Language Issues
Language Learning
Language Learning Journal
Language Teaching
Language Testing
Linguistics
New Directions for Teaching and Learning
New Zealand Journal of Educational Studies
Observer
Open Learning
Perspectives – The Orton Dyslexia Society
RASE: Remedial and Special Education
Reading
Reading Research Quarterly
Reading Teacher
Remedial Education
Research in Education
Research Quarterly
Resources in Education
Review of Educational Research
SCCC Information
SCRE Newsletter
Scottish Child
Scottish Educational Journal
Scottish Educational Review
Scottish Educational Studies
Special Children
Special Education
Support for Learning
Talk
Teacher Education
Times Educational Supplement
Times Educational Supplement Scotland

Articles

Some examples of recent research relating to specific learning difficulties are outlined below.

Acklaw J. and Gupta Yash. (1991)
Talking with parents of 'dyslexic' children: the value of skilled discussion methods.
Support for Learning. Vol. 6, No. 1, pp. 37-39.

Augur Jean (1986)
The concept of dyslexia, specific policies, strategies and techniques for its remediation and their more general application in the ordinary classroom.
Early Child Development and Care. Vol. 23, pp. 215-261.

Bailey T. (1991)
Classroom observation: a powerful tool for teachers?
Support for Learning. Vol. 6, No. 1, pp. 32-36.

Bald J. (1992)
Love and war in Letterland.
Child Education. May.

Beaver R. (1993)
Neuro-linguistic programme as practised by an educational psychologist.
Educational Psychology in Practice. July, pp. 87-90.

Beaver R., Ayre A., McGregor P. and Brightman A. (1993)
No time like the present – intervention versus assessment: the experience in Kent.
Special Children. No. 67, June/July.

Bentote P., Norgate R. and Thornton D. (1990)
Special needs: spelling – some problems solved.
Educational Psychology in Practice. Vol. 6, No. 2, pp. 76-81.

Blythe Peter (1992)
A physical approach to resolving learning difficulties.
Institute of Neuro-Physiological Psychology. 4th European Conference Paper, Chester.

Bradley Lynette (1991)
Rhyme, reason and reading.
The Observer (Schools Report). 22 Sept.

Brown Morven (1991)
Stress – the learner with a specific learning difficulty.
Centre for Specific Learning Difficulties seminar paper, June.

Brown Sally (1990)
Planning small-scale research.
Scottish Council for Research in Education, *Spotlight* 27.

Bruck M. and Treimann, R. (1992)
Learning to pronounce words: the limitations of analogies.
Reading Research Quarterly. 27 April, pp. 375-388.

Campione J. C. (1989)
Assisted assessment: a taxonomy of approaches and an outline of strengths and weaknesses.
Journal of Learning Disabilities. Vol. 22, No. 3, pp. 151-165.

Clay Marie M. (1991)
Introducing a new storybook to young readers.
The Reading Teacher. Vol. 45, No. 4, pp. 264-273.

Christensen C. A. (1992)
Discrepancy definitions of reading disability: has the quest led us astray? A response to Stanovich.
Reading Research Quarterly. Vol. 27, No. 3, pp. 276-278.

Cornelissen P., Bradley L., Fowler S. and Stein J. (1992)
Covering one eye affects how some children read. Developmental Medicine and Child
Neurology. No. 34, pp. 296-304.

Cossu G. and Marshall J. C. (1990)
Are cognitive skills a prerequisite for learning to read and write?
Cognitive Neuropsychology. Vol. 7, No. 1, pp. 21-40.

Crombie M. (1993)
The effects of specific learning difficulties (dyslexia) on the learning of a foreign language in school.
Unpublished M.Sc. thesis, University of Strathclyde.

Cudd E. T. and Roberts, L. L. (1994)
A scaffolding technique to develop sentence sense and vocabulary.
The Reading Teacher. Vol. 47, No. 4, Dec./January pp. 346-349.

Currie L. A. (1993)
English language 5-14, novel studies and the development of meta-comprehension skills.
Support for Learning. Vol. 8, No. 1, pp. 22-25.

Davidson J. (1990)
The use of speech in computer-assisted-learning programs for beginning readers.
Support for Learning. Vol. 5, No. 4, pp. 216-219.

Dombey H. (1992)
Reading recovery: A solution to all primary school reading problems?
Support for Learning. Vol. 7, No. 3, pp 111-115.

Dombey H. (1993)
Reading: What children need to learn and how teachers can help them.
Reading. Vol. 27, No. 3, pp. 1-9.

Drummond A., Godfrey L. and Sattin R. (1990)
Promoting parental involvement in reading.
Support for Learning. Vol. 5, No. 3, pp. 141-145.

Ehri Linnea C. and Robins C. (1992)
Beginners need some decoding skills to read words by analogy.
Reading Research Quarterly. Vol. 27, No. 1, pp. 13-26.

Ellis N. (1990)
Reading, phonological skills and short-term memory: interactive tributaries of development.
Journal of Research in Reading. Vol. 13, No. 2, pp. 107-122.

France L., Topping K. and Revell K. (1993)
Parent-tutored cued spelling.
Support for Learning. Vol. 8, No. 1, pp. 11-15.

Francis M., Taylor S. and Sawyer C. (1992)
Coloured lenses and the dex frame: new issues.
Support for Learning. Vol. 7, No. 1, pp. 25-27.

Gale A. (1991)
The school as organisation: new roles for psychologists in education.
Educational Psychology in Practice. Vol. 7, No. 2.

Given B. (1993)
Breakthrough learning: integrated strategies instruction through individual learning styles.
George Mason University, Fairfax, Virginia.

Goddard S. (1992)
The effects of reflex activity upon oculo-motor and visual-perceptual functioning.
Institute for Neuro-Physiological Psychology (INPP), occasional paper, Chester.

Goodman K. S. (1992)
I didn't found whole language.
The Reading Teacher. Vol. 46, No. 3, pp. 189-199.

Goswami U.(1994)
The role of analogies in reading development.
Support for Learning. Vol. 9, No. 1, pp. 22-26.

Gregory E. (1993)
What counts as reading in the early years' classroom?
British Journal of Educational Psychology. No. 63, pp. 214-230.

Griffith P. L. and Olson M. W. (1992)
Phonemic awareness helps beginning readers break the code.
The Reading Teacher. Vol. 45, No. 7, pp. 516-523.

Gross J. and Garnett J. (1994)
Preventing reading difficulties – rhyme and alliteration in the real world.
Educational Psychology in Practice. Vol. 9, No. 4.

Hansen, Elaine (1990)
Cooperative teaching between learning support and subject teachers.
Support for Learning. Vol. 5, No. 3, pp. 128-135.

Hewson, Jan (1990)
Paired spelling
Support for Learning. Vol. 5, No. 3, pp. 136-140.

Johnston R. S., Rugg M. D. and Scott T. (1987)
Phonological similarity effects, memory span and developmental reading disorders: the nature of the relationship.
British Journal of Psychology. No. 78, pp. 205-211.

Johnston R. (1992)
Methods of teaching reading: the debate continues.
Support for Learning. Vol. 7, No. 3, pp. 99-102.

Kelly M. (1991)
The role of learning support: a trefoil catalyst?
Support for Learning. Vol. 6, No. 4, pp. 170-172.

Kirtley C., Bryant P., MacLean M. and Bradley L. (1989)
Rhyme, rime, and the onset of reading.
Journal of Experimental Child Psychology. No. 48, pp. 224-245.

Lane Colin (1987)
Aiming ARROW at learning targets.
British Journal of Special Education. Vol. 14, No. 3.

Lawrence D. (1985)
Improving self-esteem and reading.
Educational Research. Vol. 27, No. 3, pp 194-200.

Lewis G. and Powell-Jones M. (1993)
Dealing with dyslexia.
Special Children. No. 67.

Lovitt T. C. and DeMier D. M. (1984)
An evaluation of the Slingerland method with learning difficulties youngsters.
Journal of Learning Disabilities. Vol. 17, No. 5, pp. 267-272.

Lowenstein, L. F. (1990)
Dyslexia – fiction or reality? Recent investigations and directions in the study of dyslexia.
Education Today. Vol. 40, No. 1.

Martlew M. (1992)
Handwriting and spelling: dyslexic children's abilities compared with children of the same chronological age and younger children of the same spelling level.
British Journal of Educational Psychology., No. 62, pp. 375-390.

McKeown M. G., Beck I. L., Sinatra G. and Loxterman J. A. (1992)
The contribution of prior knowledge and coherent text to comprehension.
Reading Research Quarterly. Vol. 27, No. 1, pp. 79-93.

Miner M. and Siegal L. S. (1992)
William Butler Yeats: dyslexic?
Journal of Learning Disabilities. Vol. 25, No. 6, pp. 372-375.

Moseley D. (1989)
How lack of confidence in spelling affects children's written expression.
Educational Psychology in Practice. April.

Mould S. (1993)
Chaos in the classroom – attention deficit disorder.
Special Children. No. 66, pp. 8-11.

Moyle D. (1991)
Methods of teaching reading: the debate resolved.
Support for Learning. Vol. 6, No. 3, pp. 108-111.

Newman S., Fields H. and Wright S. (1993)
A developmental study of specific spelling disability.
British Journal of Educational Psychology. No. 63, pp. 287-296.

Pumfrey P. D. (1990)
How can the testing and teaching of reading in the primary school be better integrated?
Support for Learning. Vol. 5, No. 3, pp. 146-151.

Newman S., Wright S. and Fields H. (1990)
Identification of a group of children with dyslexia by means of IQ-achievement discrepancies.
British Journal of Educational Psychology. No. 61, pp. 139-154.

Prance Jean (1992)
Making a good recovery (reading recovery).
Special Children. February.

Presland J. (1991)
Explaining away dyslexia.
Education Psychology in Practice. Vol. 6, No. 4, pp. 215-221.

Pumfrey P. D. (1991)
Identifying and alleviating specific learning difficulties: issues and implications for LEAs, professionals and parents.
Educational Psychology in Practice. Vol. 6, No. 4.

Rack J., Snowling M. and Olson R. K. (1992)
The non-word reading deficit in developmental dyslexia: a review.
Reading Research Quarterly. Vol. 27, No. 1, pp. 29-53.

Reason R., Brown B., Cole M. and Gregory M. (1988)
Does the 'specific' in specific learning difficulties make a difference to the way we teach?
Support for Learning. Vol. 3, No. 4, pp. 146-151.

Reid G. (1991)
Stress factors in teaching children with specific learning difficulties.
Occasional paper, Centre for Specific Learning Difficulties, Moray House, Edinburgh.

Reid G. (1986)
The perceptions and attitudes of learning support teachers to specific learning difficulties and dyslexia.
Scottish Learning Difficulties Yearbook. pp. 2-4.

Reid G. (1988)
Dyslexia: a case for training.
Times Educational Supplement. 26 February.

Reid G. (1991)
Supporting the support teacher – stress factors in teaching children with specific learning difficulties.
LINKS. Vol. 16, No. 3. pp. 18-20.

Reid G. (1994)
Dyslexia and Metacognitive Assessment. Accepted for publication. *Links* II.

Rhodes J. (1993)
How pupils and staff experienced a peer-tutoring project involving paired reading.
Reading. Vol. 27, No. 3, Nov. pp. 14-19.

Riding R. and Douglas G. (1993)
The effect of cognitive style and mode of presentation on learning performance.
British Journal of Educational Psychology. No. 63, pp. 297-307.

Royer J. M., Cisero C. A. and Carlo M. S. (1993)
Techniques and procedures for assessing cognitive skills.
Review of Educational Research. Vol. 63, No. 2, pp 201-243.

Sawyer C., Taylor S. and Wilcocks S. (1994)
Transparent coloured overlays and specific learning difficulties.
Educational Psychology in Practice. Vol. 9, No. 4, pp. 217-220.

Seymour P. H. K. (1987)
How might phonemic segmentation help reading development
European Bulletin of Cognitive Psychology. Vol. 7, No. 5, pp. 504-508.

Siegal L. S. (1989)
IQ is irrelevant to the definition of learning disabilities.
Journal of Learning Disabilities. Vol. 22, No. 8, pp. 469-477.

Siegal L. S. (1992)
An evaluation of the discrepancy definition of dyslexia.
Journal of Learning Disabilities. Vol. 25, No. 10, pp. 618-629.

Sinatra G. M. (1990)
Convergence of listening and reading processing.
Reading Research Quarterly. Vol. 15, No. 2.

Singleton C. H. (1988)
The early diagnosis of developmental dyslexia.
Support for Learning. Vol. 3, No. 2.

Smith C. J. (1993)
Problems with reading.
Support for Learning. Vol. 8, No. 4, pp. 139-145.

Smith J. (1979)
How can parents help?
Dyslexia Review. Vol. 2, No. 2, pp. 24-25.

Solman R. T., Singh N. N. and Kehoe E. J. (1992)
Pictures block the learning of sightwords.
Educational Psychology. Vol. 12, No. 2.

Spiegal D. L. (1992)
Blending whole language and systematic direct instruction.
The Reading Teacher. Vol. 46, No. 1, pp. 38-44.

Stanovich K. E. (1988)
Explaining the differences between the dyslexic and the garden-variety. Poor reader; the phonological-core variable-difference model.
Journal of Learning Disabilities. Vol. 21, No. 10.

Stanovich K. E. (1991)
Discrepancy definitions of reading disability: has intelligence led us astray?
Reading Research Quarterly. Vol. 26, No. 1, pp. 7-29.

Stone J. and Harris K. (1991)
These coloured spectacles: what are they for?
Support for Learning. Vol. 6, No. 3, pp. 116-118.

Stuart Morag and Coltheart M. (1988)
Does reading develop in a sequence of stages?
Cognition. No. 30, pp. 139-181.

Swanson H. L. and Ramalgia J. M. (1992)
The relationship between phonological codes on memory and spelling tasks for students with and without learning disabilities.
Journal of Learning Disabilities. Vol. 25, No. 6, pp. 396-407.

Swanson H. L. and Ramalgia J. M. (1992)
The relationship between phonological codes on memory and spelling tasks for students with and without learning disabilities.
Journal of Learning Disabilities. Vol. 25, No. 6, pp. 340-350, 371.

Thomas D. P. (1991)
A framework for teaching reading.
Support for Learning, Vol. 6, No. 3, pp. 103-107.

Thomson M. (1987)
Psychological and academic difficulties facing the dyslexic child.
Education Today. Vol. 37, No. 3, pp. 4-13.

Thomson M. (1987)
Psychological and academic difficulties facing the dyslexic child.
Education Today. Vol. 37, No. 3.

Topping K. J. and Lindsay G. A. (1992)
The structure and development of the paired reading technique.
The Journal of Research in Reading (UKRA).

Topping K. J. and Lindsay G. A. (1992)
Paired reading: a review of the literature
Research Papers in Education Policy and Practice. Vol. 7, No. 3, pp. 199-246.

Topping K. J. (1992)
Short- and long-term follow-up of parental involvement in reading projects.
British Educational Research Journal. Vol. 18, No. 4, pp. 369-378.

Topping K. (1991)
Achieving more with less: raising reading standards via parental involvement and peer tutoring.
Support for Learning. Vol. 6, No. 3, pp. 112-115.

Turner M. (1991)
Finding out.
Support for Learning. Vol. 6, No. 3, pp. 99-102.

Turner M. (1993)
Testing times.
Special Children. April.

Turner M. (1993)
More testing times.
Special Children. May, pp. 12-14.

Vaughan J., Underwood V., Weaver S. and House G. (1992)
A comparison of students' learning styles as determined by the learning styles inventory (Dunn, Dunn and Price) personal learning power.
Research Report No. 2. Texas Center for Learning Styles, East Texas State University.

Wasik B. A. and Slavin R. E. (1993)
Preventing early reading failure with one-to-one tutoring: a review of five programs.
Reading Research Quarterly. Vol. 28, No. 2, pp. 179-199.

Watt J. M. and Topping K. J. (1993)
Cued spelling: a comparative study of parent and peer tutoring.
Educational Psychology in Practice. Vol. 9, No. 2, pp. 95-103.

Weedon C. (1992)
Specific learning difficulties in mathematics.
Research report, Department of Education, University of Stirling and Tayside Region.

Wendon L. (1990)
Synthesis in Letterland: reinstating phonics in a 'whole language' setting.
Early Child Development and Care. Vol. 61, pp. 139-148.

Wendon L. (1992)
Love and war in Letterland.
Child Education. pp. 40-41.

Wendon L. (1993)
Literacy for early childhood: learning from the learners.
Early Child Development and Care. Vol. 86, pp. 11-22.

Whittaker E. M. (1992)
Specific learning difficulty (dyslexia) and neurological research.
Educational Psychology in Practice. Vol. 8, No. 3, pp. 139-144.

Wiener J. and Siegal L. (1992)
A Canadian perspective on learning disabilities.
Journal of Learning Disabilities. Vol. 25, No. 6, pp. 340-350.

Wright A. and Prance J. (1992)
The reading recovery programme in Surrey Education Authority.
Support for Learning. Vol. 7, No. 3.

Wright A. (1992)
Evaluation of the first British reading recovery programme.
British Educational Research Journal. Vol. 18, No. 4, pp. 351-368.

Wright J. and Cashdan A. (1991)
Training metacognitive skills in backward readers: a pilot study.
Educational Psychology in Practice. Vol. 7, No. 3, pp. 153-162.

Yopp Hallie Kay. (1992)
Developing phonemic awareness in young children.
The Reading Teacher. Vol. 45, No. 9, pp. 696-783.

Section 6 –

Conclusion

Comments and Conclusion

THE QUESTION 'What is **the answer** for dyslexic children?' is often asked. That in itself is not altogether surprising; after all dyslexic children often display real difficulty, performing in an expected manner within the conventional system – and in many cases within that system they fail.

To the scientific mind, or indeed to the concerned enquirer, problems and difficulties need to be matched with remedies and solutions. What, therefore, are the solutions to the barriers that prevent dyslexic children from achieving academic fulfilment and educational success?

The reader should by now be aware that the field of dyslexia has many facets. The term 'the dyslexias' refers to the need to recognise the concept of dyslexia as one incorporating a range of difficulties. Dyslexic children can display a variety of difficulties within that range and similarly display a range of strengths and abilities. This emphasises the importance of acknowledging the individual needs of dyslexic children, in order that appropriate teaching programmes can be identified, and curriculum and support approaches developed. This handbook has described research studies which have helped professionals acquire an understanding of the concept of dyslexia; assessment strategies and materials which can provide for early and effective identification; teaching programmes and support approaches which illustrate the abundance of resources available to help dyslexic children.

It is hoped, therefore, that this handbook will help professionals provide the appropriate support to assist the dyslexic student to achieve self-sufficiency and success in learning.

It is of the utmost importance that unfortunate experiences of the type illustrated by the extract below (sent to me by a teacher who is also a parent of a dyslexic son) are altogether avoided.

He has arrived at school and is in class waiting for the day's lessons to begin. The teacher has been doing multiplication tables with the class and he has been trying to learn these at home with the help of his parents, but finds the task exceptionally difficult. It is his turn to perform the tables – he begins and very quickly loses the place. He starts again, pauses and begins yet again. He thinks to himself, 'Did I really learn these last night?' – HE HAS FAILED.

The yellow library van arrives in the playground. The class troops out to select a book. The boy wanders aimlessly around the van. He finds a book about aircraft and looks carefully at the pictures. The teacher feels the text is too difficult. He then looks at some other books with stories which he feels he might manage. A friend looks over his shoulder and says, 'That's a baby book!' He leaves the van without a book saying that he could not find one he liked. – HE HAS FAILED.

Next comes maths. Today's page is about measurement. The teacher explains what to do on the first part of the page. The boy measures carefully the length of his rubber, his pencil, his ruler and the desks and records the answers correctly in his workbook. – SUCCESS.

The next part consists of problems based on the previous practical work. Find the difference between the length of . . .' The boy cannot read the question. He sharpens his pencil, looks out of the window, his attention diverted by the janitor busy clearing the playground of autumn leaves. The interval bell rings. He has not finished the task. – HE HAS FAILED.

After the interval the class watch a short television programme about transport. The boy watches and listens intently. Afterwards the teacher discusses the programme with the class. The boy knows more than anyone else and answers well. – SUCCESS.

They are then asked to write a little in their topic books about the programme and to illustrate their work. The boy sets to work on his drawing with great enthusiasm. His illustration is very mature and shows great attention to detail. Later the teacher looks at his work and says, 'What a great picture. You really do know a lot about aeroplanes!' – SUCCESS.

'Perhaps you could have written a little more'. – HE HAS FAILED.

After lunch it is time for language study. The teacher has written some work on the blackboard. There are ten sentences. The boy looks at the board time and time again, but keeps losing the place. After three sentences he gazes out of the window. He feels tired. He hears the teacher's voice. 'The children who are finished may choose an activity until PE time!' His friends head for the big Lego box. The boy has not finished. – HE HAS FAILED.

PE follows. He changes quickly and enters the gym. His shoes are on the wrong feet. Today's game is shipwrecks. The boy is quick and nimble. He is the only one who can climb to the top of the ropes with ease. – SUCCESS.

At the end of the school day he knows that he will probably have to take his unfinished language work home. There is one small consolation, today was not his group's day for reading.

He arrives home. His Mum asks him to go to the shops for her. 'Run up and get me a dozen brown rolls, a bottle of vinegar and a bag of plain flour'. The boy sets off reluctantly. Ten minutes later he returns. He has six white rolls and a bottle of vinegar. 'What was the other thing you said Mum?' His mother groans. – HE HAS FAILED.

The boy begins his homework. He needs some help. 'How are you doing with your homework', his mother asks. He looks upset. 'I can't do it,' he yells, 'I'm thick.' He quickly leaves the room. His mother looks bewildered. – HE HAS FAILED.

(Adapted from personal correspondence from E. Jane Smart)

With KNOWLEDGE, TRAINING, CONFIDENCE and SUPPORT the barriers described in the above extracts, can be positively tackled.

The abundance of resources described in this handbook demonstrates that **knowledge** is there and available. The desire of teachers to obtain **training** appears to be inherent in teachers' acceptance of their role. Teachers, it seems, possess a commendable, almost insatiable, appetite for further **training** and professional achievement. This desire, despite the financial climate of restraint and priorities, is recognised by the national and local bodies and indeed by schools themselves, and instils **confidence** in the profession, in parents and, most of all in children.

To give dyslexic children this **support** is a debt we owe them all.

References

Aaron P. G. and Joshi R.M. (1992) *Reading Problems – Consultation and Remediation.* Guildford Press.

Aaron P. G. (1989) *Dyslexia and Hyperlexia.* London, Kluwer Academic Publications.

Ackerman T., Gillet D., Kenward P., Leadbetter P., Mason I., Mathews C., Tweddle D. and Winteringham D. (1983) Daily teaching and assessment – primary aged children. In *Post Experience Courses for Educational Psychologists.* 1983-84, pp. 33-52. University of Birmingham, Department of Educational Psychology.

Adams M. (1990) *Beginning to Read: Thinking and Learning About Print.* Cambridge MA: MIT Press.

Ainscow M. and Tweddle D. (1984) *Preventing Classroom Failure: An Objectives Approach.* Chichester. Wiley & Sons.

Allen J., Brown S., and Munn P. (1991) *Off the Record: Mainstream Provision for Non-Recorded Pupils.* Scottish Centre for Research in Education Report, Edinburgh.

Alston J. and Taylor J. (1992) *Handwriting Helpline.* Dextral Books.

Alston J. and Taylor J. (1992) *Writing Lefthanded.* Dextral Books.

Alston J. (1993) *Assessing and Promoting Writing Skills.* NASEN Publishers.

Ames E. (1991) *Teach Yourself to Diagnose Reading Problems.* Macmillan Educational.

Aram D. M. and Healy J. M. (1988) Hyperlexia: A review of extraordinary word recognition. Obler, L K and Fein, D (eds) In *Exceptional Brain.* New York, Guildford Press.

Arnold H. (1992) *Diagnostic Reading Record.* Hodder & Stoughton (1992).

Arnold H. (1984) *Making Sense of It.* London, Hodder & Stoughton.

Aubrey C., Eaves J., Hicks C. and Newton M. (1981) *Aston Portfolio.* LDA.

Augur J. (1992) *This Book Doesn't Make Sense.* Bath. Educational Publishers.

Augur J. and Briggs S. (1992) *The Hickey Multisensory Language Course.* London, Whurr.

Ayres A. J. (1979/92) *Sensory Integration and the Child.* Los Angeles, CA: Western Psychological Services.

Baddeley A. (1987) *Working Memory.* Oxford. Clarendon.

Bandler R. and Grinder J. (1990) *Frogs into Princes:Introduction to neurolinguistic programming.* Eden Grove.

Bannatyne A. (1974) Diagnosis: a note on the re-categorisation of the WISC scaled scores. *Journal of Learning Disabilities*. 7,272-3.

Bar-Tal D. (1984) The effects of teachers' behaviour on pupils' attributions: a review. In Barnes, P., Oates, J., Chapman, J., Lee, V. and Czerniewska, P (eds) *Personality, Development and Learning*. Sevenoaks, Hodder & Stoughton.

Barthorpe T. and Visser J. (1991) *Differentiation: Your Responsibility and In-service Training Pack for Staff Development*. Nasen Publications.

Beard R. (1990) *Developing Reading 3-13*. Hodder & Stoughton.

Becker W. C. (1977) Teaching reading and language to the disadvantaged – what we have learned from field research. *Harvard Educational Review 47*: pp. 518-43.

Bell J. (1993) *Doing Your Research Project*. Open University Press.

Bell N. (1991) Gestalt imagery: a critical factor in language comprehension. *Reprint from Annals of Dyslexia, Vol. 41*. Baltimore, Orton Dyslexia Society.

Bell N. (1991) *Visualizing and Verbalizing for Language Comprehension and Thinking*. Paso Robles, CA. Academy of Reading Publications.

Bender M. L. (1976) *The Bender-Purdue Reflex Test*. San Rafael, CA: Academic Therapy Publication.

Bergeron B. (1990) What does the term 'whole-language' mean? Constructing a definition from the literature. *Journal of Reading Behaviour. 22*: pp. 301-329.

Berry R. (1986) *How to Write a Research Paper*. Oxford. Pergamon Press.

Biggar S. and Barr, J. (1993) The emotional world of specific learning difficulties. In Reid G. (ed) *Specific Learning Difficulties (Dyslexia) Perspectives on Practice.*, Edinburgh, Moray House Publications.

Blagg N., Ballinger M., Gardner R., Petty M. and Williams G. (1988) *Somerset Thinking Skills Course*. Blackwell/Somerset County Council.

Blau H. and Loveless E. J. (1982) Specific hemispheric routing – TAKV to teach spelling to dyslexics: VAK and VAKT challenged. *Journal of Learning Disabilities. 15*,8, 461-6.

Blight J. (1986) *A Practical Guide to Dyslexia*. Egon Publishers.

Bloom B. S. (1976) *Human Characteristics and School Learning*. New York, McGraw-Hill.

Blyth P. (1992) *A Physical Approach to Resolving Specific Learning Difficulties*. Chester, Institute for Neuro-physiological Psychology.

Boder E and Jarrico S. (1982) *Boder Test of Reading-Spelling Patterns*. New York, Grune and Stratton.

Bradley L. and Huxford L. M. (1994) Organising sound and letter patterns for spelling. In Brown, G D and Ellis, N C (eds) *Handbook of Normal and Disturbed Spelling Development, Theory, Processes and Interventions*. Wiley.

Bradley L. and Bryant, P. (1991) Phonological skills before and after learning to read. In Brady, S. A. and Shankweiler, D.P. (eds). *Phonological Processes in Literacy*. London: Lawrence Erlbaum Associates.

Bradley L. (1990) Rhyming connections in learning to read and spell. In Pumfrey, P D and Elliott, C D (eds) *Children's Difficulties in reading, spelling and writing*. London, Falmer Press.

Bradley L. (1989) Predicting learning disabilities. In Dumant, J. J. and Nakken, H. (eds) *Learning Disabilities. Cognitive, Social and Remedial Aspects*. Vol. 2. London, Academic Press.

Bradley L. (1989) *Specific Learning Disability: Prediction-Intervention-Progress*. Paper presented to the Rodin Remediation Academy International Conference on Dyslexia, University College of North Wales.

Bradley L. (1980) *Assessing Reading Difficulties: Diagnostic Remedial*. NFER Nelson.

Bradshaw J. R. (1990) A service to ourselves or our clients? *Support for Learning* 5,4,205-210.

Brady S. and Shankweiler D. (1992) *Phonological Processes in Literacy*. York Publishers.

Brand V. (1989) *Spelling Made Easy – A Multisensory Structured Spelling*. Egon Publishers.

Brand V. (1985) *Remedial Spelling*. Egon Publishers.

Brereton A. and Cann P. (eds) (1993) *Opening the Door – Guidance on Recognising and helping the Dyslexic Child*. London. British Dyslexia Association.

Brierley M., Hutchinson P., Topping K. and Walker C. (1989) Reciprocal peer tutored cued spelling with ten year olds. *Paired Learning*. 5,136-40.

Brown G. D. and Ellis N. C. (1994) *Handbook of Normal and Disturbed Spelling Development, Theory, Processes and Interventions*. John Wiley & Sons.

Brown M. (1993) Supporting learning through a whole-school approach. In Reid G. (ed) *Specific Learning Difficulties (Dyslexia) Perspectives on Practice.*, Edinburgh, Moray House Publications.

Bruck M. and Treiman R. (1992) Learning to pronounce words: the limitations of analogies. *Reading Research Quarterly*. *24*(4) pp. 375-387.

Bryant P. and Bradley L. (1990) *Children's Reading Problems*. Blackwell.

Bryant P. E. (1990) Phonological development and reading. In Pumfrey, P. D, and Elliott, C. D. (eds). *Children's Difficulties in Reading, Spelling and Writing*. London, Falmer Press.

Burns R. B. (1986) *The Self-Concept in Theory, Measurement, Development and Behaviour*. London, Longman.

Burge V. (1986) *Dyslexia Basic Numeracy*. Helen Arkell Dyslexia Centre.

Burt C. (1921) *Word Reading Test*. Revised by Vernon, P. E., (1938-67) as *Burt (Rearranged Word Reading Test)*. Re-normed by Shearer, E. and Apps, R. (1975). London, Hodder & Stoughton.

Butler K. A. (1987) *Learning and Teaching Style* – In Theory and Practice. Columbia, Conn. Learners Dimension.

Buzan T. (1988) *Make the Most of Your Mind*. Pan Books.

Buzan T. (1984) *Use Your Memory*. London, BBC Publications.

Buzan T. (1993) *The Mind Map Book – Radiant Thinking*. London. BBC Books.

Caine R. N. and Caine G. (1991) *Making Connections*. Banta.

Campioni J. C. and Brown A.L. (1989) Assisted assessment: a taxonomy of approaches and an outline of strengths and weaknesses. *Journal of Learning Disabilities*. Vol. *22*. No. 3. pp. 151-165.

Capel S. (1989) Stress and burnout in secondary school teachers: some causal factors. In Cole, M and Walker, S. *Teaching and Stress*. London OU Press.

Carbo M. (1987) De-programming reading failure. Giving unequal learners an equal chance. In *Phi Delta Kappan*. November 1987. pp. 196-200.

Carbo M., Dunn R. and Dunn K. (1986) *Teaching Students to Read Through Their Individual Learning Styles*. Englewood Cliffs, New Jersey, Prentice Hall.

Carlisle J. (1993) *Reasoning and Reading – Level 1*. Cambridge MA, USA. Educators Publishers.

Cavey D. W. (1993) *Dysgraphia: Why Johnny Can't Write*. A Handbook for Teachers and Parents. Austin, Texas. Pro-Ed. Inc.

Chasty H. and Friel J. (1991) *Children with Special Needs: Assessment, Law and Practice. Caught in the Act*. London. Jessica Kingsley Publishers.

Childs S. and Childs R. (1992) *The Childs' Spelling System – The Rules*. Better Books.

Chin S. J. and Ashcroft J. R. (1993) *Mathematics for Dyslexics – A Teaching Handbook*. London. Whurr Publishers.

Cicci R. (1987) *Dyslexia: Especially for Parents*. Baltimore. Orton Dyslexia Society.

Clark D. B. (1988) *Dyslexia: Theory and Practice of Remedial Instruction*. Maryland, York Press.

Clay M. (1993) *An Observational Survey of Early Literacy Achievement*. Heinemann Education.

Clay M. (1992) *Reading: the Patterning of Complex Behaviour*. London, Heinemann.

Clay M. (1985) *The Early Detection of Reading Difficulties: A Diagnostic Survey with Recovery Procedures*. Auckland, Heinemann Educational.

Clifford V. and Miles M. (1993) *A Guide to Using Talking Computers – Helping Children to Read and Spell*. Talking Publications.

Conlan J. and Henley, M. (1992) *Word Mastery*. Oxford University Press.

Coltheart M., Masterson J., Byng S., Prior M and Riddoch M. J. (1983) Surface dyslexia. *Quarterly Journal of Experimental Psychology*. 35a ,469-95.

Conway N. F. and Gow L. (1988) Mainstreaming special class students with mild handicaps through group instruction. In *Remedial and Special Education*. 5,9,34-50.

Cooke A. (1993) *Tackling Dyslexia: Bangor Way*. London. Whurr Publishers.

Cooper M., Parker R., and Toombs S. (1991) *Reading Assessment for Teachers (RAT-pack)*. Towbridge Wiltshire County Council.

Cooper M., Toombs S. and Parker R. (1992) Reading assessment for teachers. The RAT pack course and materials. *Support for Learning*. Vol. 7. No. 2. pp.78-81

Copeland E. D. and Love V. L. (1992) *Attention without Tension: A Teacher's Handbook on Attention Disorders*. Atlanta, GA. 3C's of Childhood Inc.

Cornelissen P., Bradley L., Fowler S. and Stein J. (1994) What children see affects how they spell. *Developmental Medicine and Child Neurology (in Print)*.

Cowdery L., McMahon J., Morse P. and Prince M. (1987) *Teaching Reading Through Spelling. Diagnosis Book A*. Clwyd, Frondeg Hall Technical Publishing.

Cowdery L., Montgomery D., Morse P. and Prince M. (1984-88) *Teaching Reading Through Spelling*. Clwyd, Frondeg Hall Technical Publishing.

Cox A. R. (1993) *Foundations for Literacy. Structures and Techniques for Multisensory Teaching of Basic Written English Language Skills*. Cambridge MA. and Toronto, Educators Publishers

Cox A. R. (1985) *Alphabetic Phonics*. An organisation and expansion of Orton-Gillingham Annals of Dyslexia. 35:187-98.

Cripps C. (1992) *A hand for Spelling*. Cambridge. Institute of Education.

Cripps C. and Cox R. (1991) *Joining the ABC*. Cambridge, LDA.

Crisfield J. and Smythe I. (eds) (1993,1994) *The Dyslexia Handbook*. Reading. British Dyslexia Association.

Croft S. and Topping K. (1992) *Paired Science: A Resource Pack for Parents and Children*. Centre for Paired Learning, University of Dundee.

Crombie M. (1992) *Specific Learning Difficulties (Dyslexia): A Teacher's Guide*. Glasgow, Jordanhill Publications.

Crombie M. and Reid G. (1994) 5-14 Programme and specific learning difficulties. In Jordan, E. (ed) *A Curriculum for All? 5-14 and Special Needs*. Moray House Publications, Edinburgh.

Cudd E. T., and Roberts L. L. (1994) *A Scaffolding Technique to Develop Sentence Sense and Vocabulary*. The Reading Teacher Vol. 47, No. 4 Dec./Jan pp 346-349.

Cuff C. (1989) *Study Skills*. Cambridge Educational.

Curtis M. E. (1980) Development of Components of Reading Skills. *Journal of Educational Psychology* 5,72,656-69.

Davies A. (1992) *Handwriting, Reading and Spelling System*. (THRASS) Writetract.

De Boo M. (1992) *Action Rhymes and Games*. Scholastic Publications.

De Bono E. (1986) *CORT Thinking*. UK. Pergamon Press.

De Fries J. C. (1991) Genetics and dyslexia: an overview. In Snowling, M and Thomson, M (eds) Dyslexia: *Integrating Theory and Practice*. London, London. Whurr Publishers.

Delford D. E., Pinwell G. S., Lyons C. A. and Young P. (1987) *Reading Recovery*. Report on the follow-up studies. Columbus Ohio Technical Report Vol. 6. Columbus Ohio State University, USA.

Dellinger S. (1989) *Psycho-Geometrics*. New Jersey, Prentice Hall.

Dennison P. E. and Hargrove G. (1985) *Personalized Whole Brain Integration*. California, Educ. Kinesthetics, Glendale.

DES (1972) *Children with Specific Reading Difficulties*. Report of the advisory committee on handicapped children (Tizard Report). London HMSO.

DES (1975) *A Language for Life*. Report of the Committee of Inquiry. (Chair: Sir Alan Bullock). London, HMSO.

DES (1978) *Special Educational Needs*. (The Warnock Report) London, HMSO.

Deschler D. and Schumaker J. B. (1987) An instructional manual for teaching students how to learn. In Graden, J L: Zins, J E and Curtis, M J (eds) *Alternative Educational Delivery Systems: Enhancing Instructional Aspects for all Students*. University of Kansas, Institute for Research in Learning Difficulties.

Diniz F. A. and Reid G. (1994) *Dyslexia in Scotland*. Paper presented at the twenty-first annual conference, New York branch of the Orton Dyslexia Society. April 1994, New York, USA.

Dobie S. (1993) Perceptual motor and neurodevelopmental dimensions in identifying and remediating developmental delay in children with specific learning difficulties. In Reid, G (ed) *Specific Learning Difficulties (Dyslexia) Perspectives on Practice*. Edinburgh, Moray House Publications.

Dockrell J. and McShane, J. (1993) *Childrens' Learning Difficulties – A Cognitive Approach*. Blackwell.

Dodds D. (1993) Curriculum differentiation in the secondary school. In Reid, G. (ed) *Specific Learning Difficulties (Dyslexia) Perspectives on Practice*. Edinburgh, Moray House Publications.

Dombey H. (1992) Reading recovery: a solution to all primary school reading problems? *Support for Learning*. Vol. 7. No. 3 pp. 111-115.

Dougan M. and Turner G. (1993) Information technology and specific learning difficulties. In Reid. G. (ed) *Specific Learning Difficulties (Dyslexia) Perspectives on Practice*, Edinburgh, Moray House Publications.

Dreary I. (1993) *Speed of Information Processing and Verbal Ability*. Paper presented at the Rodin Academy for the Study of Dyslexia Conference. London.

Drummond A., Godrey L. and Sattin R. (1990) Promoting parental involvement in reading. *Support for Learning*. Vol. 5. No. 3. pp.141-145.

Duane D. D. (1991) Neurobiological issues in dyslexia. In Snowling, M. and Thomson, M. (eds) *Dyslexia: Integrating Theory and Practice.* London, London. Whurr.

Duane D. D. (1993) The meaning and utility of differential diagnoses. In *44th Annual Conference, Orton Dyslexia Society Commemorative booklet.*

Dunn R. and Dunn K. (1993) *Teaching Secondary Students Through Their Individual Learning Styles.* Boston. Allyn and Bacon.

Dunn R. (1993). Teaching students through their individual learning styles: a practical approach learning styles training workshop. Center for the study of learning and teaching styles, St John's University, Jamaica, New York.

Dunn R. and Dunn K. (1992) *Teaching Elementary Students Through Their Individual Learning Styles.* Boston. Allyn and Bacon.

Dunn R. and Griggs S. A. (1989a) Learning styles: quiet revolution in American secondary schools. *The Clearing House,* 63(1). 40-42. Washington, DC: Heldref.

Dunn, R., Dunn, K. and Price, G.E. (1975,79,85,87,89) *Learning Styles Inventory.* Lawrence, KANS: Price Systems, Inc.

Dyer C. (1988) Which support?: an examination of the term. *Support for Learning.* 3,1,6-11.

Dykes B. and Thomas, C. (1989) *Spelling Made Easy.* Sydney. Hale and Iremonger.

Edwards P. (1992) *Edwards Reading Test.* Heinemann Educators.

Ehri L.C. and Robbins C. (1992) Beginners need some decoding skill to read words by analogy. *Reading Research Quarterly.* 21(1), 13-26.

Elliot C. D. (1983) *British Ability Scales, Handbook and Technical Manual.* Windsor, NFER Nelson.

Elliot C. D. and Tyler S. (1986) British ability scales profiles of children with reading difficulties. *Educational and Child Psychology.* 3, 2 ,pp. 80-89.

Ellis S. and Friel G. (1992) *Inspirations for Writing.* Scholastic Publications.

Ellis A. (1991) *Reading, Writing and Dyslexia: A Cognitive Analysis.* Open University.

Ellis N. C. (1990) Reading, phonological skills and short term memory: interactive tributaries of development. *Journal of Research in Reading.* 13,2,107-22.

Ellis N. C. and Large B. (1981) The early stage of reading: a longitudinal study. *Applied Cognitive Psychology* 2,47-76.

Emerson P. (1988) Parent tutored cued spelling in a primary school. *Paired Reading Bulletin.* 4,91-2.

Enfield M. L. (1976) An alternative classroom approach. In *Meeting Special Needs of Children with Reading Problems.* Minneapolis, University of Minnesota. Ph.D. Dissertation.

Enfiel, M. L. and Greene V. E. (1981) There is a skeleton in every closet in *Bulletin of the Orton Society* 31:189-98.

Enfield M. L. and Greene V. E. (1985) *Project Read: Practical Spelling Guide.* Bloomington MN, Bloomington Public Schools.

Engelmann J. and Bruner E. C. (1983) *Reading Mastery I and II: Distar Reading.* Chicago Science Research Association.

Evans A. J. (1984) *Reading and Thinking.* Wolverhampton. Learning Materials Ltd.

Evans A. (1984) *Paired reading: a report on two projects.* Division of Education, University of Sheffield (unpublished paper)

Evans A. (1989) Screening at 6+. *Dyslexia Contact.* Vol. 8, No. 1.

Farrer M. (1993) Early identification – the role of the speech therapist. In Brereton A. and Cann, P. (eds). *Opening the Door.* British Dyslexia Association, Reading.

Fawcett A. (1989) *Automaticity – A New Framework for Dyslexic Research.* Paper presented at the First International Conference of the British Dyslexia Association, Bath 1989.

Feuerstein R. (1979) *The Dynamic Assessment of Retarded Performers:The Learning Potential Assessment Device, Theory, Instruments and Techniques.* Baltimore: University Park Press.

France L., Topping F. and Revell K. (1993). Parent Tutored Cued Spelling. *Support for Learning.* Vol. 8, No. 1, pp. 11-15.

Frankiewicz R. G. (1985) *An Evaluation of the Alphabetic Phonics Program Offered in the One-to-One Mode.* Houston, Texas, Neuhaus Education Centre.

Freeman A. (1989) Coping and SEN: Challenging idealism in Cole M. and Walker S., *Teaching and Stress.* Milton Keynes, OU Press.

Frith U. (1980) Unexpected spelling problems. In Frith, W (ed) *Cognitive Processes in Spelling.* London, Academic Press.

Frith U. (1985) Beneath the surface of surface dyslexia in Paterson K., Marshall J. R. and Coltheart M. (eds) *Surface Dyslexia.* Hillsdale, New Jersey, Lawrence Erlbaum.

Frith U. and Snowling M. (1983) Reading for meaning and reading for sound in autistic and dyslexic children. *British Journal of Developmental Psychology.* 1,329-42.

Fynn (1974) *Mister God This is Anna.* Collins Fount Paperbacks.

Galaburda A. (1988) *Ordinary and extraordinary brains: nature, nurture and dyslexia.* Address presented at the Annual Meeting of the Orton Dyslexia Society, Tampa, Florida. November 1988.

Galburda A. (1993) *Cortical and sub-cortical mechanisms in dyslexia.* Paper presented at 44th Annual Conference, Orton Dyslexia Society. New Orleans, LA.

Galaburda A. (ed) (1993) *Dyslexia and Development: Neurobiological Aspects of Extraordinary Brains.* Cambridge, MA: Harvard University Press.

Gardner H. (1985) *Frames of Mind.* USA. Basic Books.

Geschwind N. and Galaburda A. (1985) Cerebral lateralisation biological mechanisms associations and pathology: a hypothesis and a programme for research. *Archives of Neurology,* 42, 428-459.

Given B. (1993) *Five Domains of Learning.* Personal Correspondence.

Given B. (1993) *Learning styles.* Paper presented at two-day conference Centre for Specific Learning Difficulties June 1993. Edinburgh, Moray House.

Glynn T., Crooks T., Bethune N., Ballard K. and Smith J. (1989) *Reading recovery in context.* Report for New Zealand Department of Education, Wellington, New Zealand.

Goodman K. (1976) Reading – a psycholinguistic guessing game. In Singer, H. and Ruddell, R. B. (eds) *Theoretical Models and Processes of Reading.* International Reading Association.

Goodman K. (1992) I didn't found whole language. *The Reading Teacher.* Vol. 46. No. 3. pp 189-199.

Goswami U. (1993) Orthographic analogies and reading development. *The Psychologist.* Vol. 6. No. 7 pp. 3121-316.

Goswami U. (1992) *Analogical Reasoning in Children.* Lawrence Erlbaum Associated

Goswami, U. and Bryant, P. (1990) *Phonological skills and learning to read.* Hove, Lawrence Erlbaum Associates.

Goswami U. (1988) Children's use of analogy in learning to spell. *British Journal of Developmental Psychology.* 6,21-33.

Grampian Region Psychological Service. (1988) *Reeling and Writhing: Children with specific learning difficulties.* Grampian Education Authority, Aberdeen.

Gregorc A. F. (1985) *Inside styles: beyond the basics.* Columbia, CT. Gregorc Assoc. Inc.

Griffiths A. and Hamilton D. (1984) Parent, teacher, child. London Methuen.

Hagley F. (1987) *Suffolk Reading Scale.* NFER Nelson.

Hales G. (1990) *Meeting Points in Dyslexia.* London, British Dyslexia Association.

Hales G. (1990) Personality aspects of dyslexia. In Hales, G.(ed) *Meeting Points in Dyslexia. Proceedings of the First International Conference of the British Dyslexia Association.* Reading: BDA.

Hammill D. D. (1990) On defining learning disabilities: an emerging concensus. *Journal of Learning Disabilities* 23,2,74-84.

Harris C. (1993) *Fuzzbuzz Books/Spell/Words/Letters.* Oxford University Press.

Harrison P. and Harrison S. (1989) *Writing For Different Purposes.* Folens.

Harrison R. (1989) Cued spelling in adult literacy in Kirklees. *Paired Learning.* 5,141.

Healy J. M. (1989) *Your Child's Growing Mind.* New York. Doubleday Dell Publishing Group.

Healy J. M. (1991) *Endangered Minds.* Touchstone. Simon and Schuster.

Heaton P. and Mitchell G. (1987) *Learning to Learn – A Study Skills Course Book.* Better Books Publishing.

Heaton P. and Winterson P. (1986) *Dealing with Dyslexia.* Better Books.

Henderson A. (1989) *Maths and Dyslexics.* North Wales, St. David's College.

Henry M. K. (1993) *Words – Integrated Decoding and Spelling Instruction based on Word Origin and Word Structure.* CA. USA. Lex Press.

Henry M. K. and Redding N. C. (1993) *Word Lists: Structured, sequential, multisensory.* CA. USA. Lex Press.

Henry M. K. and Redding N. C. (1990) *Tutor 1 – Structured, Sequential, Multisensory Lessons Based on the Orton-Gillingham Approach.* CA. USA. Lex Press.

Hill J. E. (1964) *Cognitive Style Interest Inventory.* Michigan ,USA. Oakland Community College.

Hinson M. and Smith P. (eds) (1993) *Phonics and Phonic Resources.* Nasen Publication.

Hinton J. W. (1990) Stress model development and testing in Spielberger, C. D. *Stress and Anxiety.* Vol. 14.

HMG (UK) (1981) *Education Act 1981.* London, HMSO.

Holligan C. and Johnston R. S. (1988) The use of phonological information by good and poor readers in memory and reading tasks. *Memory and Cognition.* 16,522-32.

Holt J. (1964) *How Children Fail.* New York, Dell Publishing Co.

Hornsby B. and Farmer M. (1990 and 1993) Some effects of a dyslexia centred teaching programme. In Pumfrey, P D and Elliott, C D (eds) *Childrens Difficulties in Reading, Spelling and Writing.* London, Falmer Press.

Hornsby B. (1992) *Overcoming Dyslexia.* McDonald Optima.

Hornsby B. and Pool J. (1989) *Alpha to Omega: Activity Packs Stage 1, 2 and 3:* Heinemann Educational.

Hornsby B. and Shear F. (1980) *Alpha to Omega: The A-Z of Teaching Reading, Writing and Spelling.* London, Heinemann Educational.

Hornsby B. and Miles T. R. (1980) The effects of a dyslexic-centred teaching programme in *British Journal of Educational Psychology.* 50,3,236-42.

Hulme C. (1993) Short term memory, speech rate, phonological ability and reading. *Paper presented at the Rodin Academy for the study of Dyslexia Conference.* October 1993. London.

Hunt R. and Franks T. (1993) *Oxford Reading Tree Pack.* Oxford University Press.

Hunter-Carsch M. (ed) (1989) *The Art of Reading.* Oxford. Blackwell Education.

Imich A. J. and Kerfoots R. (1993) Educational psychology meeting the challenge of change *Proceedings of the Annual Conference of the British Psychological Society.* April 1993. Blackpool.

Irlen H. L. (1991) *Reading by the Colours.* New York: Avery Publications Group.

Irlen H. L. (1983) *Successful Treatment of Learning*. Paper presented at the 91st Annual Convention of the American Psychological Association. California, Anaheim.

Irlen H. L. (1989) *Scotopic Sensitivity Syndrome Screening Manual*. 3rd ed. Perceptual Development Corporation.

Javorsky J. (1993) *Alphabet Soup – A Recipe for Understanding and Treating Attention Deficit Hyperactivity Disorder*. Clarkston, M.I. Minerva Press Inc.

Johanson K. V. (1992) Sensory deprivation – a possible cause of dyslexia. *Dyslexia Research Lab (BGC)*. Oslo, Scandinavian University Press.

Johnston R. S. (1992) *Methods of Teaching Reading: The Debate Continues*. Support for Learning. Vol. 7. No. 3. pp. 99-102.

Johnston R. S., Anderson M., Perrett D. I., and Holligan C. (1990) Perceptual dysfunction in poor readers: evidence for visual and auditory segmentation problems in a sub-group of poor readers. *British Journal of Educational Psychology* 60,212-219.

Jones E. R. (1989) *The Cloze Line*. Northumberland. Ann Arbor Publishers.

Jung C. G. (1923) *Psychological Types*. London, Pantheon books.

Kaufman A. A. (1992) *Intelligent Testing with WISC-R*. Psychological Corp.

Keefe J. W. (1993) *Learning Style: Theory: Practice: Cognitive Skills*. USA. NASS Publications.

Keefe J. W. (1991) *Learning Style: Cognitive and Thinking Skills*. Virginia, NASSP.

Keefe J. W. (1987) *Learning Style – Theory and Practice,* Virginia, NASSP.

Keefe J. W., Monk J. S., Languis M., Letteri C. P. and Dunn R. (1986) *Learning Style Profile*. Reston, VA. National Association of Secondary School Principals.

Kimmell G. M. (1989) *Sound Out*. Academic Therapy Publishers.

Kispal A., Tate A., Groman T. and Whetton C. (1989) *Test of Initial Literacy (TOIL)*. NFER Nelson.

Klein C. (1993) *Diagnosing Dyslexia – A Guide to the Assessment of Adults with Specific Learning Difficulties*. London. Adult Literacy and Basic Skills Unit.

Kohl M. and Tunmer, W. (1988) Phonemic segmentation skill and spelling acquisition. *Applied Psycholinguistics*. 9,335-356.

Kolb D. A. (1984) *Learning Styles Inventory Technical Manual*. Boston, McBer and Co.

Kratoville B.L. (1989) *Word Tracking: Proverbs: High Frequency Words*. Northumberland. Ann Arbor Publishers.

Kyd L., Sutherland, G., and McGettrick, P. (1992) A preliminary appraisal of the Irlen screening process for scotopic sensitivity syndrome and the effect of Irlen coloured overlays on reading. *British Orthothalmic Journal*. Vol. 49. p. 25-30.

Kyriacou C. (1989) The nature and prevalence of teacher stress in Cole M. and Walker S., *Teaching and Stress*. Milton Keynes, OU Press.

Lane K. A. (1991) *Developing Your Child for Success*. Texas, USA. JWC Louisville.

Lannen S., and Reid, G. (1993) Psychological dimensions and the role of the educational psychologist in assessment. In Reid, G (ed) *Specific Learning Difficulties (Dyslexia) Perspectives on Practice*, Edinburgh, Moray House Publications.

Lawrence D. (1985) Improving self-esteem and reading. *Educational Research*. 27,3,194-200.

Lawrence D. (1987) *Enhancing Self-Esteem in the Classroom*. London: Paul Chapman.

Lawson J. S., and Inglis J. (1984) The psychometric assessment of children with learning disabilities: an index derived from a principal component's analysis of the WISC-R. *Journal of Learning Disabilities*. 17,517-22.

Lawson J. S., and Inglis J. (1985) Learning disabilities and intelligence test results: a model based on a principal components analysis of the WISC-R. *British Journal of Psychology*, 76,35-48.

Lees E. A. (1986) *A Cognitive Developmental Analysis of Reading Skills in Good and Poor Readers*. Paper presented at Annual Conference of Developmental Psychology Section, September 1986, British Psychological Society.

Lewkowicz N. K. (1980) Phonemic awareness training: what to teach and how to teach it. *Journal of Educational Psychology*. 72,686-700.

Levine M. (1993) *All Kinds of Minds*. Educators Publications.

Levine M. D. (1992) *Keeping A Head in School*. Educators Publications.

Lewis I. and Munn P. (1993) *So You Want to do Research*. Edinburgh. Scottish Council of Research in Education.

Liberman I. Y., and Shankweiler D.P. (1985) Phonology and the problems of learning to read and write. *Remedial and Special Education*. 6(6), 8-17.

Lidz C. S. (1991) *Practitioners Guide to Dynamic Assessment*. Guildford Press.

Locke A. and Beeth M. (1991) *Teaching Talking-Teaching Resources Handbook*. NFER Nelson.

Lovegrove W. (1993) *Visual timing and dyslexia*. Paper presented at Rodin Academy for the study of Dyslexia Conference. October 1993, London.

Lunzer E. and Gardner K. (1984) *Learning from the Written Word*. Oliver and Boyd.

Macintyre C. (1993) *Let's Find Why*. Edinburgh. Moray House Publications.

McCarthy B. (1987) *The 4-Mat System*. Excel Incorporated.

McCleod J. (1994) GAP Reading Comprehension Test. Heinemann Educators.

McCulloch C. (1985) *The Slingerland Approach: Is it Effective in a Specific Language Disability Classroom?* M.A. Thesis, Seattle, Seattle Pacific University

McKeown S. (ed) (1992) *IT Support for Specific Learning Difficulties*. NCET.

McLean B. (1993) Style Counsel – Neuro Linguistic Programming. *In Special Children*, April 1993. pp. 9-11.

McNicholas J. and McEntree J. (1991) *Games to Develop and Improve Reading Levels*. NASEN Publishers.

McRoberts R. (1984) *Writing Workshop.* Teaching Materials.

Margulies N. (1991) *Mapping Inner Space – Learning and Teaching Mind Mapping.* Tucson, AZ. Zephyr Press.

Mathews M. (1993) *Can Children be helped by applied kinesiology.* Paper presented at 5th European Conference in Neuro-Developmental Delay in Children with Specific Learning Difficulties, Chester.

Mathews M., and Thomas E. (1993) *A pilot study on the value of A. K. in helping children with learning difficulties.* Paper presented at 5th European Conference in Neuro-Developmental Delay in Children with Specific Learning Difficulties, Chester.

Meek M. (1985) *Learning to Read.* London, Bodley Head.

Meyer L. P. (1984) Long term academic effects of the direct instruction project. Follow Through. *Elementary School Journal* 84:380-94.

Miles T. R., and Miles E. (eds) (1992) *Dyslexia and Mathematics.* London, New York, Routledge.

Miles T. R., and Miles E. (1991) *Dyslexia: A Hundred Years On.* Milton Keynes, OU Press.

Miles E. (1990) *Bangor Dyslexia Teaching System.* London, London. Whurr.

Miles T. and Gilroy S. (1986) *Dyslexia at College.* Methuen.

Miles T. R. (1983a) *Bangor Dyslexia Test.* Cambridge, Learning Development Aids.

Miles T. R. (1983b) *Dyslexia: The Pattern of Difficulties.* London, Collins Educational.

Miller R. and Klein C. (1986) *Making Sense of Spelling.* London, DCLD.

Mitchell S. (1985) An investigation into the presence or absence of postural reflex abnormalities in children with speech problems. *Unpublished Pilot Study.* City of Birmingham Polytechnic.

Monteiro W. (1992) *Neuro-Linguistic Processing.* Paper presented at Helen Arkell Dyslexic Conference, Cambridge, April 1992.

Moore P. J. (1988) Reciprocal teaching and reading comprehension: a review. *Journal of Research in Reading.* 11,1,3-14.

Morgan R. T. T. (1976) Paired reading tuition: a preliminary report on a technique for cases of reading deficit. *In Child Care, Health and Development.* 2,13-28.

Mosley D. V. (1990b) Research into visual function, reading and spelling. *Dyslexia Review.*

Munn P., and Drever E. (1990) *Using questionnaires in small-scale research. A Teachers Guide.* Edinburgh. Scottish Council for Research in Education (SCRE)

Myers I. and Myers R. (1980) Gifts differing. Palo Alto. *Consulting Psychologists Press.* California.

Naido S. (ed) (1988) *Assessment and Teaching of Dyslexic Children.* London, ICAN.

Nash-Wortham M. and Hunt J. (1990) *Take Time.* Stourbridge. Robinswood Press.

Neale M. (1989). *Neale Analysis.* NFER Nelson.

Neville M. H. (1975) Effectiveness of rate of aural message on reading and listening. *Educational Research.* 1,18,37-43.

Newton M. and Thomson M. (1982) *Aston Index.* Cambridge. LDA.

Nicolson R. and Fawcett A. J. (1993). Early diagnosis of dyslexia: an historic opportunity? Keynote address presented at BDA Early Diagnosis Conference, London, June 1993.

Niklasson M. (1993) *Adding meaning to life: a matter of experience.* Paper presented at the 5th European Conference of Neuro-Developmental Delay in Children with Specific Learning Difficulties, Chester.

Nisbet J. and Shucksmith J. (1986) *Learning Strategies.* London. Routledge

Office of Her Majesty's Chief Inspector of Schools, New Zealand. (1993) *Reading Recovery in New Zealand.* A Report from the office of her Majesty's Chief Inspector of Schools. London. HMSO.

O'Hagen F. J. and Swanson W. I. (1981) Teachers' views regarding the role of the educational psychologist in schools in *Research in Education.* 29, pp. 29-40.

O'Hagen, F. J. and Swanson, W. I. (1983) Teachers and psychologists: a comparison of views in *Research in Education,* pp. 36.

Osmond, J. (1993) *The Reality of Dyslexia.* Cassell.

Orton Dyslexia Society (1991) *All Language and the Creation of Literacy.* Baltimore, Orton Dyslexia Society.

Ostler C. (1991) *Dyslexia – A Parents Survival Guide.* Godalming. Ammonite Books.

Oxley L. and Topping K. (1990) Peer tutored cued spelling with seven to nine year olds. *British Education Research Journal,* Vol. 16, pp. 63-79.

Palincsar A. and Brown A. (1984) *Reciprocal Teaching of Comprehension Fostering and Comprehension Monitoring Activities.* Cognition and Instruction 1(2), 117-175.

Pavlidis G. Th. (1990a) *Perspectives on Dyslexia,* Neurology, Neuropsychology and Genetics, Vol. 1. Chichester. Wiley.

Pavlidis G. Th. (1990b) *Perspectives on Dyslexia.* Cognition, Language and Treatment. Vol. 2. Chichester. Wiley.

Payne T. (1991) Its cold in the other room. *Support for Learning,* 6.2, 61-5.

Pearson L. E. A. and Quinn J. (1986) *Bury Infant Check.* NFER Nelson.

Peck A. (1993) The use of colour in visual reading difficulties. In *Centre for Specific Learning Difficulties, Moray House, Project Information No.2.* Summer 1993.

Peck A. Wilkins A. and Jordan E. (1991) Visual discomfort in the classroom. *Child Language, Teaching and Therapy.* Vol.7 No.2 pp.326-340.

Pennington B.F. (1991) *Diagnosing Learning Disorders: A Neurological Framework.* New York, Guildford Press.

Perrin J. (1981) *Learning Style Inventory: Primary Version.* New York. St. John's University.

Peters M. L. and Smith B. (1993) *Spelling in Context – Strategies for Teachers and Learners.* NFER Nelson.

Peters M. L. (1975) *Diagnostic and Remedial Spelling Manual.* Macmillan Education.

Peters M. L. (1985) *Spelling: Caught or Taught – A New Look.* Routledge.

Pinsent P. (ed) (1990) *Children with Literacy difficulties.* Roehampton. David Fulton Publishers.

Pinnell G. S., Deford D. and Lyons C.A. (1988) Reading recovery:early intervention for at risk first graders. *ERS Monograph, Educational Research Service.* Arlington,Virginia, USA.

Pinnell G.S., Lyons C.A., Deford D.E. (1988) Reading recovery. In *Sopris West Inc Educational Programmes that Work.* (14th edition) Colorado. Sopris West in cooperation with the National Dissemination Study Group.

Pinnell G.S., Lyons C.A., Deford D., Bryk A.S. and Seltzer M. (1991) Studying the effectiveness of early intervention approaches for first grade children having difficulty in reading. *Education Report No.16, Martha L. King Language and Literacy Centre,* Ohio State University. Columbus, Ohio.USA.

Pollock J. (1990) *Signposts to Spelling.* Heinemann Education.

Pratley R. (1988) *Spelling it Out.* BBC Books.

Pumfrey P. D. (1990c) Integrating the testing and teaching of reading. *Support for Learning,* 5,3,146-152.

Pumfrey P. D. and Reason, R. (1991) *Specific Learning Difficulties (Dyslexia) Challenges and Responses.* Windsor. NFER Nelson.

Ramsden M. (1992) *Putting Pen to Paper – A New Approach to Handwriting.* Devon. Southgate.

Raven J. C. (1992,1993) *Standard Progressive Matrices.* Oxford. Oxford Psychologists Press.

Raven J. C. (1988) *Mill Hill Manual and Vocabulary Scale.* NFER Nelson.

Rawson M.B. (1988) *The Many Faces of Dyslexia.* Maryland,USA. Orton Dyslexia Society.

Ray B. J. (1986) *A cooperative teacher education and language retraining programme for dyslexics in West Texas.* Paper presented at the Action in Research V Conference. Texas, Lubbock.

Reason R. and Boote R. (1986) *Learning Difficulties in Reading and Writing: A Teachers' Manual.* Windsor, NFER Nelson.

Reason R., Brown P., Cole M. and Gregory M. (1988) Does the 'specific' in specific learning difficulties make a difference to the way we teach? *Support for Learning.* 3,4,230-6.

Reid G. (1994) *Metacognitive assessment and dyslexia.* Paper presented at Third International Conference of the British Dyslexia Association. April 1994. Manchester. Accepted for publication. Links II.

Reid G. (1993) *Dyslexia:observation and metacognitive assessment*. Paper presented at 44th Annual Conference, Orton Dyslexia Society. New Orleans, LA, USA.

Reid G. (ed) (1993) *Specific Learning Difficulties (Dyslexia) Perspectives on Practice*, Edinburgh. Moray House Publications.

Reid G. (1993) Perspectives on reading. In Reid G. (ed.) *Specific Learning Difficulties (Dyslexia) Perspectives on Practice*. Edinburgh. Moray House Publications.

Reid G. (1993) What is reading? *Unpublished study*. Centre for Specific Learning Difficulties (Dyslexia). Edinburgh, Moray House Institute.

Reid G. (1992) *Learning difficulties and learning styles – observational criteria*. Paper presented at South East Learning Styles Conference, George Mason University, Virginia, USA.

Reid G. (1991) Supporting the support teacher. Stress factors in teaching children with specific learning difficulties. *Links* Vol.16 No.3.pp.18-20.

Reid G. (1991a) The role of learning support teachers and perceived stress. *Unpublished MA. dissertation*. Open University 1991.

Reid G. (1991b) *Stress factors in teaching children with specific learning difficulties*. Paper presented at the Second International Conference:Meeting the Challenge. British Dyslexia Association. April 1991. Oxford.

Reid G. (1990) Specific learning difficulties:attitudes towards assessment and teaching. In Hales, G (ed) *Meeting Points*. Reading, BDA.

Reid G., Carson E. and Brydon P. (1989) *A Pilot Study Investigating the Merits of Segregated Provision for Primary Pupils with Severely Delayed Attainments in Reading and Spelling*. Fife Region Psychological Service. June 1989.

Reid G. (1989) The role of the educational psychologist in the identification and assessment of specific learning difficulties. *Feedback paper*. Fife Regional Council, Psychological Service, Scotland.

Reid G. (1988) Dyslexia:A case for training. *Times Educational Supplement*. 26th February 1988.

Reid G. (1987) The perceptions and attitudes of learning support teachers to specific learning difficulties and dyslexia. *Year book of the Scottish Learning Difficulties Association*.

Reid G. (1986) *An examination of pupil stress before and after transfer from primary to secondary school*. Unpublished. M.Ed thesis. University of Aberdeen.

Retief L. (1990) A Psychophysiological approach to panic disorder. *Doctoral Thesis*.

Richards R. G. (1993) *Learn Playful Techniques to Accelerate Learning*. Tucson,AZ. Zephyr Press.

Richardson A. (1985) The effects of a specific red filter on dyslexia. *British Psychological Society Abstracts*. 56.

Riddell S., Duffield J., Brown S. and Ogilvy C. (1992) *Specific Learning Difficulties: Policy, Practice and Provision*. Department of Education, University of Stirling.

Robertson A. H., Henderson A., Robertson A., Fisher J. and Gibson M. (1991) *Quest Screening, Diagnostic and Remediation Kit.* Windsor, NFER Nelson.

Rosner J and Rosner J. (1987) The Irlen treatment:a review of the literature. *Optician.* 25th September pp.26-33.

Rudginsky L.T. and Haskell E.C. (1990) *How to Spell.* Educators Publishing Service.

Rule J. M. (1984) *The Structure of Words.* USA:Educators Publishers.

Russell J. (1988) *Graded Activities for Children with Motor Difficulties.* Cambridge Educational.

Russell S. (1992) *Phonic Code Cracker.* Glasgow, Jordanhill College Publications.

Russell S. (1993) Access to the curriculum. In Reid, G (ed) *Specific Learning Difficulties (Dyslexia) Perspectives on Practice.* Edinburgh, Moray House Publications.

Scoble J. (1989) Cued spelling and paired reading in adult basic education in Rydale. *Paired Learning.* 5,57-62.

Scoble J. (1988) Cued spelling in adult literacy: a case study. Paired reading bulletin. 4, 93-6.

Scottish Education Dept. (1978) *The education of pupils with learning difficulties in primary and secondary schools in Scotland (Progress Report).* Edinburgh, HMSO.

Selikowitz M. (1993) *Dyslexia and Other Learning Difficulties.* Oxford University Press.

Selmes I. (1987) *Improving Study Skills.* Hodder & Stoughton.

Selman M.R. (1989) *Infant Teacher's Handbook.* Oliver and Boyd.

Seymour P.H.K. (1993) *Individual variation and reaction times in dyslexia.* Paper presented at Rodin Academy for the Study of Dyslexia, October 1993 Conference. London.

Seymour P. H. K. (1987) Individual cognitive analysis of competent and impaired reading in *British Journal of Psychology.* 78, 483-506.

Seymour P. H. K. (1986) *Cognitive Analysis of Dyslexia.* Routledge and Paul Kegan.

Seymour P. H. K., and McGregor C. J. (1984) Developmental dyslexia;experimental analysis of phonological, morphemic and visual impairments. *Cognitive Neuropsychology.* 1,43-82.

Sharon H. (1987) *Changing Children's Minds.* London. Condor Press

Sherman G. F. (1993) *Biological research in dyslexia: implications for differential diagnosis.* Paper presented at 44th Annual Conference, Orton Dyslexia Society, New Orleans, LA, USA.

Siegal L. S. (1989) IQ is irrelevant to the definition of learning disabilities. *Journal of Learning Disabilities.* 22,469-78.

Silberberg N. and Silberberg M.C. (1967) Hyperlexia:specific word recognition skills in young children. *Exceptional Children.* 34,41-42.

Sillars S. (1992) *Spelling Rules OK!* Milton Keynes, Chalkface Project.

Singleton C. H. (1988) The early diagnosis of developmental dyslexia. *Support for Learning.* 3,2,108-21.

Singleton C. H. (ed) (1994) *Computers and Dyslexia-Educational Applications of New Technology.* University of Hull.

Singleton C. H. (ed) (1991) *Computers and Literacy Skills.* Hull, British Dyslexia Association Computer Resource Centre, University of Hull.

Slingerland B. H. (1993) *Specific Language Disability Children.* Cambridge, MA Educators Publishing Service.

Slingerland B. H. (1985) *Screening Tests for Identifying Children with Specific Learning Disabilities.* Educators Publishers.

Slingerland B. H. (1976) *Basics in Scope and Sequence of a Multisensory Approach to Language Arts for Specific Learning Difficulties Children.* Cambridge, MA Educators Publishing Service.

Slingerland B. H. (1971) *A Multisensory Approach to Language Arts for Specific Language Disability Children.* A Guide for Primary Teachers, Books 1-3. Cambridge, MA. Educators Publishing Service.

Smith C. (1993) Problems with reading. *Support for learning.* Vol.8.No.4 139-145.

Smith F. (1973) *Psycholinguistics and Reading.* New York, Holt, Rinehart and Winston.

Smith F. (1985) *Reading.* Cambridge, Cambridge University Press.

Smith F. (1988) *Understanding Reading.* A Psycholinguistic Analysis of Reading and Learning to Read (4th edition) Hillsdale, New Jersey:Erlbaum.

Smith J. and Bloom M. (1985) *Simple Phonetics for Teachers.* Methuen.

Snowling, M. (1990) *Dyslexia:A Cognitive Developmental Perspective.* Blackwell.

Snowling, M. (1991) *Children's Written Language Difficulties.* NFER Nelson.

Snowling, M. (1993) *Specific learning difficulties:A cognitive developmental perspective.* Paper presented at two-day conference Centre for Specific Learning Difficulties, Moray House, Edinburgh.

Snowling M. (1993) *What causes variation in dyslexic reading.* Paper presented at the Rodin Academy for the Study of Dyslexia, October 1993 Conference. London.

Snowling M. and Thomson M.(eds) (1991) *Dyslexia – integrating theory and practice.* London. London. Whurr Publishers.

Snowling M. (1990) Dyslexia in childhood:a cognitive-developmental perspective. In Pumfrey, P. D and Elliott, C D (eds) *Children's Difficulties in Reading, Spelling and Writing.* London. Falmer Press.

Snowling M. (1987) *Dyslexia: A Cognitive Developmental Perspective.* Oxford, Blackwell.

Springer S. P. (1989) *Left Brain, Right Brain.* Freeman.

Stanovich K. E. (1992) Speculations on the causes and consequences of individual differences in early reading acquisition. In Gouch P. B., Ehri L. C. and Treiman R. (eds) *Reading Acquisition.* pp.65-106. Hillsdale, N. J. Erlbaum.

Stanovich K. E. (1991) Discrepancy definitions of reading disability:has intelligence led us astray? *Reading Research Quarterly.* XXVI/I pp.7-29.

Stanovich K. E. (1988) Explaining the difference between the dyslexic and the garden-variety poor readers:the phonological core model in *Journal of Learning Disabilities* 21,10. pp.590-604.

Stanovich K. E. (1980) Towards an interactive-compensatory model of individual differences in the development of reading fluency. *Reading Research Quarterly.* 16,32-71.

Stein J. F. (1991) Vision and language. In Snowling, M and Thomson, M (eds) *Integrating Theory and Practice.* London, London. Whurr.

Stein J. F. and Fowler M. S. (1993) Unstable binocular control in dyslexic children. *Journal of Research in Reading.* Vol.16 No.1. pp.30-45.

Stephenson E. (1986) *Children with motor/learning difficulties. A Guide for Parents and Teachers.* Occupational Therapy Department Royal Aberdeen Children's Hospital.

Stevens M. (1992) *Into Print.* Edinburgh. Scottish Consultative Council on the Curriculum.

Stirling E. G. (1991) *Help for the Dyslexic Adolescent.* Better Books.

Stirling E. G. (1990) *Which is Witch.* Checklist of Homophones. North Wales, St. David's College.

Stoel Van Der. (ed) (1990) *Parents on Dyslexia.* Clevedon. Multilingual Matters.

Sutton R. (1992) *Assessment – A Framework for Teachers.* Routledge.

Thomson G. (1990) On leaving school, who tells? In Hales G. (ed.) *Meeting points in Dyslexia.* Proceedings of the first international conference of the British Dyslexia Association, BDA, Reading.

Thomson M. and Watkins W. (1990) *Dyslexia: A Teaching Handbook.* London. Whurr Publishers.

Thomson M. E. (1990) Evaluating teaching programmes for children with specific learning difficulties. In Pumfrey P. D. and Elliot C. D. (eds). *Children's difficulties in reading, spelling and writing.* London, Falmer Press.

Thomson M. E. (1989) *Developmental Dyslexia* (3rd edition) London, London. Whurr.

Thomson M. E. (1988a) *Developmental Dyslexia: Its Nature, Assessment and Remediation.* (2nd edition) London, Cole and London. Whurr.

Thomson M. E. (1984) *Developmental Dyslexia.* London, Edward Arnold.

Topping K. J. (1993) Parents and peers as tutors for dyslexic children. In Reid G. (ed) *Specific Learning Difficulties (Dyslexia) Perspectives on Practice,* Edinburgh, Moray House Publications.

Topping K. (1992) *Promoting Cooperative Learning.* London. Kirklees Metropolitan Council.

Topping K. (1992) *Paired Writing Information*. London. Kirklees Metropolitan Council

Topping K. J. (1992) Short and long term follow-up of parental involvement in reading projects. *British Educational Research Journal*. 18(4)pp.369-379.

Topping K. J. and Lindsey G. A. (1992) The structure and development of the paired reading technique. *Journal of Research in Reading*. 15(2), 120-136.

Topping K. J. (1992) *Cued Spelling Training Tape*. Kirklees Metropolitan Council.

Topping K. J. and Watt J. M. (1992) *Cued spelling:a comparitive study of parent and peer tutoring*. Paper submitted for publication. Dundee, University of Dundee.

Topping K. J. (1987) Peer tutored paired reading:outcome data from ten projects. *Educational Psychology* 7,2, pp.133-145.

Topping K.J. (1986) *Paired Reading Training Pack*. Dundee. University of Dundee.

Topping K. J. and Wolfendale S. (eds) (1985) *Parental Involvement in Childrens' Reading*. London, Croom Helm.

Traub N. and Bloom F. (1993) *Receipe for Reading*. Cambridge MA. Educators Publishing Service Inc.

Turner M. (1991) Finding out. *Support for Learning*. 6(3),99-102.

Turner M. (1993) Testing times. *Special Children*. 65. pp.12-16.

Turner M. (1993) More testing times. *Special Children*. 66. pp.12-14.

Tyler S. (1980) *Keele Pre-school Assessment Guide*. NFER Nelson.

Vail P. L. (1993) *Reading comprehension:reading for reason, the reason for reading*. Paper presented at the 44th Annual Conference Orton Dyslexia Society. New Orleans, LA, USA.

Vail P. L. (1992) *Learning Styles*. Rosemont, NJ. Modern Learning Press.

Vail P. L. (1990) *About Dyslexia – Unravelling the Myth*. USA. Modern Learning Press.

Vellutino F. R. and Scanlon D. M. (1986) Experimental evidence for the effects of instructional bias on word identification. *Exceptional Children*. 53,2,145-55.

Vernon P. E. (1979) *Intelligence: Heredity and Environment*. San Francisco, CA: Freeman.

Vincent E. and de la Mare M. (1987) *New MacMillan Reading Analysis*. MacMillan Educational.

Vincent D. and Claydon J. (1982) *Diagnostic Spelling Test*. NFER Nelson.

Vitale B. M. and Bullock W. B. (1989) *Learning Inventory Manual – Tests and Remediation*. Northumberland. Northumberland. Ann Arbor Publishers.

Vitale B. M. (1982) *Unicorns are Real. (A Right-Brained Approach to Learning)*. CA. Jalman Press.

Wade B. and Moore M. (1994) The Promise of Reading Recovery. *Educational Review Publications-Headline Series No.1*. University of Birmingham.

Waller R. J. (1992) *The Bridges of Madison County*. Warner Books Inc. New York.

Waterland L. (1986) *Read with Me: An Apprenticeship Approach to Reading.* Stroud, Thimble Press.

Webster A. and McConnell C. (1987) *Children with Speech and Language Difficulties.* Cassell.

Wendon L. (1985 and 1987) *Letterland Teaching Programme 1 and 2.* Cambridge Letterland Ltd.

Wendon L. (1994) *Letterland Writing Programme.* Personal Correspondence.

White M. (1991) *Self-Esteem – Its Meaning and Value in Schools.* Cambridge, Daniels Publishing.

Whittaker E. M. (1992) Specific learning difficulty (dyslexia) and neurological research. An educational psychologists evaluation. In *Educational Psychology in Practice.* Vol. 8. No. 3. pp.139-144.

Wilkins A. (1990) *Visual Discomfort and Reading.* Cambridge. MRC.APU.

Wilkins A., Milroy R., Nimmo-Smith I., Wright A., Tyrill K., Holland K. and Martin J. (1992) Preliminary observations concerning treatment of visual discomfort and associated perceptual distortion. *Opthalmology, Physiology, Optics.* 12,257-263.

Wilkins A. (1993) *Intuitive Overlays.* I.O.O.Marketing Ltd., 56-62 Newington Causeway, London SE1 6DS.

Wilkinson A. C. (1980) Children's understanding in reading and listening. *Journal of Educational Psychology.* 72,4,561-74.

Williams L. V. (1983) *Teaching for the Two-Sided Mind.* Simon and Schuster.

Wolf B. J. (1985) The effect of Slingerland instruction on the reading and language of second grade children. *Seattle, Ph.D Dissertation Seattle Pacific University,* USA.

Wolfendaie S. and Bryans T. (1990) *Word Play.* Stafford. NARE Publications.

Wray D. (1991) A chapter of errors: a response to Martin Turner. *Support for Learning.* 6(4),145-9.

Wright A. (1992) Evaluation of the first British reading recovery programme. *British Educational Research Journal.* Vol.18.No.4. pp.351-368.

Wright A. (1993) *Irlen – the never ending story.* Paper presented at the 5th European Conference of Neuro-developmental Delay in Children with Specific Learning Difficulties. Chester.

Wright A. and Prance L. J. (1992) The reading recovery programme in Surrey Education Authority. *Support for Learning.* Vol.7 No.3. pp.103-110.

Young D. (1989) *Non-Reading Intelligence Tests.* Hodder & Stoughton.

Young P. and Tyre C. (1990) *Dyslexia or Illiteracy: Realising the Right to Read.* Open University Press.

Biographical note

GAVIN Reid is Coordinator of the Centre for Specific Learning Difficulties at Moray House and Course Leader for the Post Graduate Awards in Specific Learning Difficulties (Dyslexia). He is committed to helping teachers develop an awareness of the learning needs and potential of dyslexic children.

Previous to his present post, he was an educational psychologist and classroom teacher, and has made a number of conference presentations on a range of themes associated with dyslexia throughout the United Kingdom and the United States.

Author index

Subject index